PINOCHET IN PICCADILLY

PINOCHET IN PICCADILLY

Britain and Chile's Hidden History

ANDY BECKETT

faber and faber

First published in 2002
by Faber and Faber Limited
3 Queen Square London WC1N 3AU

Typeset by Faber and Faber in Sabon
Printed in England by Clays Ltd, St Ives plc

A CIP record for this book
is available from the British Library

ISBN 0-571-20241-1

2 4 6 8 10 9 7 5 3 1

Contents

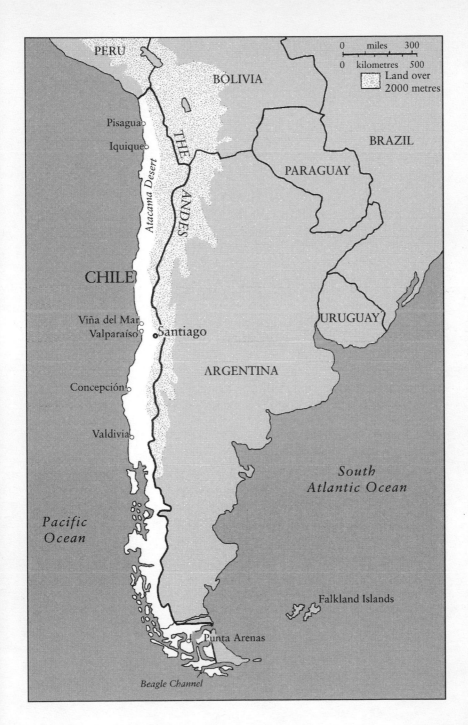

Chile and surrounding region

The Nitrate King

On the edge of south-east London, just beyond Eltham, where the lawns and dual carriageways widen and car alarms whoop in the distance, there is a vast and unexpected Victorian glasshouse. It stands behind a high wall and a screen of trees beside the A210, a pale dome flashing past between the red brick and petrol stations. But Avery Hill, as this remnant of the old estate is still known, is better viewed from the other side, on foot.

A cracked asphalt path leads uphill through dripping beeches, past approximate attempts by the council to maintain the old lawns. A few dog walkers stride and pause on the sloping grass. Beyond the treetops, the roofs of Sidcup and Chislehurst extend tidily across the horizon, pressing in on the grounds. And steadily, the glass fantasy commissioned by Colonel John Thomas North, once better known as the Nitrate King, reveals itself in full.

Its long sides rise twenty feet, then curve inwards, the panels still tilting and catching the grey light as they did in the 1890s, to a turret with a statue flouncing above. There are cracks in a few panes, taped up, and a little condensation blurs the glass, but the outlines of plants even bigger than those from the colonel's day, when he would wander tall and territorial in his slippers and pluck figs, loom dark-green and freakish inside. Between the thick rusted heating pipes, their leaves press against the walls, even the ceiling. Palm fronds droop dusty and motionless. A papery bougainvillea flowers on and on, ignoring the seasons. And the air has a strange quality: warm, but not as tropical-feeling as in most glasshouses, and somehow damp and dried out at the same time, like a desert submerged in fog. There are very few places in the world with that climate; North collected his plants from one of them, the northern coast of Chile.

For three decades, almost entirely forgotten now, he owned nitrate mines there. Their fine whitish dust was then one of the world's most desired commodities: a principal ingredient of both fertiliser and explosives. It built Avery Hill, once a hilltop riot of mock-Italian towers and competing façades, and his fortune. In Britain, North became for a time one of the best-publicised businessmen in the country, a friend of W. G. Grace and the Prince of Wales, frank and noisy in his manners, a figure of archetypal Victorian generosity and ruthlessness. In Chile, at one point, North proposed to the president that he be granted a monopoly of all economic activities in the northern half of the country, an area approaching the size of France. Then North died, quite suddenly, in 1896, after eating oysters in one of his company boardrooms in the City of London. His Chilean enterprises were revealed as verging on the fraudulent. Biographers steered away. In 1941, the Luftwaffe reduced Avery Hill, where a large quantity of butter and sugar was being stored, to the glasshouse and the mansion's shell. These days, the glasswork and palms are hired out as a backdrop for cable-television aerobics programmes, and advertisements for Sugar Puffs.

But to one person North's oversized conservatory still means much more. Sometimes, on summer mornings, Roy Rodriguez comes in at five to open up. He goes home to have breakfast at seven, then lingers late into the evening in the maze of fronds and steam, circling the tiled pathways in his damp gardener's boots and jeans, sweat in his hair and hosepipe trailing, singing nonsense to himself and thinking stray thoughts about North and Chile. He is about forty, from Gibraltar, stocky but lean, with his name tattooed on his hand and a jawline like a film star's in rough outline. He has a limp but he never pauses. He used to do farm work and golf courses; eight years ago, he moved to Avery Hill.

The glasshouse, he says, was run down when he arrived. The estate had been taken over by a teacher training college shortly after North died; that and the bombing had turned most of the buildings into a bodged-together utilitarian compound. The picture gallery and ballroom behind the glasshouse had been gutted, becoming a library for students much like any other, with plain metal shelves and, nowadays, warnings to switch off mobile phones. A solitary small bust of North, with big proud cheeks, tiny stubborn eyes and a show-off's moustache, had been left to glower at the grey carpets where once there had been mosaic floors and suits of armour. Generations of students had ducked in and out of the one surviving porch without looking up at the Chilean flags in the stonework.

Yet Rodriguez was drawn by North somehow. 'If you were in his way, he'd buy you out of the way,' he explained first, watering one afternoon in the Temperate House. He went on, in admiring fragments, interrupted by tugs on the hose behind him: 'He ended up in Chile. Saw the potential in nitrates.' Rodriguez said he collected cuttings about North and Avery Hill, and carefully produced a bundle of them, each one worn and slightly greasy with the humidity, from his tiny neat shed beneath the bougainvillea. He also kept a visitors' book. The names in it were mostly schoolchildren's, interspersed with splats of graffiti – 'Fat Pig', 'Dan G is gay'. On each page, he had painstakingly covered them up with Tipp-Ex.

'I'm doing it on behalf of the public, and for the colonel,' said Rodriguez, with a look of utter seriousness. 'The colonel would be happy with me because I would never let anything go from here.' He indicated several wide-bladed knives which he had stabbed into a piece of wood in his shed. 'I've had my shed broken into twice. Kids break in or burn things whenever they can.' The college had fitted wire mesh over the ballroom's ornamental skylights to deter burglars. He had his own methods: 'One time I came over here in the middle of the night, and I caught two thieves stealing one of the colonel's antique clocks.' His calm eyes lit with a faint excitement. 'I chased them off, and they left it behind. It had cherubs on it and everything. The college should give me a medal.'

Instead there were other rewards. In the Tropical House, there were steady crops of breadfruit and bananas, and other fruit he liked to invent names for before he ate them. Outside, along the south-facing wall of the old boilerhouse, there was a thick, cracked grapevine that had outlived North's vinery. 'It's like my Safeways here,' Rodriguez said. 'Always something to eat.' He plunged a strong wrist into the greenery. He spat one of the Nitrate King's grapes into the flower bed. 'Not ripe yet.'

Ripening is less of a problem in Pisagua. Watering is the issue. There are fat bananas on the plants clumped at each street corner in North's former nitrate port, but their leaves are burnt and ragged. No rain has ever been recorded on parts of the north coast of Chile, and the desert is there around every precious stem and tree trunk, a caramel-coloured dust in each flower bed, waiting for the town's water to be switched off.

About a hundred people still live on this stony shelf between the disused nitrate slopes and the Pacific. The level ground is not much wider than a tennis court; in front are rocks and surf and endless flat ocean; behind is a steepening ramp of black streaks and sand rising 3,000 feet to the horizon. The only road in or out zigzags up with visible desperation. A pair of headlands like pincers cuts off Pisagua to the north and south.

None of this discouraged North in the 1880s. He built a railway to follow the road inland, and bring back narrow wagons of nitrate from his mines high on the interior plateau. He constructed a dockside and jetty, and loaded sailing clippers to race to Liverpool. He acquired a house in Pisagua, and entertained the president in it. The town was important enough then, as the third biggest nitrate port in Chile, to justify its own theatre and clock tower and prison. Everything could be made of wood; the sticky morning fogs barely rotted it. Oregon pine, shipped from two continents away, was the preferred material. Two proud lines of miniature mansions – ornate terraced houses really, with fussy balustrades and balconies just like Avery Hill's – faced out to sea and the distant shareholders.

The main street, now almost the only street, is still a statement of sorts. A dozen grand houses survive, their painted fronts startlingly blue against the sand despite the bleaching sunlight. They huddle together, some well maintained, some collapsing. There are visible gaps where planks have shrunk or gone missing, as if the town were a film set in the early stages of dismantling. Yet there are people around, sitting in the shadows, casting an eye over visitors. Young men smoke cigarettes in their football shirts. Children bounce footballs. Dogs sleep. Someone has a satellite dish. There are a couple of half-built new houses. People ask for lifts.

Pisagua is a fishing village these days. Beyond the skeleton of North's jetty, nothing more now than poles marching into the sea, there are two dozen small boats at anchor. People use them to dive for shellfish. The prison has become a hotel of sorts. The theatre and clock tower have National Monument status. The former is large enough to be in Leamington Spa, prim-looking and white as waves undermine it from behind. The latter is more respectfully looked after; its prim woodwork contains the remains of Chilean soldiers, killed when Pisagua was seized from Peru in 1879 – very conveniently for North in particular.

Over the last decade, though, Pisagua has acquired another historical significance. In June 1990, three months after General Augusto Pinochet Ugarte reluctantly ceased being dictator of Chile, a mound of stones was discovered near the town cemetery. Someone had placed an artificial flower on the pile, and beside it on the bone-dry ground had traced out the number '73'. In secret, so as not to alert the local military or police, two dozen volunteers from the Solidarity Vicariate, a human-rights pressure group run by the Catholic church in Chile, began digging. Their pickaxes and shovels slowly revealed the outline of a long grave, at least eleven yards long and six feet deep. In it were nineteen bodies, clothed and blindfolded, hands tied, wrapped in potato sacks. They had been shot. They were among the very first victims of the Pinochet regime to be uncovered after it left office.

To the general, the town that North built had seemed an ideal place to make people disappear. As a junior officer, during a brief official panic about left-wingers in the late 1940s, he had himself commanded an improvised camp in Pisagua for political prisoners. So in September 1973 (hence the traced-out number), within days of his seizure of power in Chile by military coup, trade unionists, liberals and potential dissidents of all kinds again began arriving in trucks at the small military base at the north end of town. More followed in October. Some of those interned had been arrested in Iquique, the much larger capital of the local region, three barren hours' drive to the south; others had been snatched as far away as Valparaíso, the country's bustling second city, over a thousand miles away. But up here in the desert, at the end of a dirt road, in a prison of Nature's own making, there need not be many witnesses – and escape would be close to impossible. Pisagua quickly became the most significant detention centre in the region, with 500 people packed into the old jail alone at one stage. Under its hot square roof, groups of thirty-five were kept in each wooden cell of three yards by four. Women were confined separately, in a building attached to the theatre. Torture, according to a government human rights report after Pinochet stepped down, was 'systematically practised': people were electrocuted, hung by their wrists, stamped on and stung with cigarettes, subjected to mock firing squads, and forced to drag themselves by their elbows, naked, up the glass-strewn nitrate slopes behind the town.

No family or charity visitors, even from the Red Cross, were ever permitted at Pisagua. Prisoners were shot for supposedly trying to escape, or for allegedly having planned attacks on the army or police. Their trials lasted minutes: prosecution witnesses were themselves tortured into making accusations; defence lawyers were appointed by the military, and threatened if they criticised the procedures. Executions took place right next to the cemetery, sometimes after the release of the very same prisoners had been announced. Sometimes people simply died during torture. Construction of a full-scale concentration camp in the hills above the town – under the guidance, it has long been rumoured, of a German Nazi living in Chile – was begun but never completed. Pisagua was closed as a prison in 1974 after protests from the United Nations.

In the small square opposite the theatre, under a struggling palm, there is now a large mural commemorating the imprisoned and the dead. It was painted in the late 1990s by the local Communist Party, and it remains untouched by the graffiti that mocks other walls in Pisagua. The mural's main subject is a man in a blindfold, head thrown back and throat exposed. The brush strokes are a storm of black and blue and blood-red; they silence the tatty old election posters and signs for beer and ice cream nearby, like an immense war memorial on a village high street.

It is easy to find Pisagua an ominous place. Vultures actually turn overhead in the afternoon stillness. Past the mural, and the guardhouse for the local military police, a large hot rock beside it ostentatiously painted with regimental insignia, the old mansions thin out. A flat open space suddenly appears: a shadeless concrete apron covered in small whitewashed huts. They look fairly modern, but have been thoroughly emptied of any contents. They have tiny windows, high up. The remains of the local barracks are roofless and derelict and blank now. The fact that what happened in there and elsewhere in the town in the early 1970s is known at all, with all the consequences that have followed for Pinochet, is due in part to a peculiarity of local geology. The one old building at this end of Pisagua gives a clue. It is the railway station where North's nitrate wagons were unloaded, now itself slowly splintering in the sea breezes. The same deposits in the soil that North found so profitable also mummified the bodies of the general's enemies. They were so well preserved and identifiable when they were found, you could move the zips on their trousers.

2

The Mystery of General Pinochet

When General Pinochet was arrested in London in the quiet time before midnight on 16 October 1998, relatively few British people knew who he was. He had not been ruler of Chile for approaching a decade; the world since the end of the Cold War was confusingly full of ex-dictators; and Chile seemed a fairly minor and obscure place, a very long way away. Still fewer people in Britain, most likely, were aware that he was in the country. The fact had been noted here and there in the newspapers, but it was a busy time of year, and Pinochet had visited Britain just the previous autumn, and intermittently throughout the 1990s, each time attracting sparse comment. This time, it had actually taken the British press several weeks to register the general's presence at all. On 25 September, at the Dorchester Hotel in central London, he had been photographed for an interview for *The New Yorker*, the American magazine, standing bulkily to attention in a dark pinstripe suit as five bodyguards loitered off-camera around the hired suite and on its veranda. Yet it was not until 10 October that a Foreign Office confirmation of Pinochet's 'private visit' to Britain appeared as three paragraphs in the *Guardian*. And when the Pinochet issue of *The New Yorker* came out, three days later, the parts of the interview that mentioned Britain were still regarded as a surprise and a scoop and were quoted as such in British newspapers.

As for why an eighty-two-year-old South American, of French descent and seemingly alien politics, who spoke almost no English, should regard Britain as his second home – this remained most mysterious of all in the autumn of 1998. Before his arrest, and in more detail immediately afterwards, a certain amount appeared about the general's British itinerary prior to the arrival of two plainclothes policemen at

7

his bedside in the London Clinic. As well as having surgery there for a spinal hernia, he had been to Madame Tussaud's. He had visited the National Army Museum and had lunch at Fortnum & Mason. He had bought books about Napoleon at Foyle's on Charing Cross Road. He had had a talk with the head salesman at Burberry.

But all this trail constituted, in a sense, was the schedule of a fairly typical wealthy tourist: some old-fashioned and eccentric shops, a museum or two, and some discreet medical treatment. Pinochet's habitual ports of call in London were places that were so specifically styled and polished for foreign consumption that they revealed only a little about the nature and depth of his attachment to Britain. The London Clinic, for example, could have been chosen for its proximity to the Chilean embassy, a couple of streets away past the actually rather un-British Marylebone mansion blocks, with their prim shutters and dusty little balconies. And apart from the clinic's brass desk lamps and milky net curtains, it was really just another immaculate and anonymous international private hospital. Pinochet's first choice had actually been in Paris, but the French refused him a visa.

What he wore while he was still at liberty in London also sent out ambiguous signals. On the one hand, in the scraps of television footage of the general benignly buying newspapers and admiring passing red buses, there was his jacket. It was conservatively tailored, long in the back and generous in its vents and lapels, and of the precise shade of country brown, achieved with small checks of beige and black and chocolate, found only in English gentlemen's outfitters. There was also his shirt (pale and striped), and his tie (bright red). With his white moustache and pinkish face, his odd broken blood vessel and cannonball head, Pinochet could have passed for a retired British colonel of a certain sort. Or at least from the waist upwards: in his shiny black shoes and spotless chinos he was perhaps a little too dapper, and in his walk there was a grandness, an almost ceremonial deliberation in each slow, heavy step. It suggested parade grounds, but not the part-time British sort.

Once he was under guard, Pinochet's presence in Britain felt all the more like a borrowing from a strange novel. There was his brief convalescence at the clinic, as armed policemen tried not to alarm its many floors of recovering millionaires, and the first besieging stockades of anti-Pinochet protesters arranged themselves raucously around the entrances. On the same crammed pavements, there were the first counter-demonstrations by Pinochet's supporters, who looked bafflingly like ladies from Chelsea. Next, there were his undignified few weeks at Grovelands, a private nursing home in north London. It looked grand behind railings in the middle of parkland, but the suburb around it (Southgate) was modest enough, with its semis and out-of-date shops, to seem like a punishment. And the Grovelands staff, it was rumoured, did not find the general the easiest or most convincing patient; in the end, the self-styled 'saviour of Chile' had to be told he was better and asked to leave.

And then there was Wentworth. The feared former dictator confined to an executive home, on a vainglorious private estate designed for golfing tycoons. From the winter of 1998 until the early spring of 2000, among the pines and electric gates of primest Surrey, with the clatter of protesters' pots and pans carrying through the trees every Saturday, and jets leaving Heathrow airport droning tauntingly low overhead . . . Pinochet read his books on Napoleon and surfed the Internet. Only once did he attend a brief court hearing, at a high-security prison in south London. As he was driven there and back, his bodyguards held up jackets against the car windows to protect him from photographers. A beige blanket was draped over his head, as if he were a rapist or a paedophile.

The rest of the time, at Bow Street Magistrates' Court and the House of Lords and the High Court, on all the airless stage sets of this melodramatic and unprecedented episode of international litigation, the general was a ghost. As the case veered erratically about, his name was invoked so often it became more of a moral shorthand. His actual person became less familiar than the papier mâché version.

Until, abruptly, he was gone. On the damp grey morning of 2 March 2000, before anyone could get more than a glimpse of the back of a blue people carrier and an escort of police cars, Pinochet had been slipped up one of Wentworth's private roads and out of an unattended side entrance towards the motorway. By eleven o'clock, the blank little motorcade was well on its way, between wet fields and Lincolnshire hamlets, to a remote RAF base and a Chilean jet keeping its engines warm behind the perimeter fencing. On the radio, a perplexed presenter was saying: 'Two years ago I wouldn't have dreamed of asking this, but do you, as chairwoman of the National Association of Women's Institutes, have a line on General Pinochet?' By lunchtime, the ex-dictator had taken off into the mist. Another presenter was summarising wearily, as if at the end of a long royal procession: 'So, there we are, the departure of Augusto Pinochet from this country.' Rain dotted the lenses of the few cameras present. The lunchtime news programmes turned away without offering a conclusion.

The mystery of General Pinochet has endured pretty intact since. The idea that his 503 days in British custody were prompted and steered by anything other than foreign grievances and chance – a lucky initiative from a Spanish magistrate investigating old abuses against his fellow citizens, a country that happened to be receptive, an area of international law where there happened to be no consensus – has not been entertained much. The Pinochet case, it has been generally agreed, was about state torture and murder in a far-off land; the incompatible interests of those who suffered or approved; and how the law, Spanish or British or Chilean or international, might help these competing groups to live with each other in a narrow strip of land on the other side of the Andes. The moral enormity and legal complexity of all this, and the further unexpected developments in the Pinochet case since he returned to Chile, have been more than enough to take in. But every now and again, there have also been hints of an additional dimension.

In October 1999, the Prime Minister, Tony Blair, while insisting that the question of Pinochet's extradition to Spain would be decided by his government on purely legal grounds, also told the Labour Party conference that he found him 'unspeakable'. Peter Mandelson, a politician not noted for his outbursts, publicly declared that if Pinochet evaded extradition it would be 'gut-wrenching'. And Jack Straw, who as Home Secretary was personally in charge of the case, turned out to have another Chilean connection: in the late 1960s, as a left-wing student, he had spent several enthusiastic weeks in the country, meeting the sort of liberal Chileans that Pinochet would spend the next decade persecuting. The daughter of the most famous of these, Salvador Allende, Marxist president of Chile from 1970 until the general's coup killed him, was invited – a quarter of a century later – to the 1998 Labour Party conference. Isabel Allende had dinner there with the Prime Minister. 'He told me he thought my father was a hero,' she said afterwards.

Perhaps all this was just exotic coincidence, or posturing for reasons of domestic politics. But such frank interventions from New Labour, against an ogre from an altogether different era of left-wing politics, did seem startling. Why should they still care about Pinochet? How could Allende's 'Marxism with a human face' make him the 'hero' of the eagerly pro-business Blair? These were un-ideological times, it was usually said, and Labour in particular was supposed to have abandoned all its old convictions. What was it about Chile in the 1970s that stirred these careful modern politicians?

Unexpected passions also flared on the British Right. Conservative newspapers felt immediately obliged, not just to criticise Labour's arrest of Pinochet and to assert that countries' internal policies were their own business – both pretty predictable Tory positions – but to defend him more broadly. Had he really been so bad? If a few thousand people had been killed and tortured – and they often disputed the figures – perhaps this had been necessary. Pinochet had 'saved' Chile: from Allende, from the communist dictatorship he had been planning, from the chaos and imminent civil war he had been provoking, from the Cold War designs of Cuba and the Soviet Union on this strategically placed strip of the southern hemisphere. And since the general had sent his tanks onto the streets in 1973, hadn't his country prospered? It had become a 'model economy', clean, busy and entrepreneurial, light in regulations and trade unions, welcoming to global investors. Chileans had become wealthier and more self-reliant: they all had privatised pensions, for example, of the sort the Conservative Party had long been hoping for in Britain. In fact Chile, according to this highly ideological but only erratically factual reading of its history and present situation, was the place where the great and successful right-wing experiment of the later twentieth century had first started, and had been carried farthest. In the dry leader columns of the *Telegraph* and *Times*, there was, on the days when the Pinochet question was addressed, a rare sense of excitement.

It was there, too, in the eyes of Britain's dominant right-wing politician. Margaret Thatcher, from the first news of this other elderly ex-leader's arrest, seemed more energised than by any single event – general elections won and lost, European summits – since her enforced retirement. She made her first speeches in the Lords for years. She wrote her first letters to newspapers for almost as long. She abandoned her surprising admiration for Blair because of the matter. She went to Wentworth, took tea with the general among his rented cream armchairs, and called a press conference immediately afterwards. And at Blackpool in October 1999, when it seemed that Pinochet's confinement might continue indefinitely, she hijacked her own party's annual gathering to demand his release.

'My friends, it is nine years since I spoke at a Conservative Party conference,' she began. What followed was fainter and less practised than her famous rhetoric as Prime Minister, and slightly flailing in places, but it made an ambitious argument. Chile was Britain's 'oldest friend in South America'. Chile had been freed from the Spanish by a British admiral called Cochrane. Many decades later, that favour had been returned: 'President Pinochet,' as Thatcher slyly rebranded him, 'was this country's staunch, true friend in our time of need when Argentina seized the Falkland Islands.'

Here, oversimplified by Thatcher's fondness for certainties, was the outline of a relationship between two countries, far more extensive, intimate and longstanding than a mere period of wrangling over an exiled general. He, for one thing, had been having tea with her in London for years. He had sent her flowers and chocolates. She had sent her chief economic adviser during the early 1980s, Sir Alan Walters, to learn from Chile's privatisations and pared-back welfare state. Pinochet had noted her handling of the miners' strike.

In fact, since Cochrane sailed to Chile in the 1820s, and even before, there has been a busy traffic in grand schemers and utopia-seekers between these two claustrophobic maritime nations. The very distance between them, the different lights and landscapes and senses of possibility offered by the two places – these have freed minds to think thoughts a little heretical at home. In the late eighteenth century, in sooty Bloomsbury, Chilean nationalists gathered in tucked-away rooms to plan the end of Spanish colonial rule. In the late nineteenth century, in the glare and open spaces of the world's driest desert, John North from drizzly Leeds tried to establish money-making monopolies impossible in Yorkshire. In the years in between, British merchants made coastal Chile their colony, complete with cricket teams.

Next, during the 1960s and 1970s, the sprawling grey capital, Santiago, became an arena first for the hopes of British socialists, drawn to Allende as a sort of revolutionary Clement Attlee, and then for the hopes of British conservatives of all stripes – from austere admirers of Pinochet's economic policies to more flamboyant creatures, tempted by the idea of a similar 'strong man' to solve the 'crisis' back home. That strong man turned out to be a woman and an elected politician, not one of the ex-army officers, of similar age and background to the Chilean, daringly proposed in certain British circles during those feverish mid-1970s summers. Yet Margaret Thatcher's first years as Prime

Minister contained mild but distinct echoes of the general: the same unyielding rhetoric, the same monetarist 'shock treatment', the same promises of carrots and sticks, of mass share ownership and riot police. And when the whole project seemed about to collapse, it was South America that saved her. The recapture of the Falkland Islands, with extensive Chilean assistance, was partly coordinated from an old British sheep farmers' outpost in southernmost Chile, Punta Arenas.

In damp British industrial towns, meanwhile, warships and weapons were being made and serviced for Chile as they had been since the days of Cochrane. In places like Glasgow and Coventry, too, refugees from Pinochet were adjusting to early dusks and puzzled glances. Several thousand Chilean dissidents – trade unionists, Maoists, left-wingers of all descriptions – settled quietly into the background of noisy urban Britain during the 1970s, just another new brown-skinned minority who worked hard and met for strange meals in each other's houses. Few of them can ever have imagined that Pinochet would follow. But the dictator, fatally, became an Anglophile – London his favourite city after Santiago, Britain his ideal country of fair play and discretion. And when he took one trip too many, the refugees were waiting.

You could say that Britain and Chile have acted as each other's political subconscious. Britain, to a certain sort of Chilean, has always looked desirably stable and mild. Chile, to a certain sort of Briton, has always looked desirably extreme and volatile. Both countries have long advertised to the world the uniqueness of their political systems and democratic traditions, while not always functioning as admirably in practice.

You could also say that British businessmen like North gave Chile its first harsh taste of international capitalism; and that Pinochet's further refinement of the recipe, a hundred years later, ended up by passing the flavour back. That both countries are now places dominated by the free market, with privatised buses and many beggars and, currently, leftish governments forced to operate in a landscape created by domineering predecessors – this is much more than coincidence or a standard consequence of globalisation.

Such relationships are probably not best traced decade by decade, or at least not in a book like this. There were many years in the mid-twentieth century when, in truth, the links between Britain and Chile had dwindled to a few forgotten Andean mines and estates and some occasional debt-collecting by Rothschilds in London. But an erratic or forgotten or never-suspected relationship can cast a revealing light on the partners concerned. The story of the connection between Britain and Chile suggests unexplored contours in the wider histories of both these countries, in particular that of modern Britain. Besides, 'the English of South America' and their northern counterparts have become involved again. The status of Chile's longest-serving leader was changed for good that night in the London Clinic. His best-known international defender became the woman who made today's Britain. This sudden revival of the closeness between these two distant countries felt unlikely to remain very public for long. So, in that unnaturally warm autumn of 1998, it seemed a good idea to start probing it.

3

A Scotsman in Valparaíso

The place in London where the anti-Pinochet protesters used to gather most often was a narrow curve of pavement next to Westminster Abbey. *El Piquete de Londres*, or the London Picket, as its Chilean organisers quickly christened it – with the eye of instinctive activists for posterity and the audience back home – assembled there at ten o'clock every morning from Monday to Friday. Or so it said on the handout.

The first time I went along, in early 1999, I got there at ten forty-five. It was a grey and blustery day. The case was in one of its lulls. Absolutely no one was standing by the abbey railings. 'There's fewer and fewer of them every day,' said the policeman in the sentry box across the road, guarding an entrance to the House of Lords, where Pinochet had not been mentioned for some weeks. He gave a politely weary look. Between the old postcard façades of the abbey and the Houses of Parliament, the usual river of taxis and coaches flowed on. Thinly dressed tourists stopped to take photographs. The wind quickly moved them on.

Then two people carrying plastic bags came round the corner. They also looked middle-aged and foreign, but they were wearing careful layers of jumpers and anoraks and zip-up jackets, and they moved with purpose. They stopped at the railings, put down their bags, and began lifting out placards and unfurling banners. There was no show about it; just their gloved and practised hands dipping into the carrier bags and into their pockets, producing rolls of brown tape, biting off pieces deadpan, and roughly fixing the corners of posters to the ancient wrought iron. The placards they expertly bent between the railings. In about fifteen minutes, everything was in place: a long white sheet screamed 'Let Spain Try Pinochet'; a Chilean flag flew from a lamp post; a montage of small colour photos announced the protest's history so far; and it all flapped and crackled in the wind like a medieval army encamped on a hilltop.

By lunchtime, there were a dozen protesters. They formed a single ragged line of figures and faces, all Chilean, unfamiliar on demonstrations in Britain since the 1970s. There were dark, hatchet-cheeked young men with beards and long black ponytails. There were paler middle-aged women of a certain width, sitting beneath faded black-and-white portraits of 'disappeared' Chileans. There was a stout plump-faced man, about the same age, in a smart muted green jacket of the sort favoured by Santiago businessmen. And there was a wiry old man wearing a Che Guevara badge and corduroys. He seemed keenest to talk.

'The Lords are playing with the psyche of the prisoner,' he began, in quick whispery English, his small busy eyes lighting at the thought. 'He's lost twenty kilograms. He can't sit down.' He waved dismissively with a bony hand: 'The situation for him is so humiliating.' A few pedestrians stopped to listen. There were leaflets to offer them, and a visitors' book to get them to sign. The old man said he could only give me a few minutes.

He had been on the picket every day, almost from the beginning. Each morning, he got the bus across the river from the estate where he lived in Lambeth. He had been there since 1992; before that, he had been in Coventry for twelve years as a metalworker, and before that – the details rattled past like melodramatic plot summary – he had been in Chile as a member of Allende's left-wing coalition government and, later, a political prisoner of Pinochet's viciously right-wing one. He pointed at the gut of his bright red polo neck; he said he had been shot. 'My community was 200 yards from Pinochet's barracks.' Between 1973 and 1976, he had been locked up; Pinochet or no Pinochet, he did not want to go back. 'I prefer living here. I have some very good friends. In Chile I have nothing to do,' he said, quite matter-of-factly. 'I'm just a foreigner.' And then he walked off to mind the visitors' book. 'If the case carries on until the sixteenth,' he added in parting, one shoe sole flapping loose in the puddles, 'that means he's been stuck here another month.'

Two months later, Pinochet was still in Britain, and the picket was still finding the mornings difficult. It was noon and it was raining; the only sign of the protesters was their soggy sticker remnants on the railings. So I ducked into the abbey to learn about Cochrane.

In the gloom, near the centre of the nave, there was a large pale memorial slab set in the floor. It had a few black spots of damp on it, and a few chips had been knocked out. But it was quite legible. In large, jammed-together capital letters, it tried as grandly as possible to summarise his life:

HERE RESTS IN HIS 85TH YEAR
THOMAS COCHRANE
TENTH EARL OF DUNDONALD
BARON COCHRANE OF DUNDONALD
OF PAISLEY AND OF OCHILTREE
IN THE PEERAGE OF SCOTLAND
MARQUESS OF MARANHAM IN THE
EMPIRE OF BRAZIL
G.C.B. AND ADMIRAL OF THE FLEET
WHO BY THE CONFIDENCE WHICH HIS GENIUS
HIS SCIENCE AND EXTRAORDINARY DARING
INSPIRED, BY HIS HEROIC EXERTIONS IN THE
CAUSE OF FREEDOM AND HIS SPLENDID
SERVICES ALIKE TO HIS OWN COUNTRY
GREECE, BRAZIL, CHILI AND PERU
ACHIEVED A NAME ILLUSTRIOUS THROUGHOUT
THE WORLD FOR COURAGE PATRIOTISM
AND CHIVALRY
BORN DECEMBER 14TH 1775
DIED OCTOBER 31ST 1860

A row of chairs almost covered the end of the inscription. A couple of people were resting on them in the cool, ignoring it. Cochrane is not remembered much in Britain. There have been very sporadic biographies. There used to be a strip called 'Fighting Tom Cochrane' in *Victor*, the old-fashioned boys' comic. The maritime novelist Patrick O'Brian has used a daring naval officer called Jack Aubrey as a character, in whom elements of Cochrane may be discerned. During the 1930s, there was a run-down naval supply facility in Rosyth named after him, when other admirals got battleships. But as for the idea that a Scotsman liberated Chile – when Margaret Thatcher invoked his name on stage in Blackpool, in a hired cinema hot with Conservative Party delegates waving Chilean flags and cheering for all things Chile-connected, there were completely blank looks in the audience.

Nelson may make it difficult for most Britons to remember any other nineteenth-century naval heroes. And Cochrane was probably never quite senior enough in rank, too abrasive and erratic in character, and too far-flung and bizarre in his achievements, to sustain a posthumous reputation in Britain for long. He was from a family of mercurial aristocrats. The Cochranes had held land in Scotland since the thirteenth century. During the fifteenth, one of them became 'architect-courtier' and royal favourite of James III of Scotland, and was given an additional title that so enraged the more established nobility that they hanged him from a bridge. They refused his last wish that they use one of his favourite silk cords. In the seventeenth century, one of the family's younger sons was implicated in a rebellion against James II; only a large bribe from his father steered away the King's investigators. During the eighteenth, five Cochranes were killed in foreign wars. The ninth earl, Cochrane's father, after surviving unsuccessful careers in the navy and the army, decided to become an inventor; thus, commented the local historian Bishop Burnet, 'completing the impoverishment of the ancestral estates'.

Beneath the wooded slopes of the family seat at Culross, just across the Firth of Forth from Edinburgh, there ran a seam of coal. It was already mined on a small scale; the earl converted it to coke in an experimental kiln he had built, and sold the coke to local ironworks. Maintaining the turrets and the Inigo Jones façades of the Cochrane residence absorbed more income than the family could conventionally acquire. Around 1780, the earl began wondering if the thick black residue of his coke-making process, coal tar, could also be profitably used. During his brief spell in the navy (the discomfort of a cruise up the coast of Guinea was too much for him), he had become aware of a perennial problem with the wooden warships of the era: worms slowly ate them from the keel up. If he could refine his coal tar sufficiently, he convinced himself, it could be used to coat ships' hulls, and would blunt the teeth of worms and creditors alike.

For the next decade, with his young son brought along to learn, the earl built more kilns, borrowed more money, acquired the patent for coal tar, and tried to persuade the Admiralty to adopt his innovation. It worked in tests, but – in a lesson not lost on the junior Cochrane – it failed politically. The shipbuilders and their naval clients were corruptly intertwined. The income from the repairs that the worms made necessary was distributed to too many people for the coal-tar scheme to be practical. Not, at least, for another forty years: by then, Culross had been sold and the earl was a debt exile in Paris, too concerned with drink and his mistress to make the Admiralty pay up for adopting his patent. He had long abandoned coal tar for doomed schemes to manufacture salt, and to make bread for the poor from potatoes.

In the summer of 1793, shortly after the outbreak of the Napoleonic Wars, his son left Scotland to join the navy. Cochrane was seventeen, vulnerably thin and tall, with irreverent eyes and a slight pout. His father could give him a gold watch and nothing else to take to sea; another relative had to lend Cochrane a hundred pounds for his first uniform.

His early career was not very glorious. For nearly five years, he was sent to the fringes of the war: first Norway, where there were rumours of pirates in the fjords, and of a French convoy sneaking home by a cold, secret route; then Nova Scotia, where there were fishing grounds to protect and, a little further south, a newly independent United States to be intimidated. Cochrane never saw a single enemy ship emerge from the fog. Yet he learned about fickle coastal waters and weather and how they could be exploited. He also developed an appetite for philosophy, and for flippancy towards superior officers. These qualities would be fully developed by the time he got to Chile.

Before that, in barely half a dozen years, he assembled a reputation for reckless success as a sea captain. In 1799, in his very first naval action, he boarded a pirate ship off Gibraltar single-handed. In 1801, he captured a Spanish frigate with seven times the firepower of his own tiny ship, the *Speedy*, which he had disguised as a neutral Danish vessel. In 1805, he captured so many Spanish treasure ships in a ten-week spell that his personal share of the prize money was £75,000. He became quite famous. The newspapers in British naval towns recorded his successes like sporting fixtures. Pamphlets were published describing them in detail. And Cochrane's ambitions began to turn towards politics.

At sea, he had got used to exceeding orders, to ignoring the conventions of naval warfare of the time by attacking suddenly, by using trickery, by exploiting supposedly impossible odds as a form of surprise. Back on land, he would inevitably be reprimanded and denied prize money. Escalating feuds with his superiors were set in motion. His suspicion of the Admiralty, already a family instinct, swelled sharply during 1802 and 1803, when a temporary halt in the war enabled Cochrane to start poking around again in the practices of the dock-yards. The blatant bribery and overcharging he identified, and took to be symptomatic of British government as a whole, made him sympathetic to the favourite new cause of ambitious young men at the time: Reform. He stayed with the radical politician William Cobbett in Hampshire. He studied political philosophy at Edinburgh University under the famous liberal academic Professor Dugald Stewart. Then, still in his mid-twenties, beaky and red-haired and awkward, he decided to run for Parliament.

In 1805, with a general election nearing, Cobbett appealed for a Radical candidate to stand in Honiton in Devon. Cochrane saw the opportunity to transform his temporary status as a war hero into something wider and more permanent. On 8 June, he arrived at the hustings 'accompanied by two lieutenants and one midshipman in full dress', as the *Naval Chronicle* reported, 'followed by another [carriage] containing the boat's crew, new rigged and prepared for action.' Cobbett sat beside Cochrane on stage, beneath the rival candidates' flags and bunting. Cochrane had put on his blue-and-gold captain's uniform. And he stood up, before a crowd of prosperous farmers, accustomed to placing their votes with whichever candidate would pay them five pounds or more apiece, and made a high-minded speech about naval corruption. Hecklers shouted that he should 'spend his money sailor-fashion'; Cochrane responded that he was standing 'on patriotic principles' – a euphemism for refusing to bribe voters. Soon after that, somewhere in the crowd, a riot started. Sailors fought voters, Cobbett and Cochrane's opponent exchanged libellous insults, and Cochrane just screamed vainly for order. He lost the election.

But he learned. In the autumn of 1806, Honiton was contested again, and again Cochrane arrived with his carriages full of seamen and noble-sounding intentions. Yet this time his apparent naivety was a decoy. After the previous election, without warning, he had announced that those few people who had voted for him would receive ten pounds each, twice what the victorious candidate had paid. Second time round, a rumour spread through Honiton that the foolish captain would be as generous again. It was enough to win Cochrane the seat, without him ever actually promising to pay out. When voters approached him during his victory celebrations for their anticipated ten pounds, he calmly told them he had made no such offer, which was anyway against his principles; the payment last time had simply been a reward to those who had refused the bribes of his opponent.

This sly mixture of piousness, defiance and calculation made Cochrane a vivid presence in the otherwise dour politics of repressive, Napoleonic War Britain. In 1806, the Admiralty sent him back to sea to keep him from attending Parliament. He used the war as politics by other means, mounting an amphibious raid on the French coast, blowing up a fort, and raising his profile once more. In 1807, he stood in yet another election, this time in Westminster (Honiton was never going to forgive him), where the electorate was the largest and least susceptible to bribes in the country. It was also the best-publicised constituency: the famous cartoonist Gillray drew Cochrane as a priggish, bolt-upright megalomaniac in a scrum of other grotesque candidates, with a great mob of voters stretching to the horizon. Cochrane won, immediately put down motions in Parliament to expose the corruption he now saw everywhere, then sailed off to be hit in the face by a stone fragment from another fort he was busy capturing.

Gradually, though, his multiplying enemies at home began to frustrate him. In Parliament, when he was present at all, Cochrane's overheated rhetoric left him isolated and ridiculed. The Admiralty learned to give him assignments with less opportunity for glory. In 1812, in frustration, he wrote directly to the Prince Regent with a grandiose 'Plan for the Destruction of the Naval Power of France', involving 'stink vessels' (hulks filled with burning sulphur and charcoal), 'temporary mortars' (the same but stuffed with cannon balls and animal carcasses), and the much greater use of drifting fire ships to ignite enemy vessels. But initial support for this new, much more destructive notion of war bled away: the Admiralty feared French retaliation in kind. Cochrane had to put away his excited inventor's diagrams until he got to Valparaíso.

His political strategy, in the meantime, had turned feverish. In 1810, when a fellow Radical MP was threatened with imprisonment for abusing Parliamentary privilege, Cochrane holed up with him and the other Radical leaders in a house at 78 Piccadilly, having obtained a barrel of gunpowder, supposedly for self-defence. The Life Guards were called out; Radical sympathisers took to the streets; momentarily, there seemed the possibility of some kind of revolutionary spark. One of Cochrane's comrades asked him the question that other military men would be asked in the next century – in Chile and, more quietly, in Britain: 'It will be easy enough to clear the hall of constables and soldiers . . . but are you prepared to take the next step and to go on?'

Cochrane went home. Four years later, in circumstances that remain mysterious, he was implicated in a City scandal involving a false announcement that Napoleon had been killed in battle, and the frantic trading of shares as they temporarily soared in value. The evidence against him was ambiguous: one of the conspirators had visited him at home, but Cochrane had made only a tiny profit on his share dealings during the period under scrutiny. It remains possible that the troublesome seaman was set up. Either way, by the autumn of 1814 Cochrane had been tried, found guilty of fraud and perjury, sentenced to a year in prison, and expelled from the navy and the House of Commons. His family banner was ceremonially removed and kicked down the steps of Westminster Abbey.

The following spring, with comic-strip inevitability, Cochrane managed to escape from jail by knotting together lengths of rope smuggled in by a loyal servant. He even returned to Parliament, his adoring Westminster constituents having paid off the necessary fines, and became for a time the loudest advocate of civil liberties, universal suffrage and greater aid to the poor. When petitions were delivered to the Commons by the Radical mob, they would hoist and carry Cochrane in an armchair, still sun-freckled and boyish in his early forties. But the government had turned decisively against his brand of politics. The official response to Reform turned out to be censorship, the arrest of perceived subversives and the suspension of prisoners' rights. Cochrane's Radical friends began to leave the country; their cause seemed a dead end for now. Meanwhile, he was suddenly besieged by debts. With his lack of an inheritance, his unresolved disputes over prize money, and the frequent litigation that went with political notoriety, he was close to bankrupt by the end of 1817. An unpaid bill for £1,200, from a dinner for Honiton's greedy voters back in 1806, was the final blow. Cochrane began selling off his property and thinking about a move abroad himself. He let it be known that he was open to offers.

There had been South Americans in London, murmuring about independence from Spain, for at least a quarter of a century. The disruptions of the Napoleonic War were fatally loosening Spanish control of their continent; London, as capital of one of the two blocs into which much of the world was dividing, was an obvious place for frustrated foreign nationalists to set up shop. Officially or otherwise, the British might be persuaded to help.

Chile was an especially vulnerable Spanish colony. Its remote, near-infinite strip of deserts and forests and snowfields had only ever been partially conquered during the sixteenth and seventeenth centuries. The largely impassable southern third of the country, like Scotland during the Roman occupation of Britain, remained independent, and a threat. Elsewhere, Spanish power was mostly confined to Santiago and its surrounding lung of dusty farmland, and to garrison towns, lonely beside river mouths. As in Roman Britain, again, the empire-builders' main priorities lay in other, more important nearby colonies – in this case, Peru, to the north. Frustrated and rebellious notions stirred among both the local population and the neglected Spanish settlers and administrators.

During the 1790s, the half-Irish, half-Spanish son of the viceroy of Peru, Bernardo O'Higgins, was living in London, the first person from west of the Andes to seek an English education. He studied maths and, more covertly, the ideas then circulating there about national self-determination and liberty. He started visiting 27 Grafton Way in Bloomsbury, a tall grey-brown London town house which was the home of Francisco de Miranda, a Venezuelan maths tutor and, more significantly, a pioneer of South American nationalism. In 1794, back in Venezuela, Miranda launched the continent's independence revolt, with encouragement from the British government, which welcomed the chance to destabilise a rival imperial power. There were official suggestions that such help might also be forthcoming for Chile.

Sixteen years later, belatedly and with poor timing, in 1810, the first nationalist attempt to overthrow Spanish rule in Chile began. Miranda's campaign was fading to the north. And British priorities had shifted: Spain was now Britain's ally against France. A British military expedition intended for Chile was directed instead towards Buenos Aires. The Chileans managed to declare independence regardless in 1811, but were back under Spanish control by 1814, thanks in part to divisions between O'Higgins and the other nationalist leaders. He had to flee across the Andes to Argentina with his few hundred remaining soldiers. Two years later, he tried again, this time with an Argentinian general called José de San Martin – nationality seemed curiously unimportant to these nationalists – who helped the new army thread its way through the mountains, defeat the Spanish force guarding the last pass before Santiago, and march the thirty remaining miles across the hot central plain to the capital. In the late summer of 1817, O'Higgins was elected there as the first Supreme Director of the new republic.

However, as long as the Spanish navy could patrol the cold blue-green seas off Chile, all this was provisional. Spain could continue to supply the coastal citadels of colonial rule, such as the heavily fortified estuary and town of Valdivia in the south, known as 'the Gibraltar of the southern hemisphere'. This mocked the Chileans' internationally publicised claim to be self-governing, and made a counter-attack against the fragile new regime possible at any moment. Chile was barely a hundred miles wide but was thousands of miles long; almost all its settlements and resources were within raiding distance of the coast. What the republic urgently needed, O'Higgins decided, was an effective and aggressive navy, and someone to lead it.

He had heard about Cochrane. The Scotsman's international reputation for winning sea battles against superior forces, and for mounting unlikely but successful amphibious attacks, made him sound ideal from a military point of view. The Chileans' warships were old and few in number, and Valdivia and the other Spanish fortresses had recently been modernised. Politically, too, the Chileans felt Cochrane would be sympathetic: they knew of his 'common cause with the helpless and the oppressed', as O'Higgins' representative in London, Don José Alvarez, put it. And Cochrane was used to fighting the Spanish and ransacking their imperial properties. Finally, his personal circumstances – for one thing, he had not been allowed to go to sea for almost a decade – suggested he might be ready to become a mercenary. In late 1817, Alvarez was ordered to approach him. Over 150 years later, the famous Chilean poet Pablo Neruda, a passionate nationalist and no idoliser of foreigners, thought the moment worth commemorating, in a poem called 'Cochrane De Chile':

> Lord of the sea come to us . . .
> We are a people mute and oppressed . . .
> The narrow hemisphere is lit with your unconquerable splendour!
> At night your eyes close on the high mountains of Chile.

Unfortunately, the Spanish had spoken to Cochrane first. They asked him to lead a naval expedition that was being planned to smother all the South American rebellions. He refused on principle. But before

Alvarez could persuade him to adopt the opposite cause, a third South American scheme had formed in Cochrane's restless mind, which was more grandiose, even, than his previous notions about winning the Napoleonic War with exploding warships and beginning a British revolution in Piccadilly.

He wanted to make Napoleon emperor of South America. Ever since the Frenchman's defeat at Waterloo in 1815, and subsequent confinement to the forlorn mid-Atlantic island of St Helena, Cochrane had considered Napoleon's treatment 'disgraceful', as Cochrane's wife Kitty Barnes noted later in her memoirs. (Her husband's own two-volume *Narrative of Services in the Liberation of Chili, Peru, and Brazil from Spanish and Portuguese Domination* makes no mention, interestingly, of any plans involving the exiled general.) During 1816 and 1817, Cochrane began to wonder: if the Spanish could be driven from South America by O'Higgins and the other nationalists, with help from foreign experts such as himself, then perhaps all the liberated republics could be combined under a single enlightened leader. Napoleon, 'the Greatest Man in the Tide of Time', in Cochrane's opinion, was the obvious candidate. All this strategy required was a trip to St Helena, a favourable meeting with the general, and a successful military campaign against the Spanish. Then the virtually bankrupt and disgraced Scots seaman would end up as kingmaker for an entire continent.

To get all this in motion, he decided to go along with the Chileans' request. He talked to Alvarez. He learned that Chile was having an armed steamship built in London, one of the very first anywhere, to make its navy much more potent. Cochrane offered to oversee the ship's construction and steer it across the Atlantic. But O'Higgins did not want to wait months – the docks, as usual, were working slowly – for his naval saviour to arrive. Spanish ships were sharking about off Valparaíso, and Spanish soldiers were mobilising the indigenous Chilean tribes in the far south. He told Alvarez to have Cochrane signed up and escorted to Chile as soon as possible. The British government, to sharpen the situation, had learned about Cochrane's intentions, and were threatening to pass a Foreign Enlistment Act to forbid British servicemen from working for foreign powers. So in August 1818, with Barnes and their sons, aged five months and four, Cochrane discreetly travelled from London down to the small declining port of Rye on the Sussex coast, put all of them on board a tiny fishing boat, and quietly sailed out from under the town cliffs, along the silting-up channel of the harbour, and south towards a future that would be remembered in every detail by South American museums and statues.

They crossed the Channel to Boulogne, met three of O'Higgins' officials, and boarded a ship for Chile. Cochrane was still hoping to keep to his original plan, and the Chileans seemed to have no objection. Barnes recorded: 'We embarked . . . on the anniversary of the birthday of the First Napoleon, on our way to Valparaíso, but with the intention of making for St Helena, begging for an interview, and ascertaining His Majesty's wishes as regarding placing him on the throne of South America.' However, while they were en route to the island, news reached them that a Spanish army was preparing to march on Santiago from Valdivia. The captain was ordered by the Chilean government to sail non-stop to Valparaíso. Cochrane did not immediately give up on his Napoleonic dream: several weeks after arriving in Chile, he sent one of his senior aides, an acquaintance of the Frenchman, back to St Helena to negotiate. But by then Napoleon was getting ill, and nothing was agreed. And besides, as Cochrane had neared Chile, a different excitement had taken over. Simply by serving the Chileans, he realized, he could probably satisfy his political ideals and his more worldly ambitions. 'I have every prospect', he wrote, 'of making the largest fortune.' He arrived in Valparaíso in late November, the beginning of summer.

At that time of year, the hills look red and green from the sea. Out in the bay, once the milky breakfast fog has gone, they rise in front of you as steeply as seats in an opera house, in a great sunstruck curve of slopes and ravines. The distant buildings and trees appear to be squeezed onto every piece of ground that is less than vertical. Here, halfway up the coast of Chile, there are heavy winter rains and frequent earthquakes; Valparaíso is always sliding off the country's concave rim. It is a restless place, in consequence.

Up closer, from the harbour, its skyline separates out into an impossible jigsaw: red soil and red tin roofs, walls painted yellow or blue, wooden shacks and whitewashed mansions, patches of scrub and rioting flowers, white balustrades and the remains of landslides, roads like ramps for film stunts, foundations like anti-gravity experiments, great collapsing basements abandoned to chickens, endless flights of concrete steps, the salt air corroding them, the sea wind flapping laundry, apartment blocks stubbily looming, dogs wandering, cars honking, the whole jostling lava of traffic and tiles and corrugated iron and flower-pots seeming, even on a calm day, to be flowing slowly downhill towards the old cranes and customs houses by the dockside.

Valparaíso is much larger now than when Cochrane landed – in 1818 the waterfront constituted most of the town; only a few roads tentatively pushed up the ravines – but it is less valuable to Chile. Then, before the Panama Canal, Valparaíso was the first major port for all ships travelling from the Atlantic to the Pacific by the only possible route, via Cape Horn to the south, and it was often the last place for those travelling in the opposite direction to load cargo. Nowadays, the harbour is no longer black with ships; a few slim steel-grey vessels of the Chilean navy and the odd container ship at anchor are all that remain. By day, the tight streets are busy enough, but the restaurants and shops are nervously cheap. The wooden houses are tottering fire traps. Dirty water twists down the alleys, even on dry days, and poor-looking children play among the litter regardless. The one clean and new building is the sandstone arch of the Chilean Congress Chamber, looming over the rooftops like a multiplex on steroids. Pinochet commissioned it to help revive the locality and, more importantly, to keep politicians away from the radical influences of Santiago. Yet the building's height and spotlessness – swivelling cameras and guards with machine guns see to that – only emphasise the picturesque decay all around, the sense of the city as some kind of vast and teeming open-air museum. Besides, the capital is only a two-hour commute inland: congressmen don't tend to linger in Valparaíso after hours.

The air cools sharply in the evenings. The fog creeps back in off the bay. The buses flee the port's old centre for its ever-extending fingers of shanty town and new suburb – typical distant dormitories of the modern free-market Chile. Men with red drinkers' eyes come out, to sleep on benches in the squares behind the waterfront under towering palms planted in more civic-minded times. The dogs roam more confidently, in twos and threes, crossing roads in front of cars. Up in the hills, for all their pretty necklaces of lights, there is the sound of barking, all night long.

My room in Valparaíso, in December 1999, was a top-floor sliver, right under the eaves, of the Brighton Bed & Breakfast. The road up to the thin, perching house was too narrow for the taxi. The building's cottage gables and hushed, net-curtained interior, all dark antiques and bare Victorian floorboards, felt like an old-fashioned, slightly over-dramatised version of the south coast of England. And all around, in this part of town, were similar visions. Along the clifftop from the Brighton ran a terrace of faintly Regency houses called Pasaje Atkinson, with glassed-in porches and dusty roses in their front gardens. Immaculate old Chilean ladies sat inside them, dwarfed by the ceilings. In the quiet sunny grid of streets behind, a freshly painted sign announced St Paul's Church, 'Iglesia Anglicana', a whitewash-and-tin approximation of rural English solidity, albeit protected by Wackenhut private security.

The quickest way down to the centre of Valparaíso from here, as from the city's other hilltops, was by funicular. It was not so much a railway as a box and winches, with daylight juddering through the floor and 'Smith & Sons Southwark 1887' stamped ominously on the turnstiles. More old ladies operated the machinery and took fares, between minding pot plants and hanging up washing in the ticket booths. You find the same sort of cliffside lift in Southend, I noticed later, but safely decommissioned and covered in weeds. At the end of my first funicular ride, I wobbled into the bank across the street. It was a branch of the Banco Santiago now, but inside, under the old dome and chandeliers, it said Banco de Londres. Behind the flak-jacketed private guard, a large wooden First World War memorial listed exclusively English names of Edwardian vintage: Cecil Stanley Adams, Charles John Anderson, Dudley Sutton Ashforth . . .

The queuing customers, in their careful Chilean businessmen's clothes, did not pay them a glance. Valparaíso does not often remember its British past, with the exception of one nineteenth-century Scotsman. The British section of the cemetery is obscure and distant; the papers never bother to explain why a local football team is called Everton; the ancient Twyfords urinals near the naval museum, like all the other traces, are probably of interest only to very thorough tourists. Yet in the more significant recent history of the place, bits of Britishness are always there in the background.

Pinochet was born in Valparaíso on 25 November 1915. His father Augusto, like Hitler's father, was a customs official, working for one of the port's old British trading companies, Williamson Balfour. The Panama Canal had opened the year before, and the port was beginning to struggle. While Augusto was away all day among the long grey stone British warehouses, trying to preserve a century of trade with Liverpool and London, his pale young son, with his prim centre parting and proud little nose, wore sailor suits and dreamed from early childhood of joining the military. He grew up watching the Chilean navy bands marching through the squares and along the grander boulevards, commemorating, among other things, the dates of Cochrane's Pacific triumphs.

Then, as now, Cochrane made a convenient national hero. Being foreign, Cochrane has never been strongly associated with one side or another in Chile's history of fierce and frequent internal political conflicts. Being British and an aristocrat, he has also fitted perfectly with local upper-class traditions of slightly snobbish Anglophilia. So seemingly every town and city in Chile has its Cochrane Street; quite a few have a flattering Cochrane statue; several have whole rooms dedicated to him in their local museums. And nowhere is the worship of this otherwise-forgotten mercenary better established than in Valparaíso.

Behind the main shopping street in the Plaza Intendencia, surrounded by acacias flowering purple and blue, a thick stone obelisk spikes fifty feet upwards, with 'Lord Cochrane' inscribed on its plinth in large letters. The prow of a ship, in black cast iron, thrusts out from the base. Cochrane himself, also in cast iron, stands frozen in mid-stride with long coat agape, a scarf loosely knotted around his slender neck. The whole ensemble dwarfs the square's taxi rank, dozing in the warm teatime sunlight, like one of Saddam Hussein's vast but kitsch monuments in Iraq. Only a sprayed-on red anarchy symbol spoils the effect.

The first of Valparaíso's two Cochrane museums was high above, on a hillside terrace, harder for the graffiti artists to reach. It had most recently been refurbished in 1989, with the sponsorship of Shell Chile, and reopened by Admiral Merino, the head of the Chilean navy and one of Pinochet's most senior allies. A large Chilean flag was flying over the compound of red barrack-like buildings with bars over their windows. Fat old cannons pointed out over the bay, their barrels choked with repainting.

In the hall there was a photograph of the memorial in Westminster Abbey, blown up to actual size, carefully cut out and mounted. There was a portrait of Cochrane with some dusty Chilean headland behind him, an arrogant tilt to his nose, and his hips confidently forward. Another painting showed tiny white figures scrambling up a mountain of a Spanish warship from small boats. An attendant kept a reverent eye on the exhibits as I moved from room to room. But the most sacred objects of all were elsewhere, on another hillside across town, in the Chilean navy's shrine to itself, the Museo Naval Y Maritimo.

*

History is an especially self-conscious business in Chile. It is a fairly new country, with even newer borders: a parched fragment of the far north, taken from Peru in 1879, was handed back as recently as the 1920s. The precise frontier with Argentina in the far south was only agreed in the early 1980s, after a military stand-off. More important than Chile's relative youth is probably its insularity. The Andes to the east, the Pacific's emptiest stretch to the west, the Atacama and further deserts to the north, the Antarctic to the south – the country is effectively a remote island. And in this thin, bony land, most people have been confined, since independence at least, to a few towns and cities, and a few coastal plains and valleys, by the austerity of the soil and climate.

In close-packed places like Valparaíso, surrounded by old buildings, with politicians constantly associating themselves with convenient past figures and national events, the news comes ready-framed with historical resonances. People of all incomes linger by the pavement newsstands for minutes at a time, peering through the cellophane sheets covering the morning and afternoon papers. Every aggressive front page feels intensely politicised. As a slightly severe professor of Chilean history put it, interrogating me over coffee back in England, 'Which Chilean historians have you read? . . . Don't trust any of them.'

The front of the Museo Naval Y Maritimo was as whitewashed as the exhibits inside. There were tourist coaches parked in its broad drive, and parties of tidy schoolchildren trespassing on its trimmed lawns; sprinklers flung the precious water of dry-season Valparaíso to the midday sunshine. And mounted in the grass, as if it were the green baize lining of some giant museum cabinet, were bits of famous warships. A chunk of defeated Peruvian steamship sat under a monkey puzzle, the national tree of Chile. A greyish slice of the Chilean naval vessel *Almirante Cochrane* from 1874, and the bridge of another Chilean ship of that name from 1933, both kept conscientiously free of rust, jutted up at proud angles. Both ships, a plaque noted, had been built 'en Inglaterra'.

Inside, beyond the notices urging reflection on past war heroes and the eternal glories of Chile, a series of large cool rooms opened out. The first was darker than the rest, lit only by three tall stained-glass windows: one containing the figure of O'Higgins, one Arturo Prat, a naval officer martyred by the Peruvians, and one Cochrane himself. The schoolchildren were told to hush. A small girl with her hair in buns stood beneath the Scotsman's stylised profile for some time, watching his pale pink face and dark blue uniform refract the strong sunlight.

In the next two rooms, every aspect of his career inside and outside Chile was on display, with captions (unusually for Chile) in English as well as Spanish: 'El Parlamentario'; 'El Inventor'; the Gillray cartoon from the Westminster election; a print of the Cochrane estate at Culross; O'Higgins' letter asking for help. A cannonball fired by Cochrane at a Spanish fort, like a great malignant grapefruit, had been extracted from the wall in question and mounted. Even a photograph of the unveiling of the statue in Valparaíso, and a medal merely marking the bicentenary of his birth, had been included. The latter was in 1975, two years after Pinochet's coup, when his regime's atrocities were at their most frequent, and most in need of patriotic justification. And yet Neruda, who was a communist and served under Allende, had himself just written his poem praising Cochrane. The admiral's diverse qualities – civil libertarian and chemical warfare pioneer, early democrat and devious warrior – had diverse uses in Chile.

The conclusion of the exhibition was bland: 'After lending his services to Chile,' the final caption read, 'he conserved affection and appreciation for his second motherland . . . For many years he corresponded . . .' Yet an example of that correspondence, in a small glass case nearby, was unexpectedly jarring. The letter was dated 2 August 1826, over three years after Cochrane left Chile, and was addressed to the country's president. In Cochrane's fast, boldly sloping hand, it stated, 'The pittance hitherto paid to me for official service constitutes no adequate reward.' The rest of the letter was too angry to be legible. Cochrane's time in Chile, like the kernel of most patriotic stories, was less straightforward than has been remembered since.

His initial welcome was substantial. O'Higgins came from Santiago to Valparaíso to greet him. The ceremonial dinners and their guest of honour then moved back to the capital. Cochrane, with his expertise at personal myth-making, dressed up as a Highland chief, although his family was not a Highland clan. He was given the title 'Vice-Admiral of Chili, Admiral and Commander in Chief of the Naval Forces of the Republic', and the previous head of the navy announced the Scotsman's appointment in person to the ships' crews. Cochrane was so flattered, after the hostility he had endured from the Royal Navy, that he wrote: 'I decided upon Chili as my future home.'

Not all the crewmen of his half dozen ships were delighted, however, to find a foreign nobleman suddenly their commander. In particular, a Captain Guise and a Captain Spry, both British mercenaries who had arrived before Cochrane, with a ship they had bought from the Royal Navy and sold to Chile, began telling government ministers that he was unsuitable to lead the navy of a nationalist republic. Cochrane won the argument, but a pattern was set: military success would be no more separable from politics here than it was back in Britain; in fact, in a delicate new country like this, the politics would be worse.

In January 1819, he sailed north with his scrappy fleet to attack the Spanish naval base of Callao, just over the border with Peru. But a mutiny on one of his ships delayed them, and by the time they arrived the wind had dropped and an impenetrable summer fog had formed. When it momentarily lifted, Cochrane's vessels were stuck, within range of the 160 cannon defending the mouth of the harbour. 'El Diablo', as the Spanish immediately christened him, had to extricate his ships with shot slicing the air and bits of brain wetting the decks. His element of personal surprise gone, he retreated to a nearby island, and planned an assault by other means. One of the many British subordinates Cochrane had recruited for his Chilean venture was a Mr Goldsack, a former assistant of the British rocketry pioneer William Congreve. Cochrane asked Goldsack to supervise the production of a thousand rockets, which would be packed into an 'explosion vessel' and sent drifting into the harbour. Spanish prisoners were set to work. At the same time, with his usual compartmentalised sense of morality, Cochrane composed a high-minded letter to the colonial viceroy in Peru, in which he proclaimed that 'A British nobleman is a free man, capable of judging between right and wrong, and at liberty to adopt a country and a cause which aim at restoring the rights of oppressed human nature.'

Unfortunately for Cochrane, the Spanish prisoners proved as sly as he was, stuffing the rockets with rags and sand whenever their Chilean guards stopped paying attention. Out on the damp island, in the fog, the rockets kept exploding prematurely and wounding Cochrane's men, or would not work at all. After three weeks, he finally had enough to fill the explosion vessel. The Spanish guns easily sank it.

But he had other tricks. Abandoning Callao, he opted instead for one of his favourite Napoleonic War tactics: establishing a network of sympathisers in ports, and using their information about ship movements to set ambushes. In April, in separate incidents, he captured two Spanish vessels carrying a total of $130,000 in servicemen's wages, 'treasure', and military stores. He was able to increase the wages of his informers, and land small groups of marines on the long, deserted stretches of the Chilean and Peruvian coasts, to sneak inland and seize more. All this gave the appearance of success, at least: in May, he returned to Valparaíso, where his failure at Callao, and to win a decisive victory more generally, was miraculously converted into a story of heroic adventure thwarted, and survival against the odds. The Chilean government, in truth, needed him to come back to base looking 'serenely victorious', as the National Institute of Santiago excitedly put it. The confidence to taunt the Spanish was a rare and valuable local currency in itself.

Yet Cochrane needed a real triumph to sustain his reputation, and with it the new regime. A second attempt on Callao in September, with a giant floating mortar and special rafts to launch rockets, achieved little more than the first. His sailors, he complained, were too inexperienced. The government was not granting him the resources he needed, even for uniforms and wages. Guise and Spry, he suspected, were behind a rumour that he was unfairly distributing what Spanish prize money there was – they coveted his job. Another mutiny was threatening. Cochrane's account, at this point, takes on a certain prickliness:

I was greatly annoyed . . . The bad rockets, and worse faith of the Minister of Marine in not supplying me with the promised troops, were no faults of mine . . . My instructions were carefully drawn up to prevent my doing anything rash . . . At the same time, the Chilian people expected impossibilities; and I had, for some time, been revolving in my mind a plan to achieve one which should gratify them, and allay my own wounded feelings.

The Spanish headquarters at Valdivia was about twenty miles inland, hidden round a bend of a coiling, swampy river in southern Chile. As the Spanish navy's other great Pacific base along with Callao, and as the garrison which was intended to start the country's recapture, the narrow riverside grid of the town itself was protected by earthworks and fat, cylindrical guard towers. But long before anyone might confront those, they would have to negotiate the tightening throat of the river estuary. It had forts along its dark wooded northern shore, and along the south. It had a fort on the island in midstream. It had cannon on clifftops and at water level, at every inlet and on every peninsula. Right across the estuary, and deep into it, the blue-grey water was covered with invisible but lethal fields of fire, overlapping semicircles and triangles calculated according to the newest defensive theory. And should any attacker emerge from them, each fort was its own piece of precise military geometry, star-shaped and with walls thick as a house. They could hold out for weeks, or until a counter-attack was mounted.

On 18 January 1820, Cochrane appeared at the river mouth. He had a single ship, a Spanish frigate captured the year before, and from it he flew a Spanish flag. Valdivia, he knew, was expecting a friendly frigate; he was able to sail up the estuary towards the guns, and signal for a pilot to be sent out to guide him further upriver. The pilot arrived with a formal welcoming committee – an officer and four soldiers – all of whom were quickly captured and questioned. With their information, Cochrane began nosing his ship in and out of the river's navigable channels, looking for landing sites and refuges from the forts' lines of fire. Gradually, the watching Spanish realised that something inappropriate was happening. They started firing. Cochrane withdrew out of range, out to sea.

Two weeks later, he returned with three ships and 250 soldiers borrowed from the nearest Chilean base. The frigate, in the meantime, had nearly sunk on a rock, when Cochrane, short of officers he trusted, fell asleep one apparently calm night, after days of continuously being on watch. 'With some difficulty', he persuaded the crew not to abandon ship; they had to bail out five feet of water from the cracked hold with buckets. Almost all the soldiers' ammunition was now waterlogged and useless. 'I cared little,' writes Cochrane, perhaps with retrospective bluster. 'The necessity of using the bayonet in our anticipated attack' had the advantage that 'to facing this weapon the Spaniards had . . . a rooted aversion.' After lunch on 3 February, leaving the leaking frigate out of sight, he guided his two smaller vessels, now overloaded with soldiers, towards the only beach in the estuary, right under one of the forts.

One way to understand what happened next is to look down from the walls of the Cochrane rooms of the Museo Naval in Valparaíso, with their hagiographical knick-knacks, and take in the enormous three-dimensional model that fills the middle of the first room. In painstakingly sculpted green contours, and stretches of miniature estuary, and tiny stone-grey fortifications, the battlefield is laid out for your appreciation. There is the beach where Cochrane landed his soldiers despite a sudden gale; the promontory behind which they sheltered from Spanish fire until nightfall; the steep path that half his troops climbed in silence to the first stronghold; the open ground across which the other half advanced, in the darkness, making as much noise as possible; the defences which the first group quietly infiltrated amid the shots and shouting; the courtyard where they fired their few cartridges to further panic the Spanish; and the gate through which the fort's garrison fled, assuming an assault by an overwhelming force. The rest of Valdivia's citadels are each marked on the model by a red light, and a note of the time they surrendered: 2130, 2150, 2215 . . . Cochrane's soldiers, hugely outnumbered, half-trained, set in motion an accelerating panic. One fort's Spanish troops would run terrified to the next, that fort in turn would appear to be surrounded by Chilean bayonets, both garrisons would then flee to another bastion, and so on, throughout the night, until the last one gave in to Cochrane at eight o'clock the next morning. Around the edges of the model, there were buttons to press that lit up Cochrane's startling victory in stages. The schoolchildren's fingers, 179 years after the event, still had to be prised away by their teacher.

Another way to understand these events is to go to Valdivia. Cochrane sailed for weeks to get there from Valparaíso; I flew in an afternoon, via Santiago. But much the same landscape followed us south. The dusty greens and browns of central Chile, over the 700 miles, turned darker and wetter. Volcanoes like children's sketches, with perfect cones and snow still in early summer, marched along the eastern horizon where the Andes started. The fields of the coastal plains and valleys grew richer and greener as the sun lowered and the latitude cooled.

Valdivia's airport felt like a Cotswolds station in June at the end of the weekly commute: surrounded by waist-high pasture, its single building warm from the afternoon, its Friday-evening clusters of wives and waiting children who all seemed to know each other. Only wealthier Chileans fly – everyone else must navigate the maze of privatised coach services – and those disembarking and greeting were dressed for the part: tweed jackets and checked landowners' shirts for the men, blonde rinses and Jilly Cooper earrings for the women, tousled straw hair for the immaculate children. Everybody was tall and lightly tanned – not naturally dark and generally short like those Chileans with less European blood, who make up a majority of the population, and are less likely to be prosperous, or to look favourably on the rule and legacy of General Pinochet. The body language in the airport was relaxed but grand – a sense of entitlement in every slouch, every loud conversation and lift of the sunglasses – until the mint-condition suitcases spilled onto the carousel, unlined male hands grabbed them, and the car park emptied with the crunch of impatient four-wheel drives on loose gravel, heading off for dinner in distant haciendas.

Valdivia is still a watery town overlooked by fat towers. But earthquakes have flattened the rest of the Spanish buildings. Instead there are concrete shopping streets, and the more recent mansions of nineteenth-century German immigrants, barely inhabited now, it seems, with moss on their roofs and windows as though it falls from the town's habitual lid of grey cloud. Boatyards and a tangy fish market fill the river bank; otherwise there is not much to do except sit, slightly chilled, and watch the dark green currents tug at the remains of jetties and wonder how palm trees grow this far south.

The sun set on my first evening and never came back. The only way properly to see Cochrane's forts downstream was by boat, on a pre-booked tour, the earliest of which left at one o'clock the following afternoon. So the next morning I went to look at another museum. The first room, inevitably, was Valdivia's tribute to Cochrane: medals, a model of his slim frigate, a monogrammed cane on a long red cushion, roped off on a table top. As I was peering, a woman's loud voice, with an accent somewhere between rattling Chilean and smart English, said behind me in English: 'Look. He's in Westminster Abbey. In London. And it says here all about Chile . . .'

She was blonde, fortyish, in pristine head-to-toe denim. She was talking to three equally freckled, pale-skinned young children. Behind her in the doorway was her husband, also tall and pale, wearing a light-blue polo shirt and a cream panama hat. I had seen them all on the plane. He spotted my notebook, and strode across. Was I a historian? What was I writing about? Was my book 'politically motivated'? He spoke like his wife, arms confidently folded. His eyes were very blue beneath his white hair; he stared hard as I answered, for a minute or two, and then turned without warning and walked briskly off across the old polished floorboards, into the next net-curtained room, in search of more stimulus. 'You must go to the cemetery at Punta Arenas,' he said over his shoulder. I heard their voices booming from the museum's upstairs rooms for the next half hour, drowning out the guide they had commandeered.

The tour boats left from a concrete quayside lined with small ticket booths. On their wooden exteriors were worn painted route maps and the names of the forts offered. Between the booths, men with slightly hustling manners loitered, and darted out whenever anyone passing gave the boats as much as a glance. The cheapest tour cost about £2, in something the size of a large rowing boat, and lasted a couple of hours; the most expensive was over £20, included an aperitif, lunch and *onces* ('elevenses', copied from the English but taken at teatime in Chile), and would cruise back and forth across Cochrane's battlefield all afternoon and into the evening. I paid the extra.

The first few hours did not feel terribly worth it. The big glassed-in cruiser chugged slowly downriver from Valdivia. The town slowly tapered away: muddy timberyards, more boatyards, half-built vessels rusting and forgotten in the grass, smoke struggling out of chimneys in the wet air. The stone-coloured clouds steadily lowered, first to mist and then to rain. The river widened. Endless flat islands of reeds appeared, dim forest rose along both banks, the white dots of other tour boats crept along the horizon, then disappeared into the greyness. Under Pinochet, the bodies of local leftwingers were easy to dispose of among Valdivia's waterways.

There were about two dozen people on board – mostly Chileans, a few Germans – in tables of four beside the long windows of the open-plan cabin. For a while, the younger passengers would get up and go out on deck to take pictures. But then the rain, the cabin's warmth and the approach of lunch – with much careful form-filling for our choice of main course, in the style of Chilean officialdom down the ages, democratic and otherwise – exerted a growing pull indoors. A quartet of stout middle-aged Chilean ladies played cards without once looking out of the windows. Someone else fell asleep after the heavy slabs of fried salmon. Wine came only by the bottle. The boat chugged on. And then, dead in front, was the Isla Mancera.

This was the central point of the Spaniards' Maginot Line: an all-seeing fort on a rocky black island, with cannon aimed like telescopes out over the estuary. Now it was as speedily occupied and abandoned by tour parties as by Cochrane's marines. We had to wait for another tour boat to free up a space on the jetty. Then we were landed and marched up a stony path, past another group coming down, a few pretty houses with wooden fences and chickens, and a row of souvenir stalls with the grass grown thick round their foundations. Our guide was a hurrying black-haired man who had first pressed a tour itinerary into my hand on the quayside in Valdivia. He announced several times that we had half an hour on the island, and that the boat would leave without us if necessary. In the event, he gave us about twenty minutes.

It was long enough to sense the fort's humiliation. Its high grey walls were almost pristine, except for moss and blackening by rain. No heroic siege had churned up its earthworks, or pockmarked its narrow entrance. From its thick battlements, you could identify every boat in the river mouth, even through the showers. A new-looking sign by the gatehouse still insisted on how impregnable and effective the fortress had originally been, as if the colonial troops were still in residence. On the way back down, a flock of sheep suddenly appeared in front of us on the path, and retreated skittering and jostling towards the harbour. It was hard not to be reminded of the Spanish.

A small group of damp Chilean men were changing out of nineteenth-century military uniforms when we arrived at the next fort, on the south side of the estuary. It was really raining now: the clouds were halfway down the steep hillside, inky squalls were blowing off the water. We had missed the daily re-creation of Cochrane's attack. There was just a glimpse of the approximate costumes, with their rough gold braid, long boots and tunics, and drooping triangular hats. Then rolls of *pesos* were palmed, and the men hurried off to their cars. This fort was even more musclebound and helpless than the last: walls like solid rock, long lines of dripping cannon, but its entrance fatally near the waterline. Under a pine tree, in near darkness, the black-haired man quickly explained how the Scotsman, whom he called an Englishman, had captured these battlements with so few men. People laughed under their umbrellas at the cheekiness and cowardice. Then we rushed back to the boat for *onces*. At the last minute before we boarded, though, I noticed a set of black busts on a stained white plinth beside the jetty. They were of naval heroes, predictably enough, but Cochrane did not have pride of place. After seizing Valdivia at the cost of seven dead, and appearing to secure the country's survival, his status in Chile was enormous. And that, for the new republic's more jealous politicians, and for its most egocentric warrior, quickly became a problem.

When he arrived back in Valparaíso in late February 1820, having set up an administration in Valdivia, and having decided to preserve its fortifications entirely on his own initiative, Cochrane did not receive the welcome he expected. The Minister of Marine, José Ignacio Zenteno, whom he had already confronted over the navy's thin resources, publicly scolded Cochrane for recklessness and operating too independently. The Spanish had been effectively driven from Chile, except for a few remote outposts in the islands of the far south; the victory at Valdivia had secured a loan of a million pounds for the government from the City of London; but these achievements, like Cochrane's smaller-scale triumphs in Britain, only soured relations with his superiors. The contents pages of his South American memoir, drawn out and dense with self-justifying detail, give a flavour of what ensued:

Return to Valparaíso . . . Enthusiastic reception . . . Chagrin of the ministry . . . Mutinous spirit of the seamen in consequence of their captures being appropriated by Government . . . Appointment of flag captain against my wishes . . . Corruption of parties in the Administration . . . Refusal to obey orders . . . San Martin's accusations against me . . . I demand his trial . . . The squadron taken from me . . . I accept invitation from Brazil . . .

Essentially, Cochrane wanted complete freedom as a military commander, and the right to intervene in Chilean public life when it was not to his satisfaction. (Perhaps the young Pinochet found inspiration in more than the admiral's sea battles.) As a personal headquarters, he bought a coastal estate a few miles north of Valparaíso, at Quintero. Like his father at Culross, he planned to make the land the centre of an economic empire. He ordered seeds and agricultural equipment from Britain that were entirely new to Chile. He imported machinery to roll copper for a new national coinage. And he set up the country's first lithographic printing press: his polemics were to be nationally distributed. When he also suggested that the bay of Quintero would make a safer anchorage and naval base than Valparaíso, accusations followed that he was harbouring larger ambitions: 'I was credibly informed, that as the whole population was with me, I must intend, when opportunity served, to set myself up as the ruler of the Republic!'

During 1821 and 1822, his estate came to look more and more like a rival power centre to Valparaíso and Santiago. Back on shore after expelling the Spanish from Peru, in an ill-tempered land and sea operation with the militarily cautious but politically ambitious San Martin, Cochrane spent as much time as possible in his private hills and coves. Dissidents against whichever faction was currently dominant in the

Chilean government collected around him. A general in the south of Chile began planning a coup, asked him for help. When Cochrane failed to say yes or no, the rebels started marching on the capital regardless.

While Cochrane was stalling, in November 1822, an earthquake struck Valparaíso and the area around. One church and twenty houses were left standing; Quintero and Cochcrane's half-built country house were badly shaken. His prospects in Chile seemed to be darkening. From other countries, meanwhile, came flattering pleas for help with less fulfilled independence struggles. He considered Greece; he considered Mexico; then, on the 29th, he announced he was leaving Chile to lead the naval forces of the Brazilian nationalists against Portugal. The besieged Chilean government abruptly forgot its quarrels with him, and refused to accept his resignation. But Cochrane was not going to start following orders now. He spent his last few weeks in Chile living in tents amid the ruins of Quintero, accepting requests from his junior officers to follow him to Brazil, and running off farewell messages and final polemics on his printing press. Such as:

Chilenos – My Fellow Countrymen!
The common enemy of America has fallen in Chili. Your tricoloured flag waves on the Pacific . . . Some internal commotions agitate Chili. It is not my business . . . It is now four years since the sacred cause of your independence called me to Chili. I assisted you to gain it. I have seen it accomplished. It only remains to preserve it . . . You know that independence is purchased at the point of the bayonet.

On 18 January 1823, with the rebels having almost reached Santiago and Valparaíso, and the Chilean government that had hired him within days of collapse, Cochrane sailed out of the bay of Quintero in a chartered vessel. On the way he passed the wreck of a Spanish ship that he had captured months before. It had drifted ashore while the government was deciding who to sell it to, and had been breaking up ever since, in full view of his house, 'tenanted only by shellfish'. Cochrane makes it sound like the final straw.

He was forty-seven. He promised then that he was leaving Chile 'for a time'. But though he lived another thirty-eight years, he never returned. He kept in contact almost solely to argue about money. Cochrane claimed back pay in huge amounts. Meanwhile the Chilean government demanded he first account for his naval expenditure in every detail. ('Imputed error of *one dollar*!' Cochrane writes, defending 'the purchase of 756 gals. of gin, &c. &c.') In 1845, the government agreed to pay him £6,000, yet he claimed that still left him £19,000 out of pocket from his Chilean campaign. In 1857, when Cochrane was eighty-one, President Manuel Montt made a speech to the Chilean Senate and Chamber of Deputies giving official thanks for his contribution to independence, and awarding him an admiral's pay for the rest of his life. Cochrane finally relented a little, calling Montt an 'excellent president'. But Cochrane's memoirs, published two years later, still settled scores up to the last page.

And another year later, he was dead. He had been rehabilitated by the Royal Navy by then, his family title and place in Westminster Abbey had been restored, and he had been officially cleared of the City scandal from five decades previously. After Chile, as before, Cochrane lived vividly and very publicly as a mixture of curmudgeon and tireless maverick: fighting the Portuguese in Brazil, the Turks in Greece, and then returning to England to campaign again for navy reform and new forms of warfare. During the Crimean War, a white-haired, rather broader Cochrane presented plans for a 'secret weapon' (sulphur gas) to the government. As usual, he was frustrated, but other inventions possessed him to the end: steam-engined gunboats, digging tunnels by air pressure, using bitumen to surface roads. It can seem as if his four years in Chile were just one episode out of many.

Except that Cochrane's great-great-great-grandson, the fifteenth Earl of Dundonald, would not agree with you. Since 1992, he has been Chile's honorary consul in Britain. He has organised trade fairs with the Chilean commercial attaché. He has sat on the Parliamentary Committee on Latin America. He has been officially guided on a tour of Chile: 'The navy are very helpful, *still*.' He has retained old family friends and relations there (he retains no connections in Brazil, or Greece, or Peru). And he has made speeches in the House of Lords on Chilean affairs – obscure or, more recently, much less so.

We met in a smart Edinburgh hotel in September 2000, six months after Pinochet had flown back to Santiago. It was a grey morning with summer gone, quite early (as Dundonald had briskly suggested on the phone), with the wind off the sea as chilly as a bad day in Valdivia. He was a few minutes late; Americans in thick new jumpers, today's confident world-conquerors, were chattering in the pink lobby. Lulling music played and the radiators behind the tartan armchairs were full on. The distant rippling sound of car tyres on cobbles from the square outside just made it through the double glazing.

He walked in, tall like Cochrane. His face, though, was plumper. His eyes were busy like his ancestor's, but more amiable, and he wore the loose greenish clothes of a landowning civilian. He was thirty-nine, and ran a property company. 'We've just set up an IT subsidiary,' he said, in a comfortable drawling voice. He was interested in speech-recognition technology: 'I love gadgets!' His cheeks were pink when he smiled. He ordered coffee and shortbread.

He talked about 'Cochrane' with alternating coolness and fervour. 'Everybody [commanding warships then] was in it for the money – including my ancestor. The Chileans hit him at the right time . . . They were the only country who paid him. I don't know what happened to all the cash . . .' He gave the shrugging look of someone conveying old gossip: 'I know his son was a complete spendthrift.' Cochrane, he conceded, 'must have been a very abrasive character.' But a few minutes and sips of coffee later, the romance of the Cochrane legend began to seep into his words. 'We've got a lock of Napoleon's hair at home,' said Dundonald. Then, suddenly animated, he started defending the admiral's more erratic moments: first his failed weapons innovations ('they never did a fullscale trial!') then the City scandal. 'He was a very fair man,' said the earl in a sharper voice than before, half out of his armchair, arms aloft and persuading the air. 'He'd simply left instructions with his broker . . .'

The family connection with Chile felt a safer subject. 'They're charming people as a nation,' he said, smiling again. 'You couldn't find a nicer nation. They don't have an agenda.' He had visited in 1996: 'We did a big trip, top to bottom. I thought the Atacama Desert was stunning . . . I love the deep south of Chile – Valdivia is an amazing piece of water. We were taken out on it in a Chilean navy boat.' He leaned back a little, became expansive: 'I've made quite a number of friends in the Chilean navy over the years. They've always had their officers here on training – their marines and navy, you know, were founded on British lines – and they have always bought our ships secondhand.' He looked at the plate of shortbread, half lost in thought. 'Always had a crew over here.'

It was the Chileans who had asked him to be honorary consul. Since Alvarez first approached Cochrane in 1817, there had always been 'close contact' between the family and the London embassy. But now the Pinochet affair had introduced an awkward element. 'I'm told the

Chileans are unlikely to buy anything from us for twenty-five years,' said Dundonald gravely. When the general was arrested in London, 'There were quite a lot of upset people in the secondhand-warship-selling business at the Ministry of Defence. There was a very major arms sale to Chile very shortly after the Falklands.' What did he think of Pinochet himself? He paused. The lobby was deserted except for the cleaners now. 'He probably did a lot of good for the country. Killed some people. Not a very nice guy.' Dundonald said he had grown up with news of Allende and his 'Cuban advisers . . . I remember discussions over the kitchen table about what the hell was going on in Chile. It was like a country gone mad. There were friends of the family in Chile who were pro- and anti-Allende.' At least the coup, he said, had led to a good business environment, 'a proper corporate structure there.' And, he added, 'Let's face it. Thatcher imported quite a lot of ideas from Pinochet.' His smile returned. 'A lot of people don't seem to want to know that!'

Besides speaking up for Pinochet in the Lords, he had written critical letters to Jack Straw, and had had 'lots of chats' with the Chilean ambassador about the matter. He had also been in touch with Lord Lamont, the most public British figure in the campaign for Pinochet's release after Margaret Thatcher. These contacts, and his instincts, had crystallised an argument in his mind that ambitiously placed one of the early nineteenth century's most daringly pro-democratic military liberals on the same side as one of the late twentieth century's most unyieldingly anti-democratic military dictators. 'In 1820,' Dundonald began, his voice dropping into weighty public-speaking mode, 'the British government passed the Foreign Enlistment Act to stop people like my ancestor interfering abroad. And now our government is meddling in Chile's politics.' He stopped, looking satisfied at the comparison. He suggested I refer to his speeches on Pinochet in Hansard.

It was almost lunchtime. The earl had things to do. If I wanted to meet again, he said, I should check that he was not going to be at his non-Edinburgh residence, just north of Oban on the west coast of Scotland. Or about to fly down to London for work. It sounded a nice existence. But did he ever dream of following Cochrane over the Andes for good? He answered stiffly at first: 'If we continue to go down the route of the over-nannying state, I could conceive a time of not living in Europe.' Then a trace of mischief roughened his smooth vowels. 'If you go to South America, there are not that many laws . . .'

4

'The England of the Pacific'

Among Cochrane's noisy contributions to the new Chile, there had been a quieter one. He had helped open up the country to capitalism. Given his nationality, and his home country's increasing dominance of the international economy in the early nineteenth century, there was one likely beneficiary of the removal of the Spanish. Acquisitive and adventurous Britons had been eyeing the Chilean coast for centuries for potential anchorages. At first, their interest had been mostly destructive. The shelling and burning and looting of vulnerable ports, in Chile as elsewhere in the Spanish empire, was a favoured occupation of British pirates and more official warships. Sir Francis Drake raided Valparaíso in 1578; over two and a half centuries later, visiting the small coastal towns further north, Charles Darwin recorded in *The Voyage of the Beagle* that you could still hear Chileans 'relate the atrocious actions of the buccaneers'. One old woman he was told about, who had recently been introduced to a visiting English sea captain, reportedly 'remarked how wonderfully strange it was that she should have lived to dine in the same room with an Englishman; for she remembered as a girl, that twice, at the mere cry of "Los Ingleses", every soul, carrying what valuables they could, had taken to the mountains.'

Despite, or perhaps because of the British reputation for rapacity, one of the first acts of the Chilean republic was to allow foreign traders into its ports, where before there had officially been a Spanish monopoly. Smuggling via British and other vessels had already been going on for years. By the time Cochrane arrived, there was an established colony of British merchants in Valparaíso, with a few seafront warehouses and the beginnings of a smart residential quarter in the hills above. They traded in agricultural exports, like Chilean wheat during the European winter, and all year round in the manufactured imports required by the new state. They quickly acquired local social status and national political influence. As early as 1819, there was a British traders' association, which the government consulted on economic matters. Cochrane relied on these merchants 'to obtain considerable quantities of naval and military stores'. He also persuaded them to pay a subscription towards his impoverished navy for the protection and the creation of further commercial opportunities. For the first time, an important connection had been established: between the financial health – the survival, in fact – of the Chilean government, and the prosperity of British business interests.

This unequal relationship would operate until almost the end of the century. In the mean time Chile, or at least its more prosperous urban sections, turned from a colonial backwater of dirt roads and bored garrisons to a much-envied South American state, with modern street lighting and European pretensions. The breakdown of this system would only come when the local politicians and public finally found the British influence over their country intolerable. That was during the late 1880s and early 1890s, when the Chilean ambitions of one John Thomas North, the Nitrate King, swelled to controlling the business of entire towns and regions and, according to some, deposing the president who tried to stop him.

By then, North and Cochrane had helped entrench an even deeper pattern of relations between money-making and politics in Chile. The use of force to clear the way for profit, by the military and the government, had become a reflex. Pinochet, with his combined programme of torture sessions and privatisations, would be its ultimate exponent. It was perhaps not so surprising after all that the current Earl of Dundonald should see a kinship between the general and the admiral.

In October 1821, while Cochrane's warships stopped for repairs and supplies at the Mexican port of Guayaquil, he made one of his lesser-known but more startling speeches. Addressing the local population, who, like the Chileans, had been newly liberated from the Spanish, he gave a sermon on the potential benefits of independence. In it he anticipated Pinochet's economic prescription for Chile – and the free-market policies that have since spread from there to the rest of the world – with some precision:

Let foreign merchants who bring capital . . . be allowed to settle freely; and thus a competition will be formed, from which all must reap advantage . . . Let

45

your customs duties be moderate, in order to promote the greatest possible consumption . . . Let every man do as he pleases as regards his own property . . . because every individual will watch over his own with more zeal than senates, ministers, or kings.

Cochrane did also talk about political freedoms. And his faith in free trade was hardly unusual for a British entrepreneur of the period. But it was his enthusiasm for using any military means necessary that helped start Chile's first economic surge. In 1810, an average of less than fifty ships a year had been anchoring in Valparaíso. By 1830, it was over 200. By 1870, the annual total of vessels calling at Chilean ports in general had reached 4,000. Meanwhile, the country's trade across the Andes with its South American neighbours declined. It even became cheaper to procure coal for Valparaíso from Britain than from the Chilean mines around Concepción, a town only a few hundred miles south. Chile had effectively become one colony or semi-colony among many in Britain's global maritime economy.

Like those of Canada and Portugal, Chile's currency was linked to the gold standard. Business in Valparaíso was carried out in sterling, with English as the usual language of trade. Between a third and two thirds of Chile's exports went to Britain, and between a third and a half of Chile's imports came by the same route. In 1820, the country's main customs house moved to Valparaíso. In 1822, the well-known British trading company Antony Gibbs and Sons set up an office there. In 1825, a British consulate was established. In 1830, the population of the town reached 20,000, one in six of them foreigners. In 1834, taxes on imports and exports were cut sharply, and a system of licensed warehouses was set up, where goods could be stored for years at low cost while their owners waited for their value to rise. The geographical position of the port, at the centre of the Pacific trade routes and the western seaboard of South America, made it the cramped holding pen for everything from mother-of-pearl from Tahiti to surplus English sea captains. Most months, the South American Squadron of the Royal Navy patrolled offshore, offering the local administration an additional layer of protection from the sort of attacks the British themselves had once mounted, and a reminder of Chile's subordinate status.

Visiting British observers, of course, did not much care to notice the exploitative nature of this new economy. Away from the waterfront and the British quarter, much of Valparaíso was an unplanned, bursting slum. Behind the hills, the valley estates that filled the merchant ships were worked, through the blazing inland summers and clammy winters, by a near-feudal arrangement of small tenants paying their rent to great landlords by compulsory labour. But writers such as Maria Graham, a close friend of Cochrane who compiled a *Journal Of A Residence in Chile, During the Year 1822*, preferred to focus on the novelty of British influence on the far slopes of the Andes:

Retail shops for all sorts of European goods are nearly as common at Valparaíso as in any town of the same size in England. The English shops are more numerous than any. English tailors, shoemakers, saddlers, and inn-keepers, hang out their signs in every street. The number of piano-fortes brought from England is astonishing . . . It is curious, at this distance from home, to see specimens of such people as in Miss Austin's [sic] admirable novels.

Graham went to dances. She went on picnics in the hills. The wind-bent trees and the rocky sea views and the mild coastal weather reminded her of 'the finest parts of Devonshire'. Such reassuring feelings were reinforced by the availability in Valparaíso – 'vale of paradise' in Spanish – of tea and London magazines, cricket matches and British schools, local British newspapers and local horse racing by British rules. This pleasant hilltop world, and the success of British speculators and seamen in the rougher dockside below, established a rosy British view of Chile that proved surprisingly enduring. As late as 1899, a Scottish writer called W. Anderson Smith could publish a long book entitled *Temperate Chile: A Progressive Spain*. 'This remarkable State,' he began, 'a really amiable people, with whom I found myself much in sympathy . . .' The Chileans were 'so conservative and law-abiding . . . the English of the Pacific'. They were perfectly suited, he went on, 'for the task of eventually representing us, at least in South America, in some of our most marked and valuable characteristics.'

Some Chileans agreed. Diego Portales, the dominant figure of mid-nineteenth-century Chilean politics, said that he wanted his country to become 'the England of the Pacific'. He half joked about lending Chile to Britain for a few years' tuition. In 1833, the year after the first British Parliamentary Reform Act, he announced a constitutional arrangement for Chile along similar lines: an electorate limited by a property-owning qualification to the rich, the middle classes, and skilled craftsmen; a mainly aristocratic Congress with power to regularly approve, or challenge, the head of state's budget, military spending and taxation. And as in Britain, the success of this recipe in bringing stability was proudly exaggerated to Chile's neighbours for the rest of the century.

The Englishman who did most to unravel this conservative 'model republic', as *The Times* crowned it in 1880, was one of the thousands of less exotic professionals who followed the British mercenaries, sailors and merchants out to Chile. As the Chilean economy modernised and diversified during the mid-nineteenth century, patchily but surely, so it required people who knew about industrial enterprises. Britain was the world centre for this sort of expertise. Engineers and miners, builders of canals and railways, train drivers, chemists, even carpenters and, in the wind-chilled south of the country, sheep farmers with the latest breeding and ranching techniques – all of these arrived and found easy work in Chile. 'A prosperous body of freelancers,' wrote Smith later, 'have had the ball at their feet since the independence of Chile . . . They seek to trade upon the name of Englishman . . . Succeeding by minding their own business, [they] have done much to aid in developing the country.' He added a qualification, though. 'They have done little or nothing to ingratiate themselves with the people.'

5

Desert Capitalism

The subject of North came up about half an hour into my interview with Professor Miguel Benado at the University of Chile in Santiago. It was a roastingly hot afternoon, even for the capital on the cusp of December. It was late 2000; Pinochet had long since returned to Chile from London; the professor, who taught philosophy, was free to talk about less pressing topics. I had enough time before the interview to get lost on the way to his office.

First, I had tried to cross the crumbling four-lane highway that split the university from the city centre. At every shadeless crossroads, the sun prickled and the sawteeth of the Andes, Santiago's suntrap, hazily distant, mocked me with their snowcaps. A succession of rattling old yellow buses and surging new Mercedes had failed to stop. Then, after a bolt across the potholes, there had been the distracting maze of the university itself: soupy courtyards, long corridors, dim dilapidated sections from the 1930s, a new computer block. Pinochet had shelled the campus during the coup, I remembered, to quell decades of political hubbub on these very parquet floors. Now some of the students were wearing suits. There was still a Young Socialists' noticeboard near the main entrance, as big and bright red as if Allende were still president, but it was quite empty. The less conventional-looking students, I noticed, were head-to-toe in Nike.

Benado, who was from a left-wing background, was resigned but droll about modern Chile's market-driven universities. 'I teach in many places,' he said, with a shrug in his dry voice and an overnight bag behind his chair. 'This is the standard solution for many academics in Chile.' Here, he had half an office, plain and temporary-looking except for a few shelves, a desk in a corner for his long frame to lean over, and

49

two prints of Oxford University. He had been a graduate student there in the 1980s. 'I was very active in the campaign that denied Thatcher a doctorate,' he mentioned, smiling. His lean face had the beginnings of a flattering beard, black stubble flecked with grey, that matched his slim black clothes and slim black Oxford shoes. As he spoke, he swivelled casually in his chair, facing away from his desk towards the hard, upright sofa he had gestured me to. Or else he paced the room, mock-theatrically, at one point striding to the window to insult a distant statue. There was black humour in his view of Chilean history: he brandished a paperback he had written to mark the twenty-fifth anniversary of the coup, as if it were a cheap novel. Perhaps he needed his sarcasm: his father, someone else told me, had been in Allende's cabinet. Benado's years in Oxford and elsewhere in Europe had been an enforced exile. Now he was back, his office had a perfect view – across the rushing highway and Santiago's river, foaming chocolate-brown with snowmelt – of the headquarters of Chile's privatised telephone company ENTEL, built in the shape of a gigantic mobile phone.

We had been discussing Cochrane slightly distractedly, the rush-hour noise seeping into the cool dark room, when Benado said, 'Of course, a more interesting figure than Cochrane was North. There is no street named after North. He is known only to historians.' The professor abruptly forgot about telling anecdotes. With a good lecturer's crispness, he began to explain Chile's late-nineteenth-century expansion northwards, its war in 1879 with Bolivia and Peru, its civil war twelve years later and how this prefigured the 1973 coup, its erratic early tax structure and reliance on foreign loans – much, in fact, of what had formed the country's character – all in terms of North's influence. He recommended fellow academics who had studied British mining in Chile and its consequences. And then he swivelled in his chair again, the tease re-entered his voice, and he raced off on another train of thought about Pinochet being obsessed by Napoleon.

John Thomas North, when he is remembered at all, is not thought of fondly by Chileans. Patriotic historians, and left-wing ones, have traditionally placed him at the centre of a network of exploitative, meddling foreigners during the decades following independence. Chileans are often very attached to their actual land, and North – bulky, overbearing, an easily caricatured Victorian capitalist – dug it up, crushed it up, and exported it for profit. The sweat expended in this process was almost all Chilean. The investors who benefitted were almost all in

London – or so this simple but potent argument runs. When the government belatedly tried to limit his activities, he sought to undermine it. Far from defeating the country's enemies as Cochrane did, North, indirectly at the very least, helped divide Chile. And, again unlike Cochrane, no Chilean asked him to come in the first place.

North's life before he crossed the South Atlantic was promising but unheroic. He was born in Leeds on 30 January 1842. His father was a coal merchant, comfortable enough to pay for the education of his three children. Their house was in Holbeck, just south of the city centre beyond the railway arches. The area was cramped redbrick, semi-respectable. The remains of the North residence at Meadow Lane may be glimpsed, nowadays, as rubble beneath the tyres of parked cars belonging to staff of an '87,000 sq. ft. Customer Care Centre for BT Cellnet'.

In magazine articles written after he became rich, and in his more favourable British obituaries, North's early years are always described in an approving Victorian moral shorthand: 'he rose from the humblest ranks,' was 'born in a cottage in a back street – almost a slum'. During the nineteenth century, especially in Britain, North got much more and much better press than historians would subsequently grant him. Yet the few concrete details of his early life detectable amid the rhetoric sound pleasant enough. He played cricket. He became an apprentice mechanical engineer at fifteen. He worked for Shaw, North and Watson, a firm of millwrights and shipwrights in the nearby industrial suburb of Hunslet. One of the company's partners was a cousin of his father's.

After eight years, North moved to a bigger engineering firm in Hunslet called Fowler and Company. In 1865, at twenty-three, he married Jane Woodhead, the daughter of an important Conservative member of the city council. Much later, when there was a North legend to burnish, he would describe her as someone from the next-door factory. The two of them started 'on a joint salary of twenty-six shillings a week', according to a pamphlet called *Life and Career of the Late Col. North: How He Made His Millions, as Told by Himself*, published shortly after his death in 1896. The pamphlet continues, with a pinch of melodrama: 'In the ordinary course of things, I should have worked all my life in a Leeds engineering shop.' But then in 1866, or 1867, or 1869, depending on who you believe, Fowler and Company won a contract in South America. North's account quickens into an adventure:

They considered that, as one of the best young workmen in the engine sheds, I might go out there and possibly 'better myself' . . . I offered to go out for the ordinary salary I was getting . . . namely, 18s. a week, and, penniless as I was, even offered to pay my own travelling expenses.

The contract, North claims, was to build a railway in Peru. Other accounts, more convincingly, say he actually went to northern Chile to supervise the assembly of two steam locomotives of the type Fowler and Company were famous for exporting. The border at the time was very unclear, being a line through a desert, and restless foreign entrepreneurs were constantly crossing it. Either way, North's version is worth quoting further for the quality of his self-mythologising:

Well, the projected railway didn't come to much . . . But we all got our wages and, in the mean time, I was looking around for myself . . . One day I wandered down to a creek, and there I saw a rusty old steamer which had been laid up as useless. I suddenly conceived of the idea . . . that I might trade up and down the river with it, touching with grain and various provisions at the towns and villages . . . [After buying the steamer with the last of the wages] I managed to get a cargo of goods somehow, and then I plied my tiny vessel with satisfactory results. One day, when Chili and Peru were at war, my little vessel happened to come down to the mouth of the river at the critical moment. There was a Peruvian warship on guard, and they signalled to me that they were starving . . . I was able to relieve their immediate necessities, and when the war was over I claimed some compensation . . . There came to me a concession to work a hitherto unexplored field of 'nitrates'.

The British were already prominent in Chilean mining, as in most things. By the time North became interested in such enterprises, copper and silver had been dug from the bare brown ground of the north for decades, with the help of British investors and labourers, in particular expatriate Cornish tin miners. But around then, in the early 1870s, another mineral potential was becoming obvious in the empty dry plateaux of northern Chile and the neighbouring regions of western Bolivia and southern Peru.

Starting about ten miles inland, just beyond the coastal mountain range that cut off the occasional fishing villages from the interior, a series of pale-grey deposits of sodium nitrate came close to the surface. Also known as saltpeter, the mineral could be extracted from the sandy-coloured rock that carried it, and used to make fertiliser or gunpowder. With warfare and farming becoming industrialised across the rich world during the nineteenth century, demand for these nitrates was potentially close to infinite. And they existed in commercially exploitable form nowhere else in the world.

About 1810, the Peruvians had first started mining nitrates for gunpowder. In 1830, the first shipment for fertiliser had been despatched to Europe. By 1860, a third of a million tons a year were being extracted. But much of this was being done by lone freelance miners, with sledgehammers, working in the perpetually blinding noons and cold mornings of the high desert. When they struck nitrate – and it could be several metres down – they had to break off big pieces of the seam, smash these into portable fragments, and drag them to the nearest nitrate buyer, usually no more than a man in a hot tin shed on some distant ridgeline. He in turn had to light a fire, boil water, dissolve the lumps of rock, and then pour the liquid into troughs outside, where sun and evaporation would eventually concentrate it. Once all the nitrate of sufficient purity within practical reach of the buyer's shed had been dug up, he and the miners would pack up and move on.

A less painful version of this process had been invented in the 1850s, involving steam instead of water to dissolve the nitrate, and making seams of only 30 per cent purity suddenly profitable. Chilean and British businessmen began building more permanent *oficinas*, or mineworks, in suitable parts of Peru, Bolivia, and Chile itself. Great waste heaps and clumps of industrial buildings began to stud the desert. Poor people from the Chilean countryside began to travel north to the nitrate fields in search of labouring work. The finance for the mines, and the sale of their minerals, was arranged through British bankers and brokers down in Valparaíso.

However, there remained for a time a much easier way to make money in 'El Norte Grande' (literally, 'the Big North', as the Chileans called the northernmost desert). Guano, or birdshit, from the clouds of seagulls that lived along the coast, could simply be raked off the rocks and deserted islands they favoured, and also sold as high-quality fertiliser. The Peruvian government, in particular, grew rich on the proceeds by allowing companies to harvest guano if they paid for public works. This enviable arrangement lasted until the end of the 1860s. Then the guano deposits began to thin out.

As nitrate mining increased sharply in response, so did the growth of the towns that served it. One boomed in particular. For centuries Iquique had struggled along on a stony peninsula across the border from Chile in southern Peru. It was a minor port used by fishing boats and the occasional merchant ship. Although it occupied one of the few pieces of flat land along thousands of miles of mountainous coastline, its population never managed to get above a hundred throughout the eighteenth century. When Darwin visited in 1835, he found Iquique's tiny grid of unpaved streets and unpainted wooden houses, with the coastal hills towering immediately behind and clouds off the sea trapped above, 'most gloomy'. Every essential had to be shipped in and was in short supply. The population had crept up to a thousand.

But by the early 1870s, when North arrived there, Iquique had been transformed. Rivalled only by the former fishing village of Pisagua forty miles to the north, the town was now perfectly positioned as a transport hub for the nitrate mines just inland. As the *oficinas* suddenly multiplied and their profits rose, something like a gold rush swept through these ports. Iquique grew from 3,000 residents in 1868 to 11,700 in 1871: among them shipping agents and provisions merchants, accountants for registering nitrate claims, property speculators and miners who were passing through. People fought in the streets to establish ownership over building sites. House fires were frequent in the rainless climate, and provided further opportunities for new construction afterwards. The grid of roads expanded into a messy crosshatching. In two years, a dozen separate companies were formed to exploit the local nitrate deposits.

North did not immediately plunge into this entrepreneurial shark pool. In 1871, he took a job managing a Peruvian-owned mine. Despite speaking no Spanish (he never learned), he soon spotted a truth about the industry. At this competitive stage in its development, it was a safer business supplying the *oficinas* than actually owning them. As the nitrate extraction process grew more mechanised, it became hungrier for imported tools, prefabricated pipes and boilers, tanks and chimneys. And as the mines were now established compounds, with resident labour forces, so they needed ever greater quantities of food and, above all, drinking water. North began trading in all these; in 1875, he bought a ship, the *Maranon*, which he profitably turned into a water tanker – perhaps this is the root of his story about the rusty old steamer. Three years later, he began renting more tankers from the Tarapaca Water Company, a new enterprise named by its English owners after the region around Iquique. He was now thirty-six, and had been in South America a decade. He had developed a slight North American accent from contact with other traders. And he had the experience and brazen confidence to use the opportunity that was about to present itself.

In 1879 Chile went to war with Bolivia and Peru, something that had previously happened in the 1830s. All three countries wanted to dominate the Pacific coast, and for decades they had been equipping their navies accordingly. Additional tensions were created by the large influx of Chileans into the mining areas of its two northern neighbours. The substantial Peruvian town of Antofagasta had acquired a 90 per cent Chilean population by the middle of the century. In the 1860s, Chile started to argue for its borders to be moved further north. In the 1870s, a government debt crisis and general economic downturn began to make the seizure of the nitrate fields in Bolivia and Peru – which were richer than Chile's – irresistible. Simultaneously, Peru, which had signed a secret defence treaty with Bolivia, was suffering a financial implosion of its own. The revenue from guano had dwindled; government spending had not. The only solution seemed to be the nationalisation of these same nitrate mines. Peru went ahead, to the horror of the mostly Chilean mine owners. In February 1879, the Chilean navy captured Antofagasta; in April, official hostilities began between the three countries.

Iquique was right in the middle of the contested area. Many of its entrepreneurs fled, including the owners of the Tarapaca Water Company. North did not. At first, this seemed a disastrous misjudgement: the advancing Chilean forces sank the *Maranon* and destroyed much of the company's property. Yet once the Chileans had established control over the region, North was able to present himself as the man in possession of a vital utility. He won official recognition as the water company's sole owner. Then he shamelessly claimed and won compensation for the war damage, despite the fact that few of the firm's assets had been his property at the time. It was perhaps the first example of the sharp practice that would both drive and undermine his business reputation – and a further case of British capitalism in Chile depending, very publicly and successfully, on military force for its opportunities. As Iquique patched itself up and started expanding again, North miraculously unveiled an undamaged water-condensing plant and several surviving tankers. He now held the water monopoly for a boom town in the driest place on earth.

By the end of the War of the Pacific, as the victorious Chileans have grandly known it ever since, North had mounted another, even cleverer coup. Contrary to appearances, he had not spent the entire war in Iquique. While his thickset, stubborn person was thought to be remaining bravely on the besieged peninsula – with all the credibility and other advantages that brought him – he was in fact frequently slipping off to Lima, the Peruvian capital, to buy up the certificates that the government there had issued as compensation when it nationalised the nitrate mines. With the fighting and general uncertainty, these were selling for practically nothing. As a supposed neutral, North was quickly able to acquire the certificates for a large number of the *oficinas* from their panicking owners – Peruvian, Bolivian and Chilean alike – without attracting much resentment or suspicion. As a Briton, he was able to tap into the British banking network in Valparaíso for funds. And as a man of flexible ethics and charm, he was able to recruit useful local collaborators, in particular one Robert Harvey, a famously red-faced Cornishman who just happened to have worked as an inspector of mines for both the Peruvian and Chilean governments. What North did not know about nitrates, and official attitudes to their extraction, he quickly learned.

All he needed now was for the Chileans to return the mines to private ownership. Then the certificates would effectively become documents proving ownership of the *oficinas*. To secure this outcome, he had one secret piece of leverage, in addition to all his local credentials. During the war, he had given discreet aid to the Chileans. He had lent them a steamship to carry wounded soldiers, and given them eight small boats for amphibious operations. This help would more than repay itself.

When the fighting stopped, Chile was several hundred miles bigger. A whole dry tongue of land had been added to the north, including the entire Bolivian coastline, several Peruvian provinces, and all the nitrate fields. The unusual self-confidence of the Chilean military, which has endured ever since, their sense of themselves as saviours and creators of the nation, may date from this achievement. And it was a substantial one: this territory and its mineral deposits and the tax revenues they generated would modernise the country over the next few decades, and give it a more expansive self-image for ever. Less benignly, this new desert Chile would remain a sort of armed camp long after the end of the War of the Pacific. The baking emptiness, the isolation, the necessary business of fortifying the captured towns and being suspicious of anyone who threatened them – all this helped form a certain frontier mentality, especially in the army. Pinochet spent a great deal of his early career during the 1940s and 1950s on endless patrols of the sand dunes and broken hills; watching for potential subversives in the garrison towns; accumulating vague but strongly felt resentments, of a conservative and nationalist sort, against more cosmopolitan, liberal Santiago and Valparaíso, hundreds of miles to the south.

In 1948, he records in one of his many volumes of autobiography, he was ordered as a young captain to arrest all the local communists in Iquique. There were already official lists of such people, despite Chile's public credentials as a model democracy. The newly elected president, Gabriel Gonzalez Videla, wished to bury his own left-wing connections by banning and imprisoning the country's substantial Communist Party. Pinochet was provided with sixty troops to escort roughly ten times that number of communists from an old British *oficina* where they had been assembled, to a more permanent detention camp in Pisagua, down by the coast. He collected his prisoners in a small convoy of trucks. Then they drove overnight. As the road twisted and slowly descended towards North's faded nitrate port, Pinochet took satisfaction from the cowed behaviour of his prisoners: 'I remember that those same arrogant agitators, violent and rude people who spent their time sowing hatred among Chileans, were totally changed. They didn't say a word and were frightened out of their wits.'

You still feel the narrow-eyed glances of soldiers if you visit the north now. There are frequent signs by the empty roadsides for army reservations. There are airfields in the distance, every wing tip picked out by the sun. There are barracks in seemingly every town. As you drive into the seaside sprawl of modern Iquique from the airport, there is an army compound on the southern outskirts, among the beach houses and bungalows, with high grey walls in the style of a medieval castle. It looks slightly absurd, at least until you notice the armed sentry in state-of-the-art desert camouflage. And you learn that Pinochet still keeps properties in the town. The military plane that finally flew him away from British captivity in March 2000 came from the air base nearby, carrying the dust of Iquique back to Britain as the nitrate ships had once carried North's cargo.

In 1881, the Chilean government took the decision that made this trade possible. The mines were effectively privatised – a hint of official inclinations to come in Santiago and London a century later – with the holders of nitrate certificates like North allowed to take over any premises for which they possessed three quarters or more of the certificates. The following year, all the unclaimed *oficinas* were auctioned off. As many Chilean historians have since noted, it was an arrangement so perfectly suited to the ambitions of North and the other foreign mining speculators that the whole war might have been arranged for their convenience.

Conclusive evidence of such a conspiracy has never quite emerged. But it is clear that the pro-European, pro-free-market ideas that had arrived in Chile with Cochrane were dominant in government circles by the War of the Pacific. The panels of politicians and economists that decided on privatisation were packed with enthusiasts for the confident modern capitalism represented by North. Conflicts of interest, in the manner of privatisations ever since, were not investigated with much vigour. And those Chileans with more reservations about letting foreigners carve up the fringes of their country had to acknowledge that, for now at least, Chile literally could not afford to obstruct them. As one of the British bankers who were increasingly involved in financing the republic's military and other ventures put it, in a rather self-satisfied letter to another London banker: 'Ere long Chili must be a borrower in Europe + unless the Certificate holders have been satisfied, it wd be very easy to throw insuperable obstacles in the way of her getting a penny.'

By the mid-1880s, North owned so many mines that their waste heaps spilled into one another. A new horizon of sandy-grey rubble ran alongside the railway tracks that linked the long strip of workings to each other and the coast. Each *oficina* was a functional huddle of low sheds and railway sidings; lines of tanks for dissolved nitrate, crusted with its whiteness; black smoking chimneys and telegraph poles; mean little barracks for the workers; bungalows with verandas and fenced-off gardens for the managers. Here on the inland plateau, over 3,000 feet up, with Iquique out of sight in the sea mist below, the labour-intensive business of nitrate extraction could be carried out in conditions not so far from slavery. For food and clothing and other essentials, workers were almost completely dependent on the company store. Everything it sold had been marked up, and everything they bought was deducted, in advance, from their wages. The way they earned their money can be deduced from the memorials to nitrate miners in Iquique. They show bare-chested men, straining over pickaxes and shovels. They look like prisoners breaking rocks.

In 1878, another new method of purifying the nitrate ore had been devised, which used large steam-heated troughs and a succession of filters to treat the dissolved mineral. The proportion of nitrate to rock required to make a profit dropped further, from 30 per cent to 13. However, the amount of machinery needed also increased, beyond the means of North and his banker friends in Chile. In 1882, he went back to England to look for investors. He stayed for seven years. Within months, he had acquired enough capital to form the Liverpool Nitrate Company Limited, the first British enterprise to combine the mining, transport and marketing of the commodity. The Colorado Nitrate Company followed in 1885, the Primitiva Nitrate Company in 1886. Soon there was a jostle of overlapping public companies, each with North as their chairman, each offering British investors – already accustomed by the Empire to distant ventures – the prospect of vast dividends from an obscure but exciting new industry on the other side of the globe. In its first three years, the Liverpool Nitrate Company paid annual dividends of 26 per cent, 20 per cent and 40 per cent.

Meanwhile, North continued to buy up and set up secondary businesses in Chile upon which the mines depended. He established a bank in Iquique, and took a controlling stake in the Nitrate Railways Company, whose painstakingly laid, patiently ascending and descending tracks carried the mineral to the sea. He floated his water and provisions companies on the Stock Exchange in London. His steamers and nitrate clippers clogged the tight harbour at Iquique in ever greater numbers. The scale and importance of all these enterprises, locally at least, can be gauged from the *Sketch of the City of Iquique* published in 1887 by a visiting Royal Navy captain named W. M. F. Castle:

The offices of the Nitrate Railway Company are worthy of any city in Europe. There are eighteen sets of rails running into the goods station. The engine house has accommodation for thirty-five engines. The whole depot is enclosed by three sides, and has an area of about 77,000 square yards.

Nowadays, no trains run from Iquique. Pinochet, inevitably, privatised the railways in the 1980s. Since then the country's long spindly network has been shedding its more over-extended limbs. North of Santiago, the upper half of Chile has no train services at all. Instead, air-conditioned coaches roar through the night. But no one has thought to demolish the railway stations.

The former terminus for Iquique looms at the end of a street just past the coach station, in the most decayed section of the old town. Its high pink-and-white walls have blistered a little in the sun, but most of the old compound still looks intact. Along its eastern and western sides, there are two large wooden buildings with delicate verandas. Around the perimeter there are bottle-green railings, and inside there are lines of lamp posts and a fountain in the same smooth wrought iron. There is a tall spiky clock tower like a miniature of St Pancras. On everything there is still decoration: arches and columns and lacework in the most profligate Victorian style, all mummified by the bone-dry air. A doorstep to one of the buildings reads '1883' – the year North bought his shares in the Nitrate Railway Company – in thick, confident brass.

Much of this is a shell, though. The timetables may just be readable in the gloom of the old passenger concourse, but it is now a government car park. The sand has taken back most of the central courtyard. The clock has stopped. The gas lamps have been fitted with tiny, cheap bulbs. Only one fragment of platform remains, behind a street vendor selling Coca-Cola. The cement is slowly spilling from between its great paving stones, and joining the expanse of splintery debris and abandoned railway sleepers and the smashed-up spines of other platforms that extends north of the station, where the heavy nitrate wagons once ground in and out. The tracks, where you can make them out, run for a hundred yards towards the nitrate fields before a barricade of corrugated iron cuts them off.

I turned back to the courtyard. It was surprisingly busy for a relic – and not with tourists. Men wearing dark suits despite the glare kept walking purposefully back and forth, carrying armfuls of files. A gardener was having a cigarette break in the shade, beside a surviving stretch of well-maintained lawn. Young mothers were buying cold drinks. Lots of teenage boys were hanging around, with tattoos on their bare shoulders and serious expressions. The building beneath the clock tower, I noticed, was still in use. From the cool of the doorway, a glance along the high-ceilinged corridor was enough. The offices of the Nitrate Railway Company, still white and immaculate as a station master's vision of heaven, were now the local Civil Court for Minors.

I sat in the sun and watched the boys scowl for a while. Water from a hose that the gardener had left running on the lawn flopped brightly onto the grass. Then I decided to see whether the railway tracks continued beyond the corrugated iron, and what they led to.

The first thing I found on the other side of the fence was the town prison; then some new apartments, also overlooked by guard towers: Iquique's naval quarters. The sand covering the pavement crunched noisily as I hurried past. The tracks had completely disappeared, somewhere among the barrack blocks; but I carried on northwards, following the slight inland curve I remembered from the old maps of Iquique I had studied on gloomy afternoons in the British Library. A street of tin shacks replaced the barracks, and the pavement turned to pure sand. There was nobody about now, in the hardening lunchtime light. Dust sat on the windowsill of each shack as if at the bottom of an ocean.

Then, at the end of the road, a pair of rails sliced past. They were narrow and almost buried, but they looked the right age. For the next quarter of an hour, these flat metal bands, only lightly speckled with rust, dodged and swerved and crossed roads busy with trucks, cut through an industrial estate, and climbed almost imperceptibly towards the coastal hills. The tracks skirted the Zofri, a huge duty-free shopping complex upon which modern Iquique heavily depends. Scarlet bougainvillea spilled incongruously over the endless roadside fencing, and bobbed in the exhaust from the passing stream of taxis. Each tiny Allende-era Lada was crammed with passengers, carefully splitting the small fare, as most people in Iquique need to.

Suddenly the tracks slid under a pair of large white gates. They were padlocked, but I could see past. A few feet away, resting against a set of buffers, was one of North's locomotives. It was stumpy and black, a bullock of an engine, its sides held together with big Victorian rivets. Except for two splashes of graffiti and the sand round its wheels, it might have been heaving nitrate that morning.

Past the engine, the tracks began to rise more steadily. There was another, smaller station with roses still growing in its flower beds and the precise cottagey outline of the station at Charlbury in Oxfordshire. A small pack of dogs, lying in the shade of the platform, discouraged me from any closer examination. So did the streets now to either side of the railway: the taxis had given way to abandoned cars, the duty-free warehouses to men selling T-shirts in cellophane wrappers on lonely corners. A whole hillside of small shacks revealed itself: brick and tin and breezeblock, with thin children watching from doorways and thinner dogs that barked at strangers. The sun prickled as the sea air receded behind me. The rails climbed on, straight as North's profit graphs. The occasional sleeper broke the surface, furry with nitrate, as well preserved as the bodies at Pisagua.

The shacks turned to goods yards, then scrap yards, then the bare slopes of the hills themselves. Past the last fence, there was nothing but sand and bleached beer bottles – and the flat tops of the tracks, aiming ever upwards, searching the side of each hill for the easiest incline, their metal slightly silvery in the sunshine and against the blue-green sea below, until, not far from the horizon, they turned inland and disappeared round a distant headland. I stopped and sat on a rock. The tinny sound of a radio drifted up from one of the scrap yards. Beyond them, back in the direction I had come, the frayed grid of Iquique – part historic site, part Chilean Blackpool, with its new waterfront hotels and half-built holiday apartments, its slowly disintegrating mansions in the streets behind – shimmered invitingly in the early afternoon. I caught a taxi back to my hotel. That night, I climbed out onto its temporary roof in the warm darkness, among the piles of bricks for building the next floor, and looked up at the hills. A giant clock made of lights glowed on the slopes, as did an animated billboard. After advertisements for Samsung and Marlboro, there was one for the Zofri. It ended with the silhouette of an old locomotive, ghosting across the horizon.

Officially, there is scarcely a trace of North in Iquique. Not in the museum, with its display cases of heavy miners' shovels, and its seashell collection donated by Pinochet. Not in the main square, with its white Victorian bandstand and palms that fill with vultures every evening. Not in the old theatre, with its huge dulled chandeliers and painting of Shakespeare on the lobby ceiling. Or in the grander old streets, straight and wide as Wild West film sets, with the wooden bones showing through in their balconies and the nitrate still coming up through gaps in the pavement. Or in the humbler new shopping arcades – with their cheap CDs and haircuts, and Chileans on vacation, strolling in the wash of the shop lights until late in the evening.

I never found a single statue. There were streets called Wilson and Thompson, and a Parque Lynch, but nothing named after North. There was not even a plaque. There was just a café behind the market, with a few old coins framed up on its walls; they were stamped with the name of one of his companies, for use at one of his company stores. The café called itself the Santa Laura Salón de Te, after a ruined nitrate mine said to be somewhere nearby. Beside the coins, there were a few black-and-white photographs of a great ribbed building, with a chimney high as a sailing mast, beached like a wrecked ship in a seemingly endless stony flatness. Early one morning I hired a man with a van named Victor to drive me to it.

We took the only road inland. For the first quarter of an hour, it was more of a ramp. Wheezing lorries struggled up the hillside, the gradient less forgiving than the nitrate railway's. Iquique shrank very slowly in the rear view mirror. Victor's Christmas decorations swung violently from the ceiling of the camper van, but his pale eyes remained neutral. Halfway up, we juddered past another old locomotive, dusty men with bags camped around it by the roadside. A few yards on, there was a crumbling concrete plinth. On it stood a huge, back-breaking wheelbarrow and a narrow railway carriage, both the right vintage for transporting nitrate. You could see right inside the carriage through its sliding doors: there were mean little bench seats, no windows, tight stifling walls. Someone had made a bed out of sheets of cardboard on the floor.

Up on the plateau, the air turned colder but the sun already felt burning. We passed through a windowless shanty town around a road junction; then the world became nothing but brown. Beyond the telegraph poles along the highway, there were low rust-coloured hills, shallow valleys, small monochrome ridges and spurs. There were no plants, just rocks and sand. Shadows scuttled under stones. The only other colour was an occasional nitrate whiteness in the gutters, and a single painted phrase on a rock: 'Patria Y Libertad', the name of Chile's most extreme pro-Pinochet faction, active in the 1970s but supposedly dormant now. Victor, curly-haired, probably mid-forties, old enough to remember the coup, did not comment. A David Bowie song from the early 1970s played on the radio. Then a set of railway points and a roofless hut flashed past, and a familiar silhouette appeared in the distance. Victor turned off the highway onto a dirt road.

When he stopped the engine, there was complete silence. We were parked in the shade, at the edge of a dry square; around it were the half dozen surviving buildings of the *oficina* Santa Laura; beyond them was the desert. When Victor opened his door, there was a blast of wind and heat. But all other life seemed to have long departed.

The trees by the manager's quarters were rustling skeletons. The glass had gone from his windows. No easy chairs took the air on his veranda. Across the square, the great chimney of the processing shed was only held upright with cables. We walked over to the shed and Victor began to explain its functions in quick, casual sentences, as if everyone in Iquique knew how to refine nitrate. Yet it soon became hard to concentrate. The inside of the building was like a cave, filled with strange, eroded shapes: the remains of pipes and struts, frozen conveyor belts, fallen planks of wood that were soft to the touch. Light shot in streaks through a million tiny gaps in the roof. None of the debris was labelled or cordoned off. Victor bounded up a thin gangplank to point down into one of the tanks, the red dust puffing up onto his jeans and new trainers. I followed, with my eyes averted from the drop.

The rest of the mine was like an industrial museum minus the nostalgic trappings. Chutes ended in mid-air. A vast boiler lay on its side like a fallen tree trunk. Railway tracks snaked uselessly around. An outbuilding was crammed with dead engine blocks. Everywhere, traces of nitrate had risen mockingly to the surface. But this was not simply a sign of premature closure; in fact, it was part of the reason Santa Laura had been shut down. Nitrate mining got too easy.

Santa Laura was established by the London Nitrate Company, founded in 1887 by William MacAndrew, one of North's business partners. Many of the mine owners, by now mostly British, had become accustomed to sitting on the boards of each other's firms. Although they were in theory competitors, the increasing quantities in which nitrate was being extracted, and thus the growing danger of over-supplying the market and causing the price of the mineral to collapse, meant that the entrepreneurs were beginning to form what were called, with characteristic Victorian euphemism, 'combinations' or cartels. Quotas were periodically agreed to limit production, and so maintain the price of the commodity at artificially high levels. None of this was ever mentioned, of course, on the cheery posters that sold nitrate to the world's farmers.

The brittleness of this arrangement was obvious. In order to keep paying the unusually sweet dividends that drew investors in the first place, and made this whole elaborate desert venture possible, North and the other mine owners needed very large revenues from their nitrate works. So there was a perpetual temptation – in fact, a necessity – to get round the quotas. A few weeks or even months of maximum production could always be quietly ordered before the other mine operators noticed, or the nitrate price began to fall in response. As a consequence, none of the cartels ever lasted for long.

Worse than that, a cycle began to establish itself that would undermine the industry in the long term. The more erratic the accelerations and decelerations in production became, the more difficult it was to predict how many miners to employ. There were labour shortages; the wages of the Chilean workers, while still low, began to rise sharply, and with them the labourers' sense of their own strength. In 1890, the first strike involving all the mines spread across the nitrate fields. It was one of the earliest stirrings of an organised left in Chile, which would steadily gather momentum until Allende's election eighty years later. The compliance of every bare-chested employee with the schemes of North and the rest could no longer be taken for granted. Yet buying the labourers off ate into profits, making additional surges in mining activity to compensate all the more unavoidable. At the same time, the increases in productivity resulting from the mid-century breakthroughs in extraction methods were tapering away. Further mechanisation of the process was prohibitively expensive, given the remote location of the *oficinas*. And, all the while, back in the grey canyons of the City of London, the expectations of investors were soaring regardless.

'The company promoter has only to whisper the magic word "nitrates" and the market rises at him,' wrote the *Financial News* in 1889. 'Gold can no longer conjure up premiums like nitrate. It is the spell which draws the biggest crowd, and causes the greatest flurry among premium hunters.' That January, investors rushed into a new company which had bought land for nitrate mining in South Africa – when the only 'evidence' of the mineral's presence was a similar latitude to northern Chile, and similar weather.

The City's greatest excitement was reserved for North, though. At some point during the 1880s, he started to be known as the Nitrate King. The *Financial Times* took to reprinting his speeches in full. In 1889, a popular novel was published, entitled *Romance of the Nitrate King*, with a 'Henry Cartwright of Leeds' as the tycoon looming over its young protagonists in an idealised northern Chile. Portraits and caricatures of North began to appear.

It is finally possible to describe him with certainty as he entered his mid-forties: sandy mutton-chop whiskers, cheeks coloured pink by the sun, the beginnings of a double chin and a big round forehead. His eyes were small but taunting. He liked to stand with his feet wide apart and his hands in his pockets, and to hold a level stare, as if perpetually sizing up a subordinate or a rival. He favoured surprisingly delicate pointed shoes, but also more traditional dark suits with waist-coats, whether in the desert or in London. He liked to eat. And he liked to tell heroic anecdotes about himself. His success was down to untutored intelligence, energy and directness – this was the public image he promoted as relentlessly as his businesses in the dining rooms of the hotels where he held court in London and Leeds; in his speeches to calm rowdy shareholders' meetings; in his sudden, stage-managed appearances on the floor of the Stock Exchange. If a York-shire lad could get rich from nitrates, his every flat-vowelled sentence implied, then so could the humblest investor. North wanted to be the everyman of vigorous late-Victorian capitalism.

But his reputation, in Britain and Chile, was never quite as straight-forward. In 1888, the *Financial News* wrapped a summary of his appeal around a droll warning:

Put Colonel North's name on a costermonger's cart, turn it into a limited com-pany, and the shares will be selling at 300 per cent premium before they are an hour old . . . Whatever he touches turns, if not to gold, at least to premiums. In the end there is often a considerable difference between gold and premiums, but at the outset they may be easily mistaken for each other.

The Economist, in the meantime, was questioning the prospects of the nitrate business more generally. The sector had boomed and slumped throughout its history, the newspaper pointed out. The giddy dividends and share prices of the late 1880s were unlikely to be sus-tained. Week by week, the articles suggested more and more directly that this boom in particular was the product of hype and Stock Exchange tricks, of paper manoeuvres, of the creation of an appear-ance of success in a faraway country where the authorities did not ask too many questions. The public should leave nitrate stocks, *The Economist* advised, 'to the cliques which are so busy manipulating them'. In 1889, it began mentioning North and his ventures by name.

In South America, doubts were also being raised by the end of the decade. But if some of the British commercial press thought his empire was too insubstantial, some Chilean newspapers thought it was too strong. *La Libertad Electoral*, which was published in Santiago, at a safe distance from North's territories, warned in 1889 that the British might achieve a total monopoly in nitrate production. *El Ferrocarril*, also from Santiago, also in 1889, warned that the network of British banks and water and transport concerns was squeezing Chileans out of the desert's secondary industries as well. The area was becoming an 'English hacienda . . . [like] a small part of British India, exploited by a multitude of joint-stock companies organised outside Chile'. Both papers urged government intervention – even the nationalisation of some of these businesses – to prevent the lands Chile had so recently and bloodily conquered being lost to foreigners. In truth, on the ground, this was already what was effectively happening.

By controlling the Nitrate Railways Company, North increasingly controlled the region its lines stitched together. There were other railways, with different owners, but they covered only a small fraction of the desert; most *oficinas* relied totally on North's stocky engines and goods wagons to carry their produce. His freight charges greedily reflected that fact: prices were per mile along the railway's indirect, looping routes. The success of this near monopoly also awakened him to broader possibilities. A letter from the London office of Antony Gibbs, one of North's bankers, to the managers of its branches in Valparaíso and Iquique, explains what the Nitrate King had in mind:

A grand scheme is being hatched of bringing out the whole Nitrate business as a Company, his [North's] idea being to use his power in the Railway as a lever to make all the producers, especially the small ones, to come into the Company. He would virtually say this: 'My interest in the railway is so great that I will never permit another combination to be formed to restrict production; you small people cannot live with open competition therefore you will be ruined. As, however, I am a benevolent man, I will suggest to you a way of escape, and that is to try to have a general company formed that will take your *oficinas* over.' If, however, they refuse, Mr. North proposes to arrange with the Banks to sell the *oficinas* to him as they foreclose on them.

North prepared to implement this plan by having his friend Robert Harvey, the equally red-faced mine inspector, value every nitrate mine during the late 1880s. North then intended to use his contacts and charisma to raise the necessary money from investors in London. Five million pounds would be enough, he estimated. But such ambitions had consequences beyond the Stock Exchange and the northernmost slice of Chile. Many of the politicians in Santiago were also lawyers, and many of them inevitably – given its prominence in the economy – represented nitrate companies. As North's power had grown and became controversial, so a tangle of legal actions involving him and his business rivals had taken root in the courts, entwining large sections of the Chilean establishment and fixing it in pro-North and anti-North positions. These cases then crept, with the same heavily politicised slowness, through a hall of mirrors of appeals and tactical procrastinations. The government's reliance on taxing nitrate exports as its largest single source of revenue (over 50 per cent of the total by 1890) gave it a direct interest in the eventual outcome.

The contradictory need to keep North happy while also reining him in tormented one politician in particular. José Manuel Balmaceda had been elected president in 1886. He was a lofty middle-aged man from a landed family, with a gift for oratory and a long diplomatic and administrative career behind him. He was also a nationalist: he had spent eternities at conference tables ensuring Chile's military successes were fully reflected by gains in territory. Taking office in the middle of the 'Nitrate Age', as the times were becoming known, was both a problem and an opportunity. On the one hand, Balmaceda used the extra revenue to commission new roads and hospitals, bridges and telegraph lines and better port facilities. Education was greatly expanded, and technical courses in particular. A grown-up, linked-up Chile would be created, he intended, that would be less reliant on foreigners in the future.

Yet backing the foreign exploitation of Chilean resources, however temporarily, as a means of ultimately escaping foreign influence, was too subtle and double-edged a strategy for a political culture in which acrimonious confrontation had become the norm. By 1889, Balmaceda was on his eighth cabinet and had lost his majority in the Senate. By 1890, Congress had gone to the opposition too. The dominance of the president over these assemblies, which had been accepted since independence, was at an end. As Balmaceda's popularity began to collapse, so he started to simplify his stance on nitrates. In the slightly portentous language he favoured for speeches, he echoed the patriotic anxieties of the Santiago newspapers about North and the rest: the desert had been 'abandoned' to 'strangers'; 'the treasures of our soil' were being removed 'to other lands'; Chile was losing its 'native wealth'. In early 1889, Balmaceda took the road from Santiago to Valparaíso with a large official entourage, and sailed for Iquique to see for himself.

North's kingdom and his hopes of extending it were threatened from more and more directions. But it was easy not to notice. Back in England, where he spent most of the 1880s, North made strenuous and successful efforts to dignify his aggressive Chilean ventures – and inflate the personal reputation upon which they heavily depended – by philanthropy, and by buying things.

Avery Hill was at the centre of his plans for respectability. It was just a country hilltop in Kent when he spotted it, with a sugar merchant's retreat among the trees. But the City of London was a conveniently short distance by carriage, to the north across fields and fingers of new suburb. An estate of twenty acres came with the property, and more land could be leased. North began renting Avery Hill in 1883. Five years later, he bought it for £17,500.

He immediately had the original house demolished. At an exhibition of Italian art in London, he met an architect called T. W. Cutler, in a pause between purchasing paintings by the roomful ('almost by the acre', mocked a newspaper diarist), and commissioned a replacement. What Cutler came up with was a sort of Tuscan villa, swollen monstrously by the modern comforts and eccentric extras North required. There were sixteen bedrooms and a three-roomed Turkish sauna. There was a billiard room with its own bathroom, and a musicians' gallery in a cod-Elizabethan style. There were tall square towers that could be seen for miles. There was a dome, and stained glass windows, and skylights like the roof openings of a crypt. A dim millionaire's daylight struggled in past the furnishings. Every indoor surface, meanwhile, was a frantic battle between good taste and bad: tiny green mosaic tiles, slabs of pink and black marble, cherubs, Chilean flags, gold-painted fireplaces, silk linings for the walls. Timber was shipped in from South America. A pair of gates, rumoured to have been looted from Lima Cathedral when Chilean troops captured the Peruvian capital during the War of the Pacific, was erected at the entrance to the main dining room. A stuffed bear was propped up in the hall outside, holding a silver salver for visitors' business cards.

Beyond the house was a small empire of outbuildings: the glasshouse, a coach house, an orangery, stables for the racehorses North was acquiring, kennels for the greyhounds he had started racing, then lawns and kitchen gardens and orchards, the beech trees of his newly planted parkland, and finally a high brick wall and earthworks to screen out the neighbouring landowners. North had the public road that skirted his property realigned so his drive could have a more stately curve. The complete estate took over three years to establish, while its cost steepened from £40,000 to £120,000 to £200,000. The bill was only settled after a very public court case. North, so reckless with other people's money, could be careful with his own: he had refused to pay the final £2,718.

Into this slightly overbearing environment – a sort of *oficina* for purifying his reputation – he invited the diverse people he wanted to impress. There were prominent politicians such as Lord Dorchester and Randolph Churchill, who introduced North to the Prince of Wales. There were financiers, such as Nathan Rothschild, who lent North £1,750,000 to start his bank in Iquique. There were North's major shareholders, gossip columnists, fellow racehorse owners and enthusiasts. At weekends, lunch and dinner would be for thirty. 'Glasses were not allowed to remain empty,' recorded an admiring pamphlet about North entitled *Palmy Days*. Whisky and soda was the usual drink. There was ostentatiously out-of-season fruit from under the glass. After dark, North urged guests on through marathon sessions of billiards. When he was drunk enough, and he could not feel the spines, he would sometimes attempt to climb his Chilean monkey puzzle trees. The next morning, he would conduct a formal tour of the grounds, or hold a pheasant-shooting party, as if Avery Hill was not semi-suburban north Kent but the deepest countryside. And, after all this, there was his favourite diversion of all: a competitive sprint across the lawns. North would challenge all comers over sixty yards, giving them a five-yard head start. He was famous for jumping the gun, and deliberately offputting false starts.

Every August, there was a pause in these activities. North would turn Avery Hill into an armed camp. In 1888, in search of a title, he had founded the Volunteer Regiment of Tower Hamlets, with himself as Colonel. He paid for their uniforms and equipment, and allowed them to use his estate for training. Each August they camped there for a week, with tents and food provided. At other times, when North's image required it, they were available to form guards of honour for him or announce his presence with trumpet blasts. The Volunteers were ceremonial and amateurish, but they were still a kind of private army. Chile, then and a century later, seemed to give visiting Britons an appetite for uniforms.

North enjoyed the press of a crowd around him, hanging on his gruff words. Like Cochrane, he ran for Parliament, in 1895, with hopes of converting his overseas adventures into domestic political momentum. He chose the high-profile constituency of Leeds West, also contested by

Herbert Gladstone, the Prime Minister's son. Officially, North ran as a Conservative, but really he ran as himself: riding on fire engines, with his greyhounds beside him, dyed blue, and his portrait on the handkerchiefs he gave out to voters, together with gold sovereigns. He lost by only ninety-six votes and claimed 'a moral victory'. His time in Leeds was certainly not wasted; as in the desert, his presence anywhere was a commercial commodity, carefully rationed and introduced into whichever market he thought promising. So, the election campaign offered a chance to emphasise his Yorkshire origins and impress potential investors from the north of England. Meanwhile North's more indulgent-seeming forays from Avery Hill to the racetracks – with top hat, carnation, and elaborate picnic – made his name among the great mass of people who had never heard of nitrates. His horses once won £20,000 in a single year. After a victory at Epsom, North stood on a chair and gave a speech. In 1889, two of his greyhounds shared the Waterloo Cup, the Grand National of hare coursing, a sport then at its peak of popularity. Fullerton, the quicker of the two dogs, went on to win the race for the next three years running, a record that has never been equalled. When Fullerton retired in 1892, and almost immediately ran away from Avery Hill, there was a national panic, until he was discovered foraging for food two counties away. When he died, his delicate arching frame was stuffed and placed at the Rothschilds' museum of taxidermy in Tring, where it remains. A statue based on Fullerton's skeleton is displayed each year at the Waterloo Cup.

North, however, needed public symbols of his generosity as well as his success. He gave £5,000 to Leeds Cathedral, another £5,000 to Leeds General Infirmary, and £10,000 to buy Kirkstall Abbey for the city, a disintegrating medieval landmark on a river bank below the main road to Bradford. His reward was to be made the first Freeman of Leeds, and to be remembered there to this day, just.

There is a dirty yellow road sign on the way out of town, heading west. It was erected in the 1980s, and records the fact that Kirkstall Abbey, still glowering black and damp among the trees in the near distance, was 'presented to the City of Leeds by Colonel John North'. Passing buses have half covered the words in a dark green sediment. The abbey ruins look almost as neglected – gaping windows, unmarked humps of wall, a tower like a skull – as they must have been before he bought them. But the sign is the only surviving mention of North's name in a British public place, or at least the only one that I found. Leeds General Infirmary had plaques for Victorian benefactors in its blood-red entrance hall, but nothing about North. The Leeds Civic Trust had a stuffy bookshop filled with pamphlets and hardbacks on local mayors and mill owners and railway magnates, their titles conveying a strong sense that every possible opportunity to rose-tint had been taken – *Farnley in Focus, More Memories of Leeds: Page after Page of Pure Nostalgia* – but the indexes and the polite shop assistant were quite blank about him. The Armley Mills Museum of Industry, not far from the Abbey, had long rooms of locomotives and portraits of proud men in expensive waistcoats, even an ancient black steam plough from Fowler and Company, North's old employer, and a dusty engine rescued from the Chilean desert. Yet 'probably the greatest man Leeds has ever produced', as the *Yorkshire Owl* described him on his death, did not even merit a wall caption.

As I walked back and forth between all these places, in the cold West Yorkshire drizzle, with winter blowing in along the Victorian canyons of civic stone and over-decoration that North knew, and with the modern Leeds of out-of-town cinemas and shopping-as-religion not looking quite its best, the prospect of going to Chile later in the month grew steadily more appealing. The last place I tried was the City Art Gallery. I had been told it had a couple of North portraits. But they were not on show. The curator took my name and address; a few days later, I received a photocopied page of the catalogue. There were two thumb-sized photographs of a watercolour and a sketch in ink (actual sizes, nine inches by four and seven inches by six respectively), together with a paragraph of tentative biography. 'These Leeds worthies all look much the same,' said the head of paintings on the phone. 'Moustaches and self-assurance.'

In February 1889, North took the initiative against his multiplying enemies. He had established himself in England, yet the root of his fame and wealth remained in the desert that Balmaceda and *The Economist* and the rest were now menacing. So he decided to go to Chile again, this time in a rather more publicised style than on his first visit as a young apprentice.

At a lunch party in January, North had met the famous war correspondent William Russell, now semi-retired and lame, who was about to leave for Egypt to warm his limbs for the winter. Russell had never been to South America. He had already ordered a suit for the desert from his tailor. North immediately made him an offer. Russell's account of what was said is suggestive about North's grandiose but fretful state of mind:

I was invited to go out [to Chile] that I might see and report what had been done and what was being done, and to examine the works which had transformed the desert of Tarapaca – wastes without a sign of life or vegetation – into a centre of commercial enterprise, and which had covered it with animated industry and prosperous life. It had been asserted in certain journals that commercial enterprises in that region were shams – 'swindles', indeed, would be the word to use if they were what those organs described them to be – and that a railway, in which the public had invested largely, was 'a tramway ending in a marsh' . . . I was perfectly and altogether ignorant 'in that connection'. 'So much the better!' [North said]. All I would have to do was to judge for myself and relate what I saw. There was no mystery to penetrate.

North offered to pay Russell and his wife's expenses, plus a sum estimated by various newspapers at the time as being between £3,000 and £15,000. Two other journalists were also invited: Melton R. Pryor, a staff artist at the *Illustrated News*, who happened to be a director of the Nitrate Railways Company, and Montague Vizetelly of the *Financial Times*. With another dozen North relations and underlings, the total cost of the trip, according to North himself, swelled to £20,000. And this does not include the pre-departure party that he held in London, at the Hotel Metropole.

Under the headline 'Croesus in Fancy Dress: A Famous Ball', the *Sunday Times* gave over a thick and prominent column to the detail. The 800 guests began dressing at three p.m.; coaches were still leaving the hotel at six the following morning. In between, on 'a frosty, starlight night', a crowd watched the hotel doors swing back and forth to an extraordinary assortment of powerful people in fancy dress. There were twenty-eight peers, prominent soldiers, rich men from South America and continental Europe; there were City grandees and one of the Sheriffs of London; there was a Mr Barratt as Philip II of Spain; and there was North himself, dressed as Henry VIII. 'Bluff King Hal,' wrote the *Sunday Times*, 'in outward form and manner, never had a more characteristic representative. It is also worth calculating whether Henry VIII made more money by plundering the monasteries than Colonel J. T. North has made out of a great industry.'

The photographs were taken by one of Queen Victoria's favourite portraitists. North's piggy eyes blaze out from beneath a Tudor beret.

He wears a beard with just the right cruel look to it. His hand rests on his hip. His cheeks are red and fat. He stands in a fur waistcoat, legs apart, or sits looking plump and lordly, slightly older than his forty-six years. The pictures themselves are rimmed with gold, and held in heavy black albums from which the spine clasps are only now beginning to loosen. They are kept wrapped in beige cloths by North's descendants.

North finally arrived in southern Chile in mid-March. For the next three months, he processed gradually northwards by train and boat like a visiting monarch: giving interviews to the press, attending and holding banquets, offering compliments to Chile and performing small acts of charity. All the while, he took care to see every British ally and contact he had ever made, and to have his local agents bring him reports of Balmaceda's simultaneous tour to the north. 'Public attention is divided,' reported the *Chilean Times*, 'between the progress of the president and his party, and the arrival of Colonel North and his party.' On 25 March, the two men met for an hour, halfway up the Chilean coast – as if they had subconsciously divided the country between them – in the smart seaside resort attached to Valparaíso called Viña del Mar.

The meeting was polite. Balmaceda, with his 'subtle little smile', as Russell described him, assured North that the government admired his enterprises and had no intention of interfering with them. The borrowed villa was lightly guarded to demonstrate the president's relaxed frame of mind. Yet Russell noted that there were 'signs and tokens' in the conversation that 'the guiding principles of the Government' had shifted against the perpetual expansion of private monopolies such as North's Nitrate Railway Company. Four days later, on 'a decidedly hot morning', Balmaceda saw North again, this time in Santiago, away from the British orbit of the coast. The meeting was longer; Balmaceda specifically criticised the proposed sale of a Chilean-owned nitrate mine to North, while continuing to offer platitudes about the contribution of foreign entrepreneurs to the country's development. Russell does not record North's response, but it seems likely that he kept his temper. A few weeks later, showing a shrewd grasp of the importance attached to history in Chile, and an understanding as well, perhaps, of the value of delaying tactics against a president who seemed to be slipping from power anyway, North presented Balmaceda with a salvaged piece of a famous Chilean warship and two pedigree English horses for improving the local bloodlines. With the government placated, at least in his own mind, North left Santiago for his nitrate kingdom.

The month he spent there was the last he would ever spend in Chile. It formed a spectacular and drawn-out advertisement, broadcast in glowing detail by his court chroniclers, for North's apparent ability to transform the desert. Here Russell describes a visit to an *oficina*, 3,371 feet above sea level:

The dusty, hungry, and weary traveller will find a triumph of civilisation . . . [A] hotel, good rooms for living and sleeping, and abundant meals, to which additions can be made from the store, where foreign delicacies, wines, liqueurs, aerated and mineral waters, potted and preserved meats – yea, even pâtés de foie gras and truffles of Perigord – are arrayed on the shelves.

Near the end of the month, the tour reached North's furthest outpost, Pisagua:

There were twenty-five or thirty ships of large size anchored . . . The Railway Station, storehouses, and magazines gave an air of importance to the place . . . The inhabitants atone for the want of colour in their surroundings by painting their houses red, yellow, blue, orange . . . There is in every English house a drawing-room with mirrors, easy chairs, sofas, tables covered with albums, the piano, the inevitable photograph stand, the last assortment of books, illustrated papers, magazines, flowers in vases, caged birds in the veranda . . . At night the sea breaking against the foundations of the house disturbed my rest, and I could not help thinking that it would be better if we were a little higher up the hill-side . . . I hope that neither tidal wave nor earthquake will ever visit.

Russell, though ageing and compromised, had finally sensed the fragility of it all. North's great trip really resolved nothing. While he was away, without his bellowing presence to sustain them, shares in his companies fell heavily on the London Stock Exchange. Fundamentally, the nitrate business and those built up around it were no longer good investments: there was a glut of the mineral, and there was political instability in Chile. So on his return to Britain, North turned increasingly to financial sleights of hand to sustain his commercial interests. In particular, the manipulation of share prices, which he had long been suspected of, and of which he had been intermittently guilty, usually to smooth the path of some risky new venture, now became almost his core enterprise.

North's involvement in Chile until the end of the 1880s had anticipated one side of the free-market revolution that Pinochet, Thatcher and their disciples would impose on the world: the aggressive multinational company making an 'undeveloped' country its virtual colony. From about 1890, the Nitrate King's activities also prefigured the purely speculative, paper-profit side of modern capitalism – insider trading, using companies as fronts and decoys, exploiting the loaded rules of a 'casino economy', as Thatcher's critics would later call Britain. Investor gullibility, as much as the famous white mineral, was the precious commodity North now dug for.

His method was simple – indeed, other nitrate magnates did the same thing on a smaller scale. He owned a vast and exotic range of enterprises, and was always launching more. As long as he could create excitement about them, investors would want to get involved. The share price would swell. Then, before it was deflated by the realities of extracting profit from the stony Chilean plateau, he would sell his stake in the venture. And use the money to finance another; and so on.

As a result, North paid out ever more alluring dividends. Those from one mine between 1888 and 1889 exceeded its actual profits by £50,000. Before shares went on sale in his new businesses, he would anonymously arrange for brokers he knew to buy some, to give the impression of public demand. And when the time came for him to withdraw his own money from an enterprise, he would do so secretly – tipping off his allies in the City of London so they could do likewise. After his death, it was discovered that the man whose tracks and trains held northern Chile together possessed a total of 400 shares in the Nitrate Railways Company. In 1888, he had owned 15,830.

North did not leave behind a private record of his financial affairs. The precise detail of his political entanglements in Chile remains unclear for the same reason. But what is certain is that they tightened while the country was dividing against itself in the early 1890s. As relations between Balmaceda and the opposition-controlled Senate and Congress spiralled downwards in a blur of inflammatory speeches, motions of censure, demonstrations and emergency decrees – a dynamic that would repeat itself in the early 1970s – so the question of North's desert monopolies remained a convenient issue over which to argue. Broadly speaking, the opposition had its power base in the nitrate regions, and was friendly towards the mine owners, who were mostly foreign. Balmaceda's support was concentrated in Santiago and among the landowners of the central farming belt, who were mostly Chilean and felt threatened by the nitrate barons. In January 1891, these two blocs went to war.

The navy, still influenced by Cochrane's pro-parliamentary, inter-
nationalist ideas, sailed north from Valparaíso to join the opposition.
Balmaceda's garrisons in Pisagua and Iquique quickly surrendered. The
army, however, stayed loyal to the president: it had been trained in
recent years by German advisers, and had developed a taste for the
strong, Bismarck-style presidency that Balmaceda favoured, as well as
for pale-grey uniforms and high-kicking parade drills. The soldiers
rapidly silenced his remaining critics in the capital. And then, until
August, very little happened. Without ships, the president had no way
of retaking the north, where the opposition had set up a junta. The
desert between Santiago and the nitrate fields, with its few railway lines
vulnerable to sabotage, was too deep and dangerous to cross. Meanwhile the junta, without the army's weapons, could hardly mount an
invasion of the south. As summer turned to autumn, and autumn into
winter, the two sides remained stuck in their strongholds, hundreds of
barren miles apart, desperately trying to arrange shipments of equipment from Europe and the United States, and to prevent the enemy
from doing so, via elaborate networks of agents and sympathisers in
faraway ports. The result was stalemate: it seemed to be a repetition of
the race to recruit Cochrane seventy years earlier – this time as farce.

Then the navy suddenly appeared off Valparaíso with 9,000 armed
troops on board. Within a fortnight, they had landed, destroyed Balmaceda's forces, and entered Santiago. The president fled into the
Argentinian embassy, composed farewell letters and a defiant last
address, and shot himself.

The drama and violence of all this would mark Chile. Supporters of
the dead president fled into exile abroad, just as they would in the mid-
1970s. Allende, a close student of Balmaceda's doomed but radical
presidency, would martyr himself in a consciously identical fashion.
But in 1891, the mystery of how the opposition had suddenly acquired
an army was more the issue. Within months of the end of the civil war,
another visiting British journalist had published a book about Chile; it
suggested, with some fervour, that North and the other nitrate magnates were directly responsible for the junta's victory – that the war
had in fact been fought on their behalf. It is a story that has never gone
away.

Maurice H. Hervey was a sort of junior William Russell, a 'special
correspondent' of *The Times* with a dandyish taste in cravats, who was
sent to Chile some weeks after the outbreak of hostilities. 'The war had

become a topic of considerable interest to English readers,' Hervey writes in *Dark Days in Chile*, the book he assembled from his despatches. He claims objectivity – 'I held no brief' – but his language quickly betrays other intentions. He describes the junta as 'Chilian agitators', and mocks 'their foreign sympathisers', in particular North and his promoters: 'I had not lived long enough to accept a commission as Descriptive Writer for a Nitrate King.'

Hervey saw British involvement everywhere in the war. The Chilean navy bombarded Iquique 'accompanied by a British squadron "to see fair play"'. The town's surrender was negotiated by a British admiral because 'a large proportion of the property thus reduced to ashes and ruins was British-owned.' The junta then recruited its soldiers from the one local source of large-scale manpower: the *oficinas*. 'Indiscreet was the oft-heard boast of the revolutionists that they had the whole nitrate interest at their backs,' Hervey writes, 'as well as the moral support of the British Government, and of the British navy.' Perhaps with the libel laws in mind, he tries to continue more obliquely: 'It only remains for them [the junta] to perpetrate the final indiscretion of informing the world who paid for . . . the repeating-rifles which eventually won the day.' But Hervey cannot restrain himself: 'And whilst upon the subject of indiscretion, Dr Russell was not well advised (in the light of subsequent events) in recording that, at Santiago, "one gentleman urged the Nitrate King to finance a revolution in a neighbouring State".'

Hervey's allegations attracted great attention in Britain and Chile. Their weakness, though, was their second-hand nature: he never actually went ashore in Iquique, or anywhere else in the nitrate territories. And some historians have since wondered how a man as financially stretched as North could have found the money for an army. Three years after the war, with the unthinking enthusiasm of Chilean officialdom for keeping careful records of controversial matters, the new government published accounts for the temporary junta's expenditure during the conflict. They showed no large-scale contribution from North, merely a series of everyday, unavoidable transactions with his desert monopolies. Hervey was hastily ordered back to London and criticised by his editor for bias and lack of evidence.

Yet it is hard to believe that North remained strictly neutral. It is known that he wrote at least once to the British government on behalf of the junta. And their accounts do show their heavy reliance on nitrate taxes to finance their coup – that was why the very first act of the anti-

Balmaceda coalition was to invade the mining region. In effect, albeit indirectly, North *did* pay for the rebellion. Given his history of risk-taking and political dabbling, it would have been especially odd in 1891, when his interests were directly threatened, for him merely to have observed. Moreover, the regime that replaced Balmaceda's was immediately perceived as friendlier to North, and he was friendlier to it in turn. In 1893, he opened his latest, largest nitrate works to the south of the original mineral fields. In 1894, there was a boom in the price of the commodity. North was so confident of his continued success in Chile – or, at least, he wished to be seen as such – that he expanded into a host of other countries. He bought collieries in Wales, shares in French factories and Australian gold mines, even a stake in a tram business in Egypt. Where the money came from, as always, was less than clear, but his international reputation was now such that Leopold II of Belgium approached him with two proposals.

The first was to set up a business which would discreetly manage the royal plantations in the Congo on the King's behalf. North did so. The second was more far-fetched still: the construction of a luxury resort on the cold windy coast near Ostend in western Belgium. 'North City', as the project was named by locals, was intended to include a hotel, casino and enough facilities 'to convert Ostend into the sporting arena of Europe', according to a pro-North pamphlet called *From Apprentice Boy to Millionaire*. He had 'undertaken to invest the better part of a million pounds sterling'.

But he was dead before they cleared a sand dune.

His heart attack, in truth, had probably been coming for a while. North had reached his mid-fifties. He was beginning to suffer from shortness of breath and indigestion. At Avery Hill, it had been noticed by his friends that he would turn blue after running races. He had been told to stop doing them, and had predictably refused. At his offices in the City, in dark cramped Gracechurch Street, the effort of maintaining and perpetually diversifying all his businesses in distant sun-struck places, and of managing all his interlocking scams and near-frauds, and of decorating the complicated, never-finished edifice of his reputation, would have been drainingly physical even for someone without North's predilection for large suppers and lunches. Meanwhile in Chile, his monopolies were finally being tamed: a supposedly pro-North regime, by the twisting logic of politics, could regulate where Balmaceda could not. Even worse, during 1895, the nitrate price started to collapse once more. The optimism of the economics surrounding the *oficinas*, like the unstable, ever-multiplying mounds of waste that ringed them, was becoming very obvious.

On 5 May 1896, a few days after holding a banquet for 400 guests, North spent the early morning at Avery Hill arranging the installation of a phonograph. Then he took a coach to Gracechurch Street for the board meeting of one of his nitrate businesses. He had lunch as usual at a City restaurant called The Woolpack, and ordered an extra course of oysters and stout to polish off back at the office. At three o'clock, he began a second board meeting for another of his mining concerns. Twenty minutes in, he suddenly complained of chest pains. He asked for a brandy. He started to turn pale. He requested a pen to sign the meeting's final resolution, did so, then groaned. He dropped his glasses onto the table, fell back in his chair, and died.

The City authorities refused to say whether he was dead or alive for several hours. Brokers besieged them with questions. Then the tolling of a church bell near North's offices, according to the colourful accounts of his last hours, gave the news away. By the next morning, newspapers and share prices were responding wildly. The nearest telegraph office to Avery Hill stayed open all day and all night for the next four days. Condolences arrived from the Khedive of Egypt, the Belgian king, and the Prince of Wales. After the funeral, the churchyard took five hours to clear. When the crowd had dispersed and the obituaries had been published, though, it became apparent that North still held substantial shares in only a single nitrate mine.

The implosion of a large reputation can be tricky for the descendants. It did not seem to be a problem, however, for Vera Proctor. She was North's great-niece, she referred to him on the phone as 'good old J.T.', and she was very keen to invite me for lunch. 'What he did reminds me very much of all these dot com companies,' she added brightly, in the voice of an extremely vigorous pensioner.

She lived alone in Rye, the place from which Cochrane had slipped away to Chile. In the weeks before we met, several neat, busy letters on headed paper arrived, enclosing the names of further relations and a map of the town's looping medieval streets. Mrs Proctor also mentioned in passing that she believed that Colonel Oliver North, infamous in America for illegally supplying arms to the Nicaraguan Contras in the 1980s, was a direct descendant of the Yorkshireman.

The train journey to Rye was slow and circuitous, like one of North's sly routes for transporting his rivals' nitrate. My ageing empty carriage juddered south from London to the coast, banging and clanking. At Hastings, there was a glimpse of bandstands and seaside spikes and domes, their Victorian decorations bleaching in the bright milky light. There was a faint whiff of Iquique, too, in the town's fading station where I changed trains. But this was East Sussex in the glum early summer of 2000; heading east, the clouds soon closed again overhead, and deep green woods pressed in along the embankments, and then a marshy plain revealed itself, a sort of anti-desert, with Rye on its steep hilltop in the middle just visible through the first spots of rain.

I hurried uphill from the station, over the uneven cobbles, preparing to be late. As instructed, I headed towards Church Square, at the very top of the town, its oldest and most prestigious address. The rain was thickening as I entered. But there on the far side, beyond the dimming churchyard, was the tiny, very upright figure of a dark-skinned woman, in an immaculate gold-trimmed blue suit and matching gold sandals and pearls, waiting calmly with her arms folded.

Mrs Proctor offered a delicate handshake. She had outsized dark eyes and a Latin set to her nose. She spoke like an especially poised guest at a royal garden party. 'J. T. wasn't marvellous or grand but he made waves,' she said straight away, unclipping the mossy chain that guarded her front garden. She led the way into a house of rugs and paintings and blinds pulled down. 'He was a very good showman,' she continued. 'It's a very North style.' She sat me in an armchair and began, birdlike, to dart back and forth across the big living room, fetching items. There was a file on North, an antique flower holder from Avery Hill, a recent photograph of a young woman holding one of his socially ambitious picture albums. 'My granddaughter is an absolutely typical North – red-gold hair and a civil engineer,' said Mrs Proctor. 'The Norths are doers. No learning.' She got me up to look at her fourteenth-century back garden, tumbling down behind the house towards the marshes. There were vast camellias, as in the Avery Hill glasshouse. The sea and Cochrane's escape route were lost somewhere in the mist. Mrs Proctor strode possessively about. Then she marched me to her favourite restaurant.

She was born in Iquique, she said on the way, in 1922. Her mother was Bolivian; her father was British, but from Pisagua. Vera Proctor was educated at boarding schools in England to make her seem

English, while her parents stayed in Chile, trying to make something of a copper-mining concession they had bought near Iquique. She did war service, then worked as an air hostess ('galley slave') on flights to Africa. She kept her Chilean passport. And her mother brought the desert back with her when she came to live in England too: 'My mother would watch these cowboy films, and she'd say, "That's what it was like! That's what it was like! Gambling and card games and guns."' Whenever there was a British general election, her mother would always draw the curtains, expecting a contest in the Iquique style.

Vera Proctor married and began investing in property. 'I have that North thing. You must make money!' She was keen, over coffee in the restaurant, to tell me about her current Internet stocks. But before that, in the dark-panelled dining room, as waiters greeted her by name and gave us the best table and proffered a menu that included an 'orchestration of vegetables', she told me the story of her two trips back to Chile, one under Allende and one under Pinochet.

When her father died, she inherited the family copper mine. It was a deposit of middling quality, beside the Pan-American Highway. Her father had worked it for a while, then given up. But by the early 1970s, she was making enough money from property to contemplate a dabble in mining herself. She flew out to Santiago. 'It was amazing to find the poverty just as bad as when my mother left. The little corrugated houses, millions of them . . .' Mrs Proctor paused over her fish course. What had she thought of Allende? She answered instantly: 'He'd been duly elected. Thank God these poor people had finally got a chance.' Such views were not shared, however, among the other Anglo-Chileans she met. 'At the Prince of Wales Club everyone was brown-skinned and black-haired and trying so hard to be English. They were *appalled* at the political situation. I went to the British embassy to inquire about a mining agent, and they sent me to Antony Gibbs [North's old collaborators]. They were closing their offices. They just wished me luck.'

She paid £5,000 to have her property surveyed, but was told that the north of the country was too volatile to visit. She flew back to England, intending to return during a calmer period. Yet when she did, in the mid-1970s, Chile was quiet in a way she had not previously experienced. 'I looked down from my hotel on La Moneda [the presidential palace] and it was just a shell. It was terrible, the way they had bombed it.' Nevertheless she went to see Pinochet's new department of mines: 'They were very efficient. They had remapped the whole area where our land was. They had renamed the mine Albion.' She thought again about trying to go up there. Until Santiago spooked her again, thoroughly this time: 'One night I was in the hotel on my own, and I heard some people being arrested in the street outside. There were soldiers and shouts. I reached under the bed, to hide – and it was solid, a divan!' She finished her sentence with a laugh; but the quaver of seriousness in her voice grew for the next anecdote. 'A body was fished out of the river. Our host was an Anglo-Chilean who had gone out there to work for Shell. He said, "He's probably an Indian who's got drunk."'

She left Chile again after a couple of weeks in the capital. In 1975, the mining rights expired. She never went back. For a long time her connection dwindled to buying everything Chilean that she came across in Waitrose, and to her daughter learning Spanish. 'I haven't had tea with a lace tablecloth for years and years and years,' Mrs Proctor said, suddenly wistful for Anglo-Chilean customs and looking more her real age. Through the restaurant window, there was a view of cobbles and Tudor rooftops. It was hard to believe there was anyone South American within a hundred miles.

But in October 1998 there suddenly was. 'People would ask me when Pinochet was arrested: what did I think? I said, "He shouldn't be sent to Spain, but should be sent back to be tried by his own people."' There was a flash of fierceness in her big eyes: 'He's got his just deserts.' She was not, however, going to be precisely pigeonholed on the issue. 'My daughter lives in Sunningdale, and we used to drive past the Wentworth estate. When it was raining, my daughter said, "Like good Chileans, when it gets uncomfortable, the protesters won't be here."' Mrs Proctor smiled at the wisdom of it. 'They weren't there.'

Vera Proctor is regarded by the other North relations with a certain caution. She is only the colonel's great-niece after all; yet, as she cheerily admits, 'I am always having these mad ideas' about commemorating him. At one stage, she wanted Fullerton's stiff carcass moved to Avery Hill. She has led North's great-grandchildren on pilgrimages, through the uneven grass of the nearby municipal cemetery, to his neglected gravestone. She has planted a monkey puzzle outside his misty glasshouse, in memory of her husband. She invited the Norths to the ceremony.

They have long since scattered to Scotland and the Midlands and East Anglia. Until Vera Proctor got in touch, North's great-grandchildren had not paid much attention to Avery Hill. 'We kept going past, and saying, "We must go in some time,"' said Sara Rawlings, the great-granddaughter. Her brother William North, after cancelling a couple of times, agreed to meet me in his lunch hour.

We ate a rushed sandwich in a near-deserted pub in Reading town centre. He had an office job there, commuting most days from Worcestershire – at least two hours each way. He had a slightly tired and delicate manner. The dark pinstripe of his suit made his face seem paler. He looked closer to fifty than forty, with dry pink cheeks and much smaller, less confident features than his ancestor. He spoke softly but smartly, like a Conservative MP from a more gentle era. 'I don't know much,' he began, 'about his business side. But the impression I have is that he was nouveau riche.' He gave a sudden, thin-lipped smile: 'A bit flash.'

'I was about eight or ten when I first heard about him,' he continued. 'That he was the person who discovered nitrates. And laid the foundations of the Chilean railway system . . .' He shrugged. 'OK, he exploited the situation. Isn't that what all entrepreneurs do?' I asked as decorously as I could what had happened to the profits. Another thin smile: 'I don't know. Whatever they were . . . they certainly haven't come down to this generation.' North's son was killed near the end of the First World War. His daughter had to pay a lot of tax. Things were sold. And now the surviving Norths were left with the stubborn remnants. 'We've got these huge heavy black overcoats. Massive things: fur-lined, bit moth-eaten. And shoes . . . My brother's got some huge portraits, of him and his wife, in oils.' There was more at a family property in Ireland. 'We don't know what to do with it all. It's sitting in cupboards, clogging up space.' He did not quite know, either, what to make of the modern Avery Hill: 'I find it rather disjointed now.'

After three quarters of an hour, he said he had to go. He walked me to the station, handkerchief in his top pocket, and then, with a dry handshake, disappeared under the railway bridge in the direction of a business park. Before he walked off into the colourless June afternoon, he had tentatively suggested I come to Worcestershire. But over the summer we exchanged increasingly infrequent messages. He was very busy with something at work. Dates were arranged to meet but always cancelled. And there were so many other people to interview; the autumn came and went.

Then, in November 2000, just before I was due to go to Chile again,

William North was finally free. I should come to Reading again, he explained with a new crispness on the phone. I should arrive about five in the afternoon. We would then drive to Worcestershire, where I could stay the night and be shown things, and then back to Reading very early the next morning. Provided, of course, that the record-breaking floods in both places did not worsen.

I arrived in Reading early. His office block was quick to find. It was one of several, in the gabled, sharp-edged 1980s style you could call Thatcherite, on a slice of land between a BMW showroom and the railway line. William North worked, appropriately enough, to the distant rattle and whistle of one of his great-grandfather's old fields of enterprise. Better still, William North's employer was another: a water company. And Thames Water, as he explained in the car, were moving into Chile. 'We've been getting quite involved in their water industry. We've got about 40 per cent.' A few weeks before, Thames Water had won an auction for one of the country's largest water suppliers. One recently privatised utility had taken over another; the spirit of aggressive enterprise seemed very much alive in Anglo-Chilean commerce. 'I've met our Chile representative,' North said. 'I definitely shall go there.'

But his thoughts about modern Chile ran out before we were through the Reading rush hour. Instead, as we queued for roundabouts and chased the receding evening down the motorway, he began to talk unexpectedly and expansively about modern Britain: its congestion, the need to solve it, the possibilities of park-and-ride railway lines and electric cars. His voice thickened with a sudden confidence – he sounded like a North. It turned out that his job at Thames Water was helping to prepare a bid to run the London Underground. With his hands quite relaxed on the steering wheel, he politely dismissed all the commonly held reservations about the project that I could think of. His words were very clear, as his Saab sped almost noiselessly across the middle of England. Despite – or perhaps because of – his pinstripe suit, his slight fogeyishness, and his nightly escape to the Worcestershire countryside, the unyielding logic of the current sort of capitalism, the global craze for privatisation first begun by Pinochet, seemed to come as naturally to William North as breathing. On the outskirts of Worcester, the road shrank to a causeway between black flooded fields, eerily smooth in the passing headlights. But he talked on, appearing not to see them. A few weeks later I learned that Thames Water had been taken over by a German company.

6

Jack Straw and the 'Revolution in Liberty'

During the decades after North's death, Britain and Chile became steadily less important to each other. You can see it in the cemeteries. Along the dry avenues of headstones in Valparaíso and Punta Arenas, the British names begin to peter out by the early twentieth century. By the 1930s, there are precious few of them – mostly sailors and elderly widows. Fresh flowers are a rarity at their gravesides.

The buildings and business dynasties and ways of doing things that Cochrane and North had helped to establish did not collapse, but they became Anglo-Chilean rather than British, thanks to intermarriage and distance. Two world wars and the Depression of the 1930s, and the blockages in global trade they caused, called into question the optimistic geography of the nineteenth-century links between the two countries. When nitrate exports to Europe were halted by the First World War, Germany invented artificial fertilisers in response, and the *oficinas* never really recovered. Rather than standing for exotic profits, the nitrate industry became known in Britain during the interwar years as a notorious drain on the more gullible banks in the City of London.

Meanwhile countries much closer to South America, in particular the United States, began to see the commercial possibilities in Chile, with its relatively large middle class and relatively urbanised population. And as Britain generally lost economic and imperial momentum, Argentina, which was a little like Chile but more populous, became the focus of the dwindling British commercial involvement in the region. There is something melancholy about the small successes claimed by the British Commercial Secretary at the Santiago embassy, John Ure, in an article for a *Times* supplement on Chile in 1970: 'Unilever have a prosperous soap and margarine business in partnership with Chilean industrialists . . . British Leyland assemble Minis here . . .' With a slightly bitter nostalgia, he adds:

No Englishman visiting Chile is left in any doubt about the cordiality of Anglo-Chilean relations. He soon hears the phrase 'the Chileans are the British of South America'; he is told about Lord Cochrane, and he notes the stock-broker-Tudor façades of the clubhouses and the Gieves cut of the naval uni-forms. The difficulty of the British Embassy in Chile is to put some substance into this cordiality before it evaporates in a cloud of sentiment and mutual admiration.

In Britain, attitudes to Chile were less respectful. In the 1930s, sub-editors at *The Times* famously held a competition to construct the most boring headline imaginable. The winner was 'Small Earthquake in Chile. Not Many Dead.' The few stories that did appear about Chile were usually thumbnails – 'Adios to the Noon Siesta in Chile', 'Ashtray Thrown in Budget Debate', 'Expedition to Remote Region Led by Englishman' – that suggested a colourful but insignificant country of impossible remoteness.

In fact, between 1900 and 1960, you could say Chile was the oppo-site of all these. Far from being some sort of banana republic – only Pisagua and a few other places in the far north had the climate for the fruit, after all – the country was industrious, democratic and stable, compared to the rest of its continent or, for that matter, most of Europe. Copper mining replaced nitrates as Chile's source of foreign currency. Fish-processing plants gave jobs and a greasy odour to the fading Victorian ports. The main cities acquired apartment blocks, trade unions, stadiums for football (another British import), pollution problems, great poverty, great wealth – all the ambiguous modern qualities of Manchester or Glasgow. Chilean politics seemed to reflect this mix of bustle and slight dourness: many parties, frequent elections, governments that generally tried to avoid the fundamental social ques-tions. That Chile was a young country, recently extended by war, with near-feudal arrangements persisting in its rural regions, was sometimes easily forgotten amid the respectable grey stone of Santiago's official buildings.

Yet new political currents disturbed the calm surface of the period more often than the cautious Chilean self-image admitted. In 1907, hundreds of striking nitrate workers were machine-gunned to death by soldiers in the centre of Iquique. In 1924, when relations broke down between the president and Congress as they had under Balmaceda, it took a bloodless military coup to end the stalemate. The officers went back to barracks the following year. After a brief democratic interlude, Chile lurched again in an authoritarian direction. Between 1927 and 1931, Carlos Ibáñez, 'the Chilean Mussolini', exiled political opponents, promised to eradicate 'communism and anarchism', and had several union leaders murdered. In 1932 another ambitious cluster of servicemen seized power. Unusually, they were left-wingers; they threatened La Moneda with low-flying aircraft and declared a 'Socialist Republic of Chile', the first such regime in South America. For three months revolutionary committees were formed, the bourgeoisie were alarmed, and right-wing militias threatened civil war. This time, democratic government quickly returned, but its perceived failures provoked another coup attempt, a failed one by Fascists, in 1938.

Such flirtations with the radical left and right did not end until the early 1950s. In 1938, Chile elected the only Popular Front government outside Europe. Its loose coalition of liberals and communists and socialists, including a charming young doctor from Valparaíso called Salvador Allende as minister of health, lasted three years. In 1948, Videla's similar-seeming regime suddenly turned on its communist members, and gave Pinochet his first public role as their desert jailer.

Chile, outside observers began to realise, offered the full kaleidoscope of politics, in a country small and centralised enough for every ideology to have hopes of success. Its narrow test tube of territory, its concentrated population of less than ten million, its perpetually bubbling inflation and European-style consumer booms and slumps, its endless elections – all this seemed to make it an ideal laboratory for new notions from abroad. Chile's strategic position linking the South Pacific and Antarctic offered further justification for foreign voyeurism and dreams of intervention. Finally, there was the dramatic look and atmosphere of Chilean politics: the great sunlit demonstrations along Santiago boulevards; the barricades and uniforms; the slums and distant snowcaps; the sense of stodgy parliamentarianism mingling with more reckless flavours. It reminded some people a little of Spain in the 1930s.

In 1955, when inflation reached 83 per cent, a group of American economic advisers visited Chile and persuaded the government to freeze wages. Inflation fell sharply, but the costs of this crude early experiment in right-wing economics – collapsing incomes, mass unemployment and strikes – were too high to be politically sustainable in the democratic Chile of the period. In 1959, the Americans tried another tack. They invited Pinochet, now a major, and other Chilean army officers they perceived as promising, to come to the United States for training in military and other matters. The prosperous cities the Chileans were shown, and the Cold War warnings they received about the threat to such civilisation from communism, left a lingering impression.

The reawakening of British interest in Chile was a more polite affair. It was political rather than economic, and it started later, in the mid-1960s, with the election of Eduardo Frei as Chilean president. He was a tall, angular man with a background in the mildly reformist politics of the country's Christian Democratic party. But by his election in 1964 he had decided, in his serious-minded way, that the vast divisions between rich and poor in Chilean society were threatening its stability, and needed to be challenged and narrowed in a much more substantial way than before. At the previous presidential election, a coalition led by Allende, now leader of the Socialist Party, had been defeated by a bare 33,500 votes – and only because there had been a rival left-wing candidate. In the late 1950s, the right to vote had been belatedly extended to all adult Chileans; if the lives of the poor were not improved quickly, Frei believed, the country might succumb to the revolutionary ideas now being exported all over South America from Cuba. He called his programme the 'Revolution in Liberty'.

To British ears, it had a romantic but reassuringly moderate ring about it. As Frei set about nationalising the copper industry, introducing a measure of state planning into the economy, and redistributing some of the fertile slopes and valleys of southern and central Chile to the landless peasantry, he appeared to be the South American ambassador for the brand of cautiously left-wing modernisation favoured by, among others, Harold Wilson, who was elected the same year. Admiring profiles – 'A Key Figure in Latin America', 'Chile Aiming for a Quiet Revolution' – began to appear in British newspapers. The first curious British socialists, internationalists, and other would-be radicals began to fly out to Santiago.

The British government appeared equally keen. In 1965, Frei was invited to make the first official visit to Britain by a Chilean head of state. 'The de Gaulle of Latin America', as one over-excited paper called him, was taken from the airport to Victoria station in a special train, met by the Queen and the Prime Minister, and paraded in the sunshine to Buckingham Palace in an open carriage. Over the next five days, Frei visited Cochrane's tomb at Westminster Abbey, received a chart of the bay of Valparaíso made by the Royal Navy in 1821, and sat pale and unsmiling through welcome speeches from everyone from City aldermen to members of the Greater London Council. The trip was judged a great success; three years later, the Queen was invited to Chile in return. There was another open carriage, even greater crowds, hotter sunshine. She planted a tree on a Santiago hilltop. She drove through the streets of its western slums. She shook hands at the Prince of Wales Club, the Anglo-Chileans' favoured country club in the wealthy eastern suburbs. When she visited the Senate chamber, Allende himself gave the welcome address. 'If she ran for president in 1970,' one Chilean journalist reportedly said, 'she would win hands down.'

Yet amid this passing frenzy of Anglophilia, there were a few details of more lasting – and ambiguous – significance. When the Queen spoke to a joint session of Congress and Senate, her chosen topic was the value of democracy despite its imperfections. Beneath her bland generalities, a comment on Chile could be detected. In 1968, the year of attempted revolutions everywhere, the 'Revolution in Liberty' was looking a bit threadbare. Like many moderate reformers in sharply divided countries, Frei was increasingly encountering resistance from both conservatives and radicals. Land reform inevitably made enemies of the old landowners. Limited nationalisation alarmed business *and* encouraged the left to demand more. Meanwhile, the perennial difficulty of controlling inflation – every upturn in the economy sent Chile's substantial middle class flocking to the shops, seeking imported luxuries at any price – gave the unions a perfectly justifiable reason to go on strike for better wages. That every increase tightened the inflationary spiral, which led to further strikes, and so on, was a perfectly satisfactory outcome – indeed often the planned one – for many union members: they wanted Allende to win the next election. By the late 1960s, the number of strikes was running at a thousand a year.

A less obvious restiveness was also spreading at Chile's many military bases. Defence spending had been falling since the 1950s, and there were grumblings about inadequate pay and equipment. In 1968, eighty trainee officers resigned in protest at their alleged hardship. Frei was unsympathetic; compared to the rural labourers and city slum dwellers he was worrying about, servicemen were comfortably off. But all Chile's neighbouring countries now had military governments, and there were still memories, among the older, more right-wing officers, of giddy interventions in Chilean politics during the 1920s and 1930s. Public gestures at parades; menacing the Congress chamber with sudden deployments; fake bombing runs over La Moneda – the techniques and traditions of the coup remained alive but dormant.

In 1969, they began to stir. First, a whole regiment deliberately arrived late for an official ceremony, in order to embarrass Frei. Then a general who had been retired early, on suspicion of plotting against the government, flew suddenly to Santiago, took command of one of the city's barracks, and declared a military strike. Expecting an imminent assault, Frei took symbolic refuge inside the thick nineteenth-century walls of La Moneda, promising, 'Nobody will move me from here!' The unions called a general strike in his support. Municipal rubbish trucks were parked in the wide squares either side of the presidential palace to stop tanks. The next day, the general surrendered, but soon afterwards Congress voted for a substantial military pay increase.

In these shifting circumstances, the fly-past by the air force that greeted the Queen when she first arrived at Santiago airport was not just about pretty formations. It was a demonstration of the military's pride, and its capabilities for carrying out operations, external and – Chile not having fought another country for almost a century – otherwise. The six jets that appeared as dots over the heat-hazy hills, then flashed over the modest terminal building, low as the rebel aircraft over La Moneda in the 1930s, were British-made. They were Hawker Hunters, slightly bulbous and slow by the standards of the most modern Cold War fighters, but highly popular with air forces around the world for attacking targets on the ground. Since the mid-1950s, at Suez and in Cyprus, in Borneo and in border skirmishes between Pakistan and India, the Hunter had become almost an icon of a certain sort of warfare: the bombing of guerrillas and other small groups putting up stubborn resistance against superior forces.

Chile had bought twenty-one Hunters in 1966, shortly after Frei's trip to London. The accepted rationale at the time, in a period of otherwise low military spending, was an unavoidable arms race in the region – Argentina had just bought new fighters, Peru was about to, and Chile remained suspicious of its neighbours. The Frei government even paid for the Hunters' heavy Rolls-Royce engines to be periodically sent back to a specialist factory in East Kilbride, outside Glasgow, for maintenance.

But such precautions against foreign attack did not prove necessary.

There would be no twentieth-century repeat of the War of the Pacific for these aircraft; no heroic devastation of some invading army seeking to recapture the old nitrate territories. After the Queen's visit, the next time the Hunters would be noticed by journalists, they would be small roaring silhouettes above the balconies and chimney pots of Santiago, this time with bombs on board, heading towards a familiar Chilean target.

But the signs of impending crisis during the Frei period should not be overstated. Few people were waiting for a coup. Despite all the opposition, his government continued to do well at elections. For all its political polarisation, Chile became more prosperous, and more people knowingly shared in this wealth. Even Pinochet, on returning from America in 1965, felt the need to conceal his sharpening conservatism. Seeing the professional dead ends into which the more recklessly right-wing officers were being shunted, he expressed tentative support for the Christian Democrats.

He went from major to brigadier in three years. And he was sent back to the austere desert Chile that he relished: first as the commander of a division in Iquique, then as deputy governor of the whole far north of the country. There he stayed until several months after the election of Allende as president in 1970. During these years, Pinochet made the national headlines only once: for putting down a strike at the El Salvador copper mine, up in the Andes, by ordering his soldiers to open fire on a hostile crowd of protesting workers and their families. Six miners were killed, and two of their wives.

The unions never quite forgave the Frei government. Yet despite – or perhaps because of – such incidents, Chilean democracy during his rule grew even more noisily alive than usual. In the capital and the other university cities, like Valparaíso and Concepción, a counter-culture had seeded itself. It extended far beyond the established trade unions, and the traditions of industrial militancy learned in Victorian nitrate mines. Partly inspired by events in Paris and Berkeley, partly by distinctively Chilean dissatisfactions, this counter-culture was as diverse, confused, and exciting as those in richer countries. The labyrinthine campuses, predictably, were the centre of much of the activity. They were contested, department by department, by the student wings of the Christian Democrats (who were splitting into left- and right-wing factions), the Socialists (believers in a Chilean and democratic version of

Marxism), the Communists (paradoxically more cautious believers in something similar), the brand-new Movement of the Revolutionary Left, or MIR (Cuban-inspired advocates of 'armed struggle', usually from middle-class families), and diverse right-wing groups from the *gremios* ('guilds', allied to small business), to traditionalist Catholics, and the homegrown near-fascists of Patria y Libertad.

There were sit-ins and window-smashings and grapplings for radio transmitters. People grew their hair. People grew wispy beards like Che Guevara's. And beyond the overcrowded universities, the disruption of everyday life by these and the other new rebels covered the full 1960s spectrum, from fashionable posing to small-scale terrorism. The MIR carried out bank robberies and aircraft hijacks, most of them unsuccessful. Bombs were detonated at the American consulate, several supermarkets, and the tomb of a conservative president. There were seizures of the derelict land in Chile's gap-toothed city centres by groups of squatters. There were fights between rock fans and 'squares' outside a well-known Santiago ice-cream parlour. More lastingly, a musical protest movement took shape around half a dozen young men and women with acoustic guitars and a vivid line in imagery about the Chilean poor. Victor Jara, with his sad voice and reproachful stare, would become the most famous performer of 'New Chilean Song', as the form proudly called itself. An anguished biography written by his English wife Joan, published ten years after his death, received a full-page review in the British *New Musical Express*, where most books about musicians were lucky to get a few paragraphs.

Into this agitated but seductively alive-seeming Chile, in the winter of 1966, came a bespectacled and slightly skinny nineteen-year-old from Leeds University. Jack Straw was studying law, but also had ambitions in left-wing student politics. He was curious about Chile, and when the Fund for International Student Cooperation, a now defunct offshoot of the British Council, organised a trip for twenty people from British universities to visit Viña del Mar that July and August, he asked to join the party. The plan was to help build a youth club in a poor area of the seaside resort, to meet a representative sample of Chile's politicians and public, and to take the temperature of the 'Revolution in Liberty'.

Viña del Mar was an ideal place to see the contradictions of Frei's Chile. If Iquique was the Chilean Blackpool, Viña was more the Bournemouth: leisured and prosperous-seeming, with a wedding-cake

casino, palms to cool its many pensioners on their benches, and a frost-
ing of white balconies craning for views of the Pacific. Yet at the other
end of town from the casino gardens, if you walked along the beach
and kept going north, the landscape suddenly rose and changed. There
was a mass of collapsing reddish cliffs. A single road led uphill into
them. Either side of it, after a steep climb, was the suburb of Gomez
Carreno. It was another world: cut off from Viña and the seafront, but
with glittering views of both, crammed with young working-class
Chileans and old cars, sharing sunsets with the resort but little else.

Straw and the other British students worked there for six hours a
day. They dug the youth club's foundations, mixed concrete for its
walls and floor, and heaved together its low steel framework. The sun,
unusually for the winter, shone on their backs almost continuously.
They were supervised by a local architect, and local Chilean students
laboured with them. The British were felt to be a bit high-minded, to
be testing slightly idealised notions about working-class life and
Chilean social democracy. But they worked quite hard, and they had
brought £2,000 with them, which paid for materials no one had previously been able to afford. The plain building went up fast.

Every lunchtime, work would halt for an outdoor meal. The residents of Gomez Carreno were invited. There would be stop-start conversations in English and Spanish. And late every afternoon, the
British students would leave the building site to wash off the dust and
eat dinner with Chilean host families. Straw would put on a tie for the
occasion. At weekends, when everyone went to the beach, he would
lie on the sand on one elbow, looking slightly bored.

He seemed more comfortable when the students put on their crested
university blazers and became visiting dignitaries. He inspected a
poncho factory. They met local student leaders. Some of them went to
Santiago and met Frei. Some of them, it is said, saw Allende for *onces*
in Valparaíso, where he was the senator, a few minutes along the coast
from Viña. Straw will only say now, with perhaps a touch of lawyerly
caution, that he 'met a number of Chilean students . . . and talked
about politics and other subjects . . . After thirty-two years [I] cannot
recall anything which could be defined as "political activity" beyond
that.' But when he got back to England, he managed to publish a substantial article on the Chilean political situation for *Tribune*, the left-
wing Labour Party newspaper. 'Can Frei Reform Chile?' was its
headline. Straw appeared sceptical: the president's schemes, he alleged,

were relying heavily on concealed funding from the American government (there is evidence of such support for the Christian Democrats
during election campaigns of the period). 'The entire underlying trend
in Chilean politics,' Straw continued, with the confidence typical of the
activist who has spent six weeks in one small area of a foreign country,
'is a burning desire for reform. At the last election, the Chileans decided they would prefer this reform to be brought about by the more moderate Christian Democrat party . . . But party loyalties in Chile are very
tenuous.'

In fact, much of this analysis could be disputed. Attachment to political parties was tribal and fierce in Chile compared to Britain. Much of
what was to come would violently demonstrate that. And at least a
third of Chileans were quite opposed to left-leaning 'reform'. They
would undermine all attempts at it, moderate and otherwise, between
now and 1973, and would gradually give their support to Pinochet's
subsequent counter-revolution, despite the bloodshed and breaks with
national tradition that this entailed. Yet Straw was right about one
thing. If Frei's programme appeared to stall, many voters would turn to
Allende, as 'the only choice left', and that would have very unpre-
dictable consequences.

7

Allende

Nowadays Gomez Carreno could serve as a small memorial to the
hopes of Frei and Allende. Its views have been partially erased by a line
of five new apartment towers, built at the base of the cliffs in a style
you might call high-rise Versailles, or pink-and-green Las Vegas. In
fact, the whole Viña seafront has become a middle-class resort dream
of glass pyramids and velvet lawns, boutiques and high-concept restaurants, valet parking and warm, would-be Californian sidewalks. It is a
favoured location for modern Chilean television.

But Gomez Carreno is still apart from all this. There are a dozen
four-storey blocks of flats, painted red and cream and arranged in a
tight rectangle, as if for self-defence. Their walls are a little chipped,
exposing the concrete. Old cars stew in the afternoon sunshine. Road
noise drowns out the sound of the surf below. Yet otherwise an ideal of
communal housing seems intact: there are surviving concrete benches,
an ambitious, Mondrian-style arrangement of the windows and roof
ledges, roses and geraniums instead of litter in the flower beds, shared
lawns sloping down to the cliff edge with the Pacific in the distance.
Even the graffiti seems time-warped: a CND symbol, 'I Love Pink
Floyd'. A couple of teenagers lie kissing in the shade. A pair of long-
haired gardeners turn up to fiddle with flower beds.

Immediately to the north of the estate, there is a wall, and behind it,
just visible, the roof of a communal building. The Centro Recreativo
Las Salinas has walls of glass and irregular stone blocks, in the crazy-
paved 1960s style, with cement roughly smeared into the joints. It has
an amateurish-looking floor of raw concrete slabs. And it has a roof of
exactly the same gentle pitch as the one in the photographs of Jack
Straw and the others, smiling proudly in their blazers against the big

Chilean sky, which were fleetingly printed in British newspapers while Pinochet's legal prospects were being decided in March 1999. The building is still used as a youth club – there is a basketball court and a barbecue, and crates of empty Coke bottles piled outside – but it is being refurbished more solidly. I hoped, watching the dozen workmen with their cement mixer and drills, that the lovely period optimism of its glass walls would not be compromised.

But when I walked round the club's perimeter to get a better look, through the pine trees and buttery flowers that still grew wild along the clifftop, another building came into view. It was some way away through the trees, but clearly well maintained and in use. The Viña del Mar naval hospital was built in the unmistakable boxy style favoured by General Pinochet. It dwarfed the youth club and estate as if they were back-garden experiments.

Salvador Allende was elected president of Chile in September 1970. After a day of voting in the Chilean style – streets swarming from early morning, people smartly dressed, whole families walking together to the polling stations, a pervasive murmuring – the electorate had to wait until after midnight, much longer than usual, for the result. The early spring evening was long and quite tense. The campaign had been particularly confrontational, and tanks were parked on the streets as a precaution. Radios and televisions blared from open doorways. Groups of men stood on street corners, heads cocked, as they always do in Chile at these moments, or paced the stilled pavements like expectant fathers, hands clasped, arms folded. People sat in parked cars, listening to the news. Passers-by stopped to lean in through their windows for the latest. Conversations were to the point. No alcohol was served.

Around nine o'clock, the customary sombre male voice began reading out the voting tallies, region by region, slowly assembling a new political jigsaw out of the country's thin, disconnected pieces. Allende did well in the desert, the shanty towns, and the far south. The central valley and the richer built-up areas were split between the other candidates: Jorge Alessandri, a seventy-four-year-old conservative and son of a previous president, and Radomiro Tomic, a reform-minded Christian Democrat. (Frei, like other Chilean presidents, was only allowed one six-year term). The many Chileans hostile to Allende, or persuaded to be so by his opponents' warnings of impending Marxist dictatorship, simply did not know whom to vote for. He squeaked in by 39,000, with just over 36 per cent of the vote.

The result came as a surprise to the outside world. Most foreign newspapers, with their Cold War assumptions, struggled initially with the notion of an elected 'Communist' head of state – the world's first – and also described Allende as a 'Socialist', a 'Marxist', and a plain 'President of the Left'. They compensated for their unpreparedness by emphasising his thin margin of victory, as if the outcome of the election was, at best, some sort of statistical accident, or at worst, an undemocratic conspiracy. In years to come, these lines of argument would be very popular with Allende's enemies and Pinochet's apologists, not least in Britain. After the general's arrest in 1998, aides and former subordinates of Margaret Thatcher, whose three large electoral majorities rested on a proportion of the vote not vastly higher than Allende's, would hotly deny that the left-winger had ever achieved real democratic legitimacy and therefore – there was usually a discreet pause here, to disguise the impossible leap in logic – his violent overthrow by the unelected Pinochet was quite justifiable.

Yet in Chile in September 1970, the election of Allende did not seem freakish. For one thing, he had been standing for president since the early 1950s, increasing his share of the vote almost every time. In 1964, he had actually received 39 per cent. And by 1970, after six years of increasingly left-leaning government from Frei, the Christian Democrats appeared to be following much the same path as Allende anyway. Tomic advocated 'the replacement of capitalism' in his manifesto. He got 28 per cent of the vote; added to Allende's total, it made a left-wing majority of over two-thirds.

Unfortunately for the new president, this favourable arithmetic did not translate into actual power. After the election, the Christian Democrats seemed to forget their recent radical inclinations; in Congress and the Senate they joined the right, to form large anti-Allende majorities. The story of the next three years, in a sense, was about his efforts to get around this constitutional barricade, and his long-term hopes of making such vetoes of social change by the Chilean ruling class impossible. What elevated this struggle from a local matter, from men in suits in a remote country arguing in fussy debating chambers about the rights of parliament – even the most dramatic Allende-era documentaries have their dull moments – or from being just another developing country in turmoil, with the usual demonstrations and strikes and clampdowns, was the new president's determination to get his way using only the methods of liberal democracy. 'The Chilean Road to Socialism', as Allende called his governing philosophy, with a typically canny nationalist touch, was potentially a path any democratic country could follow – a way of ending inequality quickly, of having a revolution without bloodshed, of applying Marx without the repressiveness of every previous Marxist government. Or so it appeared for a while.

Allende's speeches were central to the creation of such expectations. Many poorer Chileans were illiterate; if he could appeal to them, over the heads of the opposition politicians and the largely opposition-controlled press, he might gain sufficient popular support to swamp the landowners and old business families who had run the country for their own benefit, with only passing interruptions, since independence, and in some cases since before then. And as a keen student of other revolutions, Allende also knew the importance of attracting sympathy from abroad. If he could make his battles into political theatre – and after 1968 and Vietnam, there was an international appetite for the next radical cause – foreign aid and volunteers would follow.

At first sight, however, he was not well suited to the task. By 1970, he was sixty-two years old. He had a middle-aged figure and was not especially tall. His face was cautious and square; its most noticeable feature was a pair of heavy, black-framed glasses like twin televisions. His voice, when speaking from a platform, was a strained bark, like a mild man reluctantly roused to anger. He was a doctor by profession, and a former Director of the Chilean Medical Association. He was a freemason, following in his family tradition. Even his vices were bourgeois: wine and whisky, a long-running affair with his secretary. He had a dry, slightly detached sense of humour. No one was going to mistake him for Che Guevara.

Yet Allende's careful, hard-working image had an appeal in a country that saw itself, at least some of the time, in those terms. At the rallies and demonstrations where Chilean politics increasingly took place, he could play the straight man to the noisy thousands in front of him: wearing a V-neck jumper and jacket among the long hair and denim, looking appealingly embarrassed at the chants of support, speaking in modest tones about social upheaval.

His first public speech as president, before the great shallow bowl of the National Stadium in Santiago, with the Andes like a second bank of seating beyond the floodlights, acted as a kind of stirring trailer for all those that followed. There were sweeping declarations of intent ('Here at last Engels' vision is to be fulfilled . . . that "it is possible to conceive of peaceful evolution from the old society to the new"'), of principle ('The road to socialism lies through democracy, pluralism and freedom'), and of utopian possibility ('A new society in which men can satisfy their material and spiritual needs, without causing the exploitation of others'). There was a patriotic weaving of Chilean history into the Marxist rhetoric: 'Because of Chile's particular conditions, the social and political institutions are available to realise the transition.' There were several emphatic references to Balmaceda, 'a combatant in the patriotic effort to recover our national wealth', and more codedly, North: 'from foreign capital'. No wonder most of the Anglo-Chilean community would come to loathe Allende: he planned to upset the social and economic order they had established and prospered under. Here and elsewhere, his speech had an irresistibly melancholy undertow, acknowledging the unhappy fates of past Chilean radicals who had attempted this task. The romantic package was complete.

Allende quickly made some surprising converts. The British ambassador in Santiago, David Hildyard, a recent appointee of the new Conservative government in London, learned within weeks of Allende's election that another retired general was planning a coup. The CIA – appalled at Allende for the same reason that bedsit revolutionaries were so excited – sent the plotters arms, in the guise of untouchable diplomatic cargo for the American embassy. But when Hildyard found out, he organised 'the entire non-Communist diplomatic corps' (as the American ambassador at the time later recalled), to warn the United States that Britain and the rest of Europe would not recognise a military regime in Chile. 'Take the long view of history,' Hildyard reportedly told the Americans. 'All of Latin America probably needs to go through communism for twenty years to eliminate the glaring injustices.'

As the new regime settled in, and the sky did not fall in, despite a campaign of provocation and terror, including the assassination of the moderate head of the armed forces, General René Schneider, by fringe right-wingers, so Allende's many observers abroad began to relax and buy air tickets to Santiago. 'This is a quiet revolution,' wrote the *Daily Telegraph*'s man in Chile in March 1971, 'at first glance more reminiscent of post-war Labour Britain than Dr Castro.' He noted the price controls and rationing, the familiar nationalisation programme, the recognisably Keynesian plans for greater state spending to boost the economy; also 'the bland atmosphere' on the streets; the continuing robustness of free speech; and above all, the tangible sense of power and wealth being quietly but massively redistributed. 'For the masses these are days of euphoria,' he had to concede, not a state of affairs often depicted in his newspaper.

On the first anniversary of Allende's election, the *Daily Mail* ran a report with the headline 'Red Revolution! And Girls Are Even Wearing Hot Pants'. The even more right-wing tabloid's long history of anti-communist scares suddenly seemed as nothing: 'An astonishing experiment [is] taking place in Chile . . . a government that is half democratic and half Communist . . . It has worked well so far. If it survives, the implications will be immense for other countries torn between the two systems.' In Santiago, the visiting correspondent continued:

Allende's huge popularity is conspicuous and noisy . . . He has kept his biggest election promise by increasing wages 36 per cent, and checking inflation . . . The man in the street has more escudos in his pocket and the shops have more to sell . . . The restaurants are crammed with people eating the local seafood, washed down with one of Chile's excellent wines.

In left-wing British circles, reactions were were more measured at first. There was a sense that it might all be too good to be true. Allende, after all, had enough potential enemies *within* his government, let alone outside it: the MIR, the more impatient elements of the Socialist Party, the militant landless peasants in the south. Many people on the Chilean left did not see the need for proceeding so constitutionally, especially as the government's opponents seemed less squeamish. Yet the very tensions of this situation, and Allende's apparent ability to overcome them, exercised a greater and greater fascination among his British sympathisers. In October 1971, the Labour Party sent its radical and ambitious shadow minister for overseas development, Judith Hart, to meet the president and inspect his work.

'He is a cool, clear politician,' she wrote afterwards, 'whose emotionalism is never uncalculated, who knows that in politics it is vital to take the initiative and always does.' One of Allende's subordinates, who was involved in land reform, told her: 'We have the same amount of irrigated land as California, and we have better soil and a better climate . . . This winter the snow and rains have been marvellous. God is on the side of the Popular Front.' Hart wrote in conclusion, 'It is unique, this democratic revolution. There are no patterns to follow: it is new ground all the way.'

As the Allende government was passing its first anniversary, Dick Barbor-Might was in London, failing to finish a master's degree. He was already in his mid-thirties. He had been involved in student politics during the 1960s. At Leicester University, he had been president of the student union. There had been a sit-in in 1968 – 'I, in a sense, led it.' He was a good organiser: affable but relentless, crisp on detail, with persuasive eyes beneath his kind, creased forehead. But this moment of apparent possibility had passed, and three years later, he found himself at the London School of Economics, on his third degree. The unsatisfied, slightly melancholy side of his character was asserting itself. 'I was looking around for something significant to do, to be honest.'

His political beliefs had been drifting leftwards for years. Once, he had been a civil servant, happy to arrange weapons purchases for the British armed forces. But Vietnam and his Catholic conscience had ended that; then the books he read as a mature student at Leicester, analyses of the destructiveness of empires, had radicalised him further. Now he had settled into a vague left-wing internationalism, with a strong anti-American element. His friends saw the world similarly. One day towards the end of 1971, he remembers, 'One of us said, "What's going on in Chile?"'

From the modest amount he could learn from the papers, Allende's Chile sounded like Attlee's Britain in the late 1940s: 'the welfare state with knobs on'. America's evident hostility made the situation more interesting. In April 1972, confidential records from the American telecommunications firm ITT were published in the United States, showing that the company, which had substantial investments in Chile, had repeatedly tried to sabotage Allende's prospects. During the 1970 election campaign, and in the weeks after the result was announced, ITT had frantically lobbied the CIA, the American government, and other American companies with business in Chile, to do anything to stop Allende taking office. 'We are prepared to assist financially in sums up to seven figures,' one Washington foreign policy official had been promised over the telephone by an anonymous ITT representative.

During the summer of 1972, Barbor-Might edited a British edition of the 'ITT papers', as these collected revelations became known. His activist energies reawakened. He went to see the Chilean embassy in London: 'We hit it off. They said I should mobilise support for the Popular Front in the UK. I should encourage students to help.' At the same time, a quiet, self-contained British woman called Pat Stocker, whom he knew and wanted to know much better, left for Santiago. She had intended to study the boisterous new popular culture of Allende's Chile, but when she got there was quickly drawn into the almost daily drama of demonstrations and counter-demonstrations, workers' committees and shanty-town expeditions, emergency decrees and rumours of conspiracies. She began working as an interpreter for the pro-government unions, and describing what she saw in letters back to the distracted graduate student she knew at the LSE.

'Pat's letters educated me,' Barbor-Might says now. 'The notion that anti-capitalism could happen without Leninism, without violence, without repressing political freedoms . . .' His voice, usually still brisk, softens and trails off at the wonder of it. For the rest of 1972 and the first half of 1973, he tried to find reasons to go to Chile. He wrote an article on the ITT affair for the *New Statesman*. He acquired press credentials and a commission to do another piece for the magazine, this time from Santiago. He considered writing a book on the newly nationalised Chilean copper industry. And, more usefully than either, he managed to get himself entrusted with the delivery to Chile of letters from two prominent British trade unionists, inviting their South American counterparts to make an official visit to Britain to raise funds and support. In early August, Barbor-Might finally flew to Santiago.

'Pat met me at the airport. We got a taxi into the city. I remember as we drove along the sheer quality of the light.' It fell first on fields, flat against the mountains and fresh with the early spring; then on walled vineyards and farm workers smoking at crossroads; then on the first distant, sunlit tower blocks; the first juddering yellow backs of buses on the dual carriageway; the first squatters' encampments of mud and corrugated iron and old cars; the windowless pastel houses of Santiago's outer suburbs; the corner shops like busy caves; the bright crowded pavements, and the palms along the central reservation; the traffic thickening to a honking, jostling crawl; the buildings growing heavier and taller; the red banners strung from their grey facades along the Alameda, the capital's enormous main boulevard; young Chileans sitting and talking on its public lawns – the clean-edged Pacific light, it seemed, fell on a city more alive than any city Barbor-Might had ever been to before.

'Pat was living in a sort of courtyard house,' he remembers. It was just off the Alameda, opposite an old Franciscan church, about 200 yards from the presidential palace. There were half a dozen people sharing her flat, including two more English women and an English man on an international scholarship called Adrian Jansen. Barbor-Might immediately felt a charge: 'There was a way of using space. There was an ease – an eye contact – between men and women. There was a colour, a gaiety, a kindness that was entrancing.' And, under it all, 'There was a sense of belonging to something very large and powerful. That could make changes.'

After a few days acclimatising and being shown around, he ventured out into the city on his own. He had been invited to dinner with a French 'worker-priest' on the other side of Santiago. His account of the evening still has a solemn, step-by-step rhythm to it: 'I walked through the city. There was no transport. I was hours late. We had dinner. They had no English. I had vestigial French. We struggled through.' Barbor-Might pauses, untypically, and loses his thread for a moment. 'I was a Christian then . . . I've no words to describe the feeling in that priest's flat. The Christ-like aspect . . . I had one of the most profound experiences of my life. A sense of being taken to a political level without falsifying the human.'

Once he had delivered his letters of British support to the Chilean trades union organisation, the CUT, he was treated like a visiting dignitary. He was taken to a factory that had been occupied by its workers. He met Victor Jara. He was given good access to government officials for his *New Statesman* article, including several appointments at La Moneda. In its hidden interior courtyards and rings of high, shuttered offices, 'Everything was quiet and calm. There were fountains. Everyone was going about their business.' On the rare occasions when the purpose of it all became too much, he and Pat would escape from the smoggy bowl of Santiago. 'Once we went up to the Andes. We got right up to the snow line.' He loved the sharp black-and-white peaks, receding as if to infinity; the empty, cleansing landscape. But the revolution's appetite for participants, and vice versa, always drew them back.

'In early September, I was drinking with Pat in a bar in Santiago, when there was suddenly something like a river of people outside.'

They joined it with barely a thought, as it flowed down the Alameda towards the presidential palace. There were loudspeakers set up in the trees at the roadside, calling for Allende to come out. There were trucks and buses full of Allende supporters, advancing with the crowd. 'I've got a picture in my mind of being in front of a great cement-mixing lorry. The lorries would stop and give you a lift. There was a feeling of creativity and straightforwardness.'

Everyone hurried to the deep square in front of La Moneda, where the march had stopped and spilled into a human lake: hundreds of thousands of people, perhaps even half a million. Barbor-Might and Stocker squeezed their way to within a few yards of the palace. Then Allende appeared on a balcony above them. He gave a brief, downbeat speech. 'Pat translated. He said something like, "I am running out of options. It will be for you, for your generation, to find the solution." Then everything went completely silent. Everyone walked away in total silence. Me and Pat went to a basement bar, and I wept. Which was something I'd never done before.'

There is a slight wetness beneath Barbor-Might's thick, greying eyebrows as he finishes the story. 'Emotionally I am still in seventies mode,' he says, characteristically shifting into self-criticism, 'although in my head I know things have moved on.' He looks down at the table, at our mugs of coffee, which have gone cold. He is in his mid-sixties now. His health is not perfect. It is over a quarter of a century, and many political revolutions, since the few weeks in Santiago he has been describing. 'You can't have history a second time,' he adds.

But it is obvious he does not really believe this. A few sentences later, his big eyes dampen again. 'I remain a socialist very strongly,' he says, in the manner of someone stating their faith. 'If I'm on my own, which I am a lot, I go through what I experienced in Chile a lot. The re-creation of the feelings and convictions of that era is crucial . . .' His voice lifts: 'To bring it to a younger generation.'

We are sitting in his narrow living room, in his first-floor sliver of a flat, in a tight terraced street in Birmingham with mattresses and weeds in people's front gardens. It is April 2000; a month since Pinochet went back to Chile. It is sleeting outside, as inner-city Birmingham hurries past with its bags of shopping. The gas fire has been on all afternoon behind Barbor-Might's net curtains.

In the fug of sunken armchairs and old carpets and old files about

Chile, on shelves that extend out into the corridor, Allende and Pinochet and all the rest still seem quite real. Violeta Parra, one of the founders of the New Chilean Song movement, is singing on the spotless CD player. Her voice is slightly like Edith Piaf's, roughening the edges of her words and relishing her r's as the guitar hums and clicks beneath her, but with a trembling, more vulnerable quality. 'She's got a lovely voice,' says Barbor-Might with a faraway look, rolling his thumbs on the table in time with the rhythm. 'You can find her in the Santiago General Cemetery, near to Salvador Allende's grave.'

When I arrived in Birmingham, around lunchtime, Barbor-Might had met me by the side gate to his flat with the news that he was composing a letter to the Chilean president. The wet snow was settling on his shoulders and hair, which was still thick and bowl-shaped like a 1960s schoolboy's, but he had been too preoccupied to put a coat on. He shook my hand eagerly and led me upstairs, limping slightly. In the living room, another man of similar age, with spectacles on a cord round his neck, was helping Barbor-Might compose. They continued for a few minutes: Barbor-Might typing rapidly with two fingers at the desk in one corner of the room, hitting the computer keys hard, and the other man making suggestions, sometimes met with brisk rejections. Their letter was crisp, with both particular and general points to impress on the current incumbent, Ricardo Lagos (once a subordinate of Allende, now more of a South American Blairite): that the prosecution of Pinochet should continue; and that the political murders of certain named individuals under his rule should be further investigated. The general might have got away for now, but the Birmingham Group for the Disappeared in Chile was not going to be giving up.

It is one vehicle of many that Barbor-Might has used to pursue his great cause across the decades. When he lent me one of his files on Chile, its yellowed pages were so squeezed in and numerous that the ragged edges of the holes for the ring binder had intertwined, locking the paper into a single block. There were urgent lobbying letters he had written to British ministers, and accounts of the stonewalling meetings he had secured with them; there was a three-page statement of support secured from Neil Kinnock in 1977; a smudged photocopy of a picture of Denis Healey, then deputy leader of the Labour Party, at a vigil for Chile in 1981; details of the disappearance of a senior MIR member some time during 1973 or 1974; even, rather startlingly, a letter from Margaret Thatcher's private office on the eve of her first election victory: 'Mrs Thatcher has been kept informed about the unhappy case referred to . . . Let there be no doubt in your mind that the next Conservative Government will give the whole question of human rights top priority . . .'

Beside Barbor-Might's desk, I noticed, there was a new black briefcase, standing ready for the next meeting. Even a dispiriting trip back to Chile in 1998, his first and only one, had not discouraged him for long. After a fortnight in Santiago and Valparaíso, investigating the privatised pension system and avoiding nostalgic locations, he had concluded that 'The [Lagos] government was operating policies it had adopted wholesale from the Pinochet era. It seemed to me that there had been a fundamental shift: the country wasn't going to become a socialist country again.' But then, a few months later, Pinochet was arrested, and the old hopes returned, and Barbor-Might was hammering out letters again.

It is past seven o'clock before I can pause the interview and mention my train back to London. He kindly offers to call a taxi. We wait a quarter of an hour for it to come, as the chill deepens outside, and the gas fire hisses. 'I saw a great strength in Chile in '73,' Barbor-Might has time to re-emphasise. 'People who were in the Spanish Civil War speak of the quality of human relations . . .'

One evening in Valparaíso, a few months earlier, I had got a hint of what he meant. It was towards the end of the presidential election campaign that, along with Pinochet's detention in Britain, had been preoccupying the Chilean newspapers for most of 1999. Lagos, cautious and elderly-looking, was standing against a man with very white teeth called Joaquin Lavin, who was mayor of Las Condes, the wealthy eastern part of Santiago, and who had once been an adviser to General Pinochet. There had been much obvious potential for the refighting of old battles – Lagos had even been imprisoned by Pinochet – but the campaign had mostly avoided them. Both sides had recognised a long-established truth about Chilean politics. The Left and the Right each have the loyal support of about a third of the electorate, on an instinctive, almost tribal basis. The precise ideologies and voting preferences of the rest of the public are as blurred and shifting as the shoal of small centre parties that have flitted through Chile's political history. So the way to win power, democratically at least, has been to build coalitions and claim to stand for the whole nation. Even a radical like Allende had to do it. In the 1999 election, this traditional strategy meant not saying anything contentious about Pinochet, for or against, and concentrating instead on looking kindly and wise, if you were Lagos, or young and businesslike, if you were Lavin.

All this highly televisual moderation, however, had an unexpected consequence. Lagos had long been favourite for the presidency: the parties backing him had been in power since Pinochet had been forced to retire as national leader in 1990, and the country was not generally felt to be ready for a president with links to the dictator. Yet as Santiago began putting out its summer furniture, Lavin suddenly started to catch up in the opinion polls. His smile and spouse became more prominent on news broadcasts, always surrounded by mobs of similar Chileans: light brown and prosperous-looking, of mainly European rather than local ancestry, exuding the clean-living aspiration associated with Las Condes. Lagos, meanwhile, always seemed to be visiting farms, and holding earnest conversations with filthy workers. He began to look like the past.

By December, Lavin had narrowly passed him in the polls. In Britain, there was excitement in the parts of the right-wing press that had developed a sudden interest in all things Chilean. Lavin, it was assumed, would demand Pinochet's return with more vigour than Lagos, whose attitude to the general's foreign incarceration seemed to vacillate between official unhappiness and quiet satisfaction. Lord Lamont, Pinochet's most tireless ally in London, wrote an article in the *Spectator* predicting success for Lavin on the basis that his election posters were more numerous. Or at least, they had been in the areas of Santiago that the Pinochet Foundation had recently invited the former Conservative Chancellor of the Exchequer to visit.

But Chilean newspapers drew a different conclusion from Lavin's apparent strength – the Chancellor's political judgement, after all, had never been flawless. The closer the Right seemed to power, the argument went, the more likely it was that every grey-bearded Marxist, and former MIRista, and collector of Allende memorabilia would come out and vote. Perhaps for Lagos; or perhaps, to punish his many compromises with Pinochet's Chile, for the Communist Party's own candidate, Gladys Marin. She was a woman of high profile and an embattled charisma. Her husband had been martyred under the dictator. Her party still had a certain status, and significant support. During the last week of the campaign, her long and handsome Andean face started to appear in the papers with increasing frequency. Her final rally was planned for Valparaíso, on 9 December.

I heard about it from a scrawl of red spray-paint on a rock. 'GLADYS PLAZA VICTORIA 9 DEC 1800', it read in urgent letters, on a section of the cliff face underneath the Brighton Bed & Breakfast too steep even for the local builders. It was my very first day in Valparaíso; I had been clambering up and down hills in search of Cochrane all afternoon. When I saw the graffiti, it was past five o'clock, and I was aching my way up the last incline to my room. I carried on to the Brighton, and lay down on my thin bed, wondering whether to bother. Then a truck went by below my window. It was playing a song at great volume. Through the distortion, and the screeches of the other traffic, and the port's general honk and rattle, the word 'socialist' was just identifiable, ending every line of the song. I put my shoes back on.

When I got to the Plaza Victoria, where the young Pinochet once used to play between the trees and bandstand, I immediately saw a youngish man in a Che Guevara T-shirt. Up closer, I realised it was advertising an American rock band. But on the far side of the square, facing down Valparaíso's main shopping street, there was a stage of respectable size. Its backdrop was a great white sheet with 'Gladys' printed on it next to an outline of her fierce smiling face, and, off to one side but slightly larger, a picture of Allende. Although he had never been a member of the Communist Party, and had often argued with them when they governed together, his thick glasses and grandfatherly cheeks evidently did not require a caption.

Along the sides of the street, which had been closed to traffic, a trestle table and other makeshift stalls had been set up. A man who would barely have been born in the early 1970s was selling Allende posters from the table, as I passed, to a young mother and daughter who definitely would not have been. Another stall was selling bootleg tapes of Victor Jara, and a Chilean protest album against the Vietnam War. At the kerbside, teenagers proffered Chilean flags with Allende's face superimposed, and bags of confetti made with white paper and a hole puncher.

There were a few hundred people in scattered clumps. It was almost six o'clock; most of the shops were still open in the warm evening sunshine, and the McDonald's was doing good business. A few of those waiting for the rally to begin were middle-aged or older, with black berets and beards and sunglasses, but most of the people talking and sitting on the kerb looked nothing like figures from documentaries on the 1970s. There were lots of children and teenagers, tidy men in tweed jackets, a pair of young men with management consultants' haircuts and armfuls of textbooks, even a couple of passing soldiers. The main difference from Lavín's supporters was in everyone's faces: big cheekbones, black hair with no blonde rinses, outdoor skin rather than poolside complexions. They looked like the people you saw wearing servants' uniforms in Las Condes.

By seven o'clock, the first of several songwriters was strumming stiff-armed in the distance. Some of the gaps in the crowd had disappeared. People were standing on the stumps of benches (street furniture can have a hard time in Valparaíso) to get a better view. Other people chalked slogans on the tarmac, or unfurled long red banners. Hammers and sickles were popular, still, and the names of militant shanty towns from the Allende and Pinochet periods, now somewhat less legendary.

The sun dropped behind an apartment block. The night-time chill started to come in off the harbour. There were speeches being made on stage now – in more than usually percussive Chilean Spanish – but no sign of Marín. Then, at about seven-thirty, I belatedly registered a faint drumming. It was accelerating in tempo all the time, and coming from the opposite direction to the stage, which I had been facing from what I thought was the mid-point of the crowd. I looked round, and saw a horizon of flags. The entire wide street behind me, as far as I could see, was suddenly solid with people. And at the centre of this mass of red and black and white, among the slicing flags and bobbing heads and the confetti fluttering down through the remaining shafts of sunlight, like an arriving monarch in one of the Royal Shakespeare Company's more epic productions, was Gladys Marín on the roof of a bus.

As it crept forward, the cleverness of the symbolism became obvious. The bus was the battered boxy sort still used by working-class commuters, Allende-era in design, the perfect vehicle for demonstrating the exclusion of most Chileans from the imminent good life of leisure and private assets long promised by the Right. An improvised metal platform had been bolted on top of the bus; Marín stood at the front of it, as if at the prow of a ship, waving. She was wearing jeans and a casual orange top, and squeezed up there with her was a radio journalist shouting commentary into a microphone, several less modestly-dressed women, dancing, a paunchy bald man of unclear purpose, another middle-aged man with a beard, and a whole crowd of other unselfconscious workers' representatives. When the bus stopped in front of the stage, Marin had to climb down a ladder, brushing the confetti from her hair.

Her opening mention of Allende drew crackling applause. The first reference to Pinochet – the 'criminal de Londres' – got cheers and whistles. Then there was an attack on Lagos for his 'neoliberalisme'; outrage at the consequent 'milliones e milliones' of Chileans in poverty; old-fashioned talk of 'el pueblo' (the people); hoarse pleas for a return to the 'collectivo'. Marin rolled up her sleeves, pointed her strong fingers, and scolded modern Chile. Half an hour in, she was still picking up speed. A few people were talking among themselves, but most people were raising their heads to catch every word.

Afterwards, on my way back to the Brighton, I went to an old fish restaurant. It was a long brown room, its walls hung with swords and anchors and models of sailing ships. There were a few other diners. A middle-aged couple with an academic look about them were sharing half a bottle of red. A man of about fifty was sharing a plate of chips with a woman in tight jeans, who might have been his daughter. Each pair was staring at the other. But up to now, their evenings had not been so different. The academics had a pile of Gladys Marin stickers on their side plates. And the man of fifty was picking white confetti out of the young woman's hair. Under her thigh, she had a rolled-up red flag for safe keeping.

That night, I lay awake for a while listening to Marin's supporters drive round the town, chanting, 'Gla-dys! Gla-dys!' But in Chilean politics, at least, it is probably unwise for foreigners to become too excited in their expectations. When the election result was announced a few days later, Lagos had won narrowly. Marin got 3 per cent of the vote.

8

The Coup

The success of Allende's first year was partly an illusion. His government had inherited a budget surplus from Frei. It had been handed an economy in an understretched condition. The all-important harvest had been sown before the election, and all the disruptive political pressures its result would release in the farming areas of the dry central valley and damp south.

So Allende had been able to jolt Chile awake by sharp increases in state spending, welfare payments and working-class wages without running out of money or overstimulating the economy and causing inflation. During 1971, unemployment halved in the spider's web of industrial suburbs around Santiago. The gross national product leapt by 8.5 per cent. And inflation actually fell, from 35 to 22 per cent. When such statistics have been the result of the application of free-market principles, at that time or since, they have usually been hailed by right-wing economists as a 'miracle' or a 'model'.

The grey austerity that wealthy Chileans and many foreign observers expected when Allende was elected – during September 1970 the cool lobbies of Santiago banks clattered with well-dressed people transferring assets to foreign capitals – did not immediately materialise. The sudden and substantial improvement in the incomes of the majority of Chileans meant, for the first time, that they could share a little in the consumerism long considered a birthright by the prosperous. People could afford cheap televisions, even cars, and eat red meat on a more regular basis. Some of them stopped working as domestic servants in favour of the better-paid and unionised jobs being created by the state. Part of the outrage about the direction of the country that would spread in Las Condes and similar areas in the coming months was generated, indirectly, by this redistribution of opportunities. Chile, as it had developed so far, was a narrow, relatively unproductive place – for all its Californian weather and famous agricultural estates, a lot of produce had to be imported – and greater social equality meant shortages. The matrons of Santiago were not accustomed to queues and items in the shops selling out. By 1972, both would be regular occurrences.

The government's popularity had peaked by then. In April 1971, at the local elections which Allende encouraged voters to treat as a referendum on his administration, his Popular Unity coalition won 49.7 per cent of the vote across Chile as a whole. It was a very high figure for any democratic contest: in Britain such a mandate would be considered exceptional in any country-wide election. Unsurprisingly, this sort of comparison – indeed any mention of the 1971 elections at all – was absent from the many speeches and letters, otherwise dense with newly acquired historical expertise, composed by Lord Lamont, Margaret Thatcher and Pinochet's other British allies during his detention.

In Chile in the early 1970s, however, the result was more than a debating point. To Popular Unity, it was a vindication, and an encouragement to be more radical. It seemed that 'the people', so often invoked rhetorically, were actually ready to accept more aggressive socialist policies. Rather than continuing to nationalise slowly by legislation, for example, Allende began to take over businesses using an old legal loophole that allowed the state to requisition important private enterprises whose production was failing. All that was needed was a prolonged strike or factory occupation, and workers were increasingly happy to oblige.

Meanwhile, he began to talk about creating a new political structure. 'At an appropriate time,' he told Congress in 1971, 'the replacement of the present liberal constitution . . . with a constitution of a socialist orientation' would take place. Given that Allende spent so much time resisting requests from the MIR and the more dogmatic Socialist Party members to abandon democratic methods, it is improbable that what he had in mind was authoritarian; most likely it was the creation of a single-chamber parliament, with less ability to obstruct popular left-wing presidents. But the opposition parties began to fear, or to claim that they feared, an imminent one-party state. At the same time, outside Congress, the wealthy and military and variously right-wing foes of Popular Unity began to worry about the regime for the opposite reason: its apparently growing popularity meant it might win the next presidential election as well. If the revolution promised by Allende was to be halted, other methods might be required.

For all these reasons, during 1972 and 1973 Chile's supposedly reliable democratic machinery went into reverse. Far from generating consensus, it began to produce distrust, not the usual parliamentary frictions, but a corrosive and spreading tension. At some speed, and despite the many politicians and voters – until the last few weeks, almost certainly a large majority – who were committed to democracy, Chile spiralled into civil war. The fact that this could happen in one of the developing world's apparently most modern and moderate countries, seemingly beset with the same problems – inflation, panics about essential services, growing militancy on the Left and Right – as many a developed one during the early 1970s, gave the news from Santiago great symbolic and practical interest abroad. 'What concerns us most directly,' wrote the *Sunday Telegraph* in October 1972, in a long article that abandoned the previously relaxed view of Chile in its daily counterpart, 'is the message Allende carries for the rest of the world and especially for Britain.' Soon, the example set by Pinochet would make them even more animated.

In Santiago, between his epiphanies, Dick Barbor-Might was becoming uneasy. He knew about the French Revolution and the Spanish Civil War and the ultimate directions they had taken. He sensed a similar polarisation, and felt it would not favour people like Allende.

One day Barbor-Might visited one of the local committees that had been established to control the distribution of essential foods and prevent the increasing hoarding of them by shopkeepers:

It was in a hall. There were four people sitting in a row of chairs. In front of them were two or three shopkeepers, looking dejected while they were told off. I didn't particularly like the feeling of it. They were being browbeaten . . . Then, suddenly, a vast crowd of people poured in, following a man who was shouting and waving his arms at the committee. The committee shouted back. Then they gathered up their papers and left. Afterwards, I recall being told that there had been a row over an election, and the man who was shouting had been sidelined. I got the sense that there was no superior authority. It was whoever could impose his authority.

He pauses and tries for a more urgent description. 'The hatreds in that room. I felt like the door was opening into a pit.'

On another occasion, he went to a worker-occupied factory that had been just raided and searched by soldiers looking for arms. By 1973, such aggressive initiatives and counter-initiatives were common. Even parts of the countryside hundreds of miles from the contested cities were being battled over, by peasants and landowners who for opposite reasons found the pace of land reform unacceptable. Allende, determined to move the country leftwards by consent, was more and more trapped between these sorts of interest groups, aroused with possibilities now and readying their weapons for the confrontation that they felt would soon come.

The factory Barbor-Might saw was a large one. 'It was full of party banners. Trade union leaders were getting up and speaking. But they had no response to what had been done. They had no counter.' Unlike the armed forces, even the most revolutionary workers had limited access to guns and were unsure about using them. Except for the MIR, most left-wing Chileans believed that the massed working class would spontaneously defend Allende if or when the Right sought to depose him. 'People were just defending with their hearts,' says Sergio Rueda, who was in the MIR at the time. One night, he was involved in trying to guard an occupied factory: 'I was in charge of the Molotov cocktails. I did not smoke, so I did not have any matches.'

A similar impotence increasingly afflicted the government. Some of its difficulties had outside origins, not always of its own making. For all the interest Allende had created abroad, foreign investment in Chile almost ceased after his election. The price of copper, the country's main export, had one of its cyclical collapses during the early 1970s. And after pressure from America, international aid and loans to Chile shrank drastically. The World Bank refused a request for a loan in October 1971, for example, saying that Chile lacked 'creditworthiness'. At the time, inflation was half the rate Allende had inherited, and the country's industrial output was up 23 per cent on the same month a year before.

Yet the experimental economic policy that produced such results was not sustainable. It was only a matter of time before all the new public and private money released into the economy during Popular Unity's first year in office began to push up inflation again. From that October, it rose continuously, first fairly slowly – 19 per cent in November 1971, 22 per cent in December, 25 per cent in January 1972; then in dizzying jumps – 77 per cent in August, 150 per cent in November, 304 per cent by August 1973. The gains most Chileans had made under Allende in their wages and welfare benefits disappeared at the same rate. For the last two years of his presidency, the country had the highest annual inflation in the world. The *Daily Mail*'s visiting correspondent, once so positive, now looked on in horror: 'Cash is useless . . . Housewives carry bundles of banknotes on shopping trips . . . Most necessities can only be bought on the black market. Chile is probably the world's first nation to establish a black market in lavatory paper.' Like the *Sunday Telegraph,* he concluded with a warning: 'The experiment [has] pointed up the dangers a relatively prosperous country faces when it seeks to reform overnight. And Britain has stood on the brink of just such rapid change frequently since World War II.'

This was debatable. But to British observers who were enduring electricity blackouts and inflation and shortages of their own, because of strikes and other forms of industrial protest by, among others, power workers, dockers, miners, dustmen, and Post Office employees, the Chile of Allende's final months did not seem so distant from Britain under Edward Heath's flailing Conservative administration. In both countries, it appeared that the struggle for resources between different social groups, always there below the surface of politics, had now burst out into the open. Picketing and lockouts, placards and police charges, raised hands at factory gates, official states of emergency – these were the symbols and rituals, the pictures on television, of civil conflict in Sheffield and Santiago alike. And the disruption of everyday life in both societies, however liberating and exhilarating for some, inevitably also disrupted economic activity, which made the resources that were being struggled for scarcer, which made the struggle between social groups ever fiercer, and so on. In Chile, it seemed, the whole process had simply gone further, and was nearing its logical conclusion.

Industrial output, more and more hampered by factory occupations, began to fall in September 1972, and did so continuously from then on. Agricultural output, increasingly affected by farm occupations – there were almost 1,500 illegal land seizures in 1971 alone, many of them encouraged by the MIR's rural organisers – dropped by 4 per cent in 1972 and by almost a sixth in 1973. The more intrepid foreign correspondents travelled south from the capital to find a semi-anarchy of squats, improvised collective farms and miniature kingdoms among the deep green forests and wind-stung sheep pastures of the lower third of the country. Proud former farm labourers with Kalashnikovs gave indiscreet interviews and strode round their new territories. Their kind of militancy, like the factory workers', had some sympathy with Allende's goals; it was just that his mild-mannered radicalism, as interpreted down here, seemed an invitation to settle ancient grievances against landlords and pursue almost millenarian fantasies of freedom and equality. The MIR were delighted to be of assistance. In the south, as far as they were concerned, the popular 'armed struggle' against traditional Chile for which they had been waiting had now started.

Other Chileans, however, were beginning to protest and strike and defy the law for a very different set of reasons. In December 1971, five thousand women in pearls and generally prosperous clothes walked through the centre of Santiago, banging saucepans together to complain about food shortages. The 'March of the Empty Pots' was the first of a swelling wave of middle-class actions against Allende: some spontaneous, some set up by his enemies on the Right, and some discreetly supported by the Americans.

In October 1972, the National Truckers' Confederation went on strike. The supposed spark was a government plan to set up a state lorry firm in a distant southern region, where private hauliers were failing to provide a sufficient service, in the view of the local governor. But the speed with which truckers down the entire length of the country stopped driving, and the equal swiftness with which the opposition parties and newspapers backed them, made the dispute look distinctly political. The long, narrow spine of tarmac – often a single road – that ran from the desert to the snowfields via Chile's overcrowded, hungry cities, was the obvious point of vulnerability for an already wheezing economy. For the next eleven months, the truckers menaced it: pulling their trailers off the road, arranging them into stockades on the verges and nearby hilltops. At its peak, the action involved 23,000 vehicles, and it never completely ceased while Allende was in La Moneda. Money from ITT kept the strikers in food and cigarettes. They were joined in their mass stoppage, at various points, by thousands of shopkeepers, bank clerks, taxi drivers, dentists, doctors, lawyers and architects, in a coordinated revolt of the self-employed and professional classes. For the government, the sense of a country under siege was as damaging as the worsening shortages that resulted.

The memory of it all still resonates in some quarters. In September 2000, on the twenty-seventh anniversary of the Pinochet coup which the Chilean truckers did so much to hasten, another left-leaning government was nearly swamped by a campaign by lorry drivers. Tony Blair hardly qualified as an Allende, but when British hauliers abruptly blockaded every oil refinery in the country, a few months before the anticipated date of a general election, on the apparently flimsy premise that fuel prices, which had been high for years, were suddenly now unacceptable, left-wingers who knew their history flinched a little. 'Let me remind you,' John Monks, the General Secretary of the Trades Union Congress, told his annual conference, 'of another occasion that trucks and lorries were used by the self-employed and the far Right to attack democracy. That was in 1973 in Chile, and it started a chain of events which brought down the Allende government.'

Some commentators thought him a bit melodramatic. Yet a similar-seeming coalition of enemies to Allende's quickly joined the British truckers: farmers and taxi drivers, pro-hunting landowners and wealthy 'countryside commuters', right-wing politicians and newspapers with a sudden taste for the civil disobedience that they usually condemned. As petrol stations imposed queues, then rationing, then agreed only to serve essential workers, then closed altogether, a slight sense of the early 1970s began to spread along the empty roads.

I was at home quite a lot that week, planning a trip to Chile. North-east London, usually beeping and roaring, was as still as Santiago on the days of the biggest anti-Allende protests. There were a few traffic cones blocking the entrance to the nearest petrol station, no explanation needed. A sleepy hot sun, unusual for the time of year, fell on the deserted forecourt. There was a sense of normal life suspended, of strange possibilities. I wondered whether I had been reading too many books about Chile. One stuffy evening I went to a commemoration of Allende and his overthrow, and sat in a room of Chilean exiles watching newsreels from the 1970s and drinking *café con leche*, as the central London rush hour dwindled ominously early outside the open windows. When I got home, there were reports on the radio of stand-offs at distant fuel depots. Rumours of the police refusing to act. Of foreign oil corporations content to see Blair struggle. Imminent food shortages. Hoarding. A truck advance on Parliament. 'Will this bring the government down?' asked a presenter on the BBC. 'Could it?'

In Chile, during the middle months of 1973, a new sort of worker was in evidence in the places worst affected by the crisis. The *colero* made money by standing all day in the queues, or *colas*, in order to buy and then sell anything scarce. There were other sights that were or were taken to be ominous: ostentatious gatherings of officers at military funerals, advisers arriving for Allende from Cuba. Dick Barbor-Might was riding in the back of a truck one day when he saw a small boy form a rifle with his hands, and sweep the hillsides they were driving through with its imaginary sights. He asked the boy what he was doing. 'Looking for MIRistas,' came the reply.

A coup attempt was widely seen as inevitable. It came in late June. In the middle of the morning rush hour, three columns of tanks and armoured cars rolled out of their barracks in Santiago, surrounded the Defence Ministry and La Moneda, and commenced firing. The palace guards fired back. For two hours, both sides were pinned in their positions, the walls of La Moneda and the tank armour protecting them, exchanging machine-gun fire across the lethally open spaces around the palace. At least twenty-two people were killed and at least fifty wounded, most of them civilians trying to flee or shelter. A Swedish television cameraman was shot by a tank as he filmed it.

But the rest of the army did not join the rebels. By mid-morning, its commander-in-chief General Carlos Prats, who remained faithful to Allende as the elected head of state, had persuaded most of the plotters that they were trapped and should surrender. The president had not even been at the palace; instead, on hearing of the attack, he had successfully appealed to his supporters to flood the centre of the capital 'with whatever material [you] have at hand'. The contrasting incompetence of the coup plotters was symbolised, it was felt afterwards, by a misfortune suffered by one of the tanks: it had to stop at a petrol station to fill up.

It was briefly possible to believe that Allende would survive. His government still had substantial popular support: in March, at the congressional elections, it had won 44 per cent of the vote. And the crisis could be exaggerated. Nobody was starving. Unemployment in Santiago remained around 3 per cent, the lowest rate in history. Allende made emollient approaches to the military high command and leading conservative figures, asking them to join his cabinet. On 9 August, Prats and three other commanders representing the three services did so. On 22 August, Prats recorded in his diary that another senior comrade had reassured him by telling him about a recent conversation with Allende. 'President,' the man in question had announced, 'be aware that I am ready to lay down my life in defence of the constitutional government that you represent.' The man in question was General Pinochet.

He had remained up in Iquique for the first few months of the Allende government, watching the border rather than the revolution. Then he was summoned to Santiago and promoted to be commander of the capital's garrison. The switch reflected great trust in him. So did the additional tasks given to him by the regime. He went to Moscow several times to negotiate arms purchases – a role he would relish for decades ahead, although not without consequences – and he even escorted Allende on official visits abroad.

It is not recorded how the slightly stiff and priggish general got on with the president, with his fondness for dinner parties. (At one such occasion in the weeks before the coup, Allende asked a British journalist, 'Does this look like *The Last Days of Pompeii*?') But they were photographed side by side: Allende short and dapper, in a slightly baggy suit and adventurous tie, a questioning tilt to his spectacles; Pinochet taller, rigid as a flagpole, a pale grey army tunic of nineteenth-century cut buttoned all the way up. His hands are hidden behind his back and he is wearing sunglasses.

In 1972, as the country polarised and people who shared his undeclared conservative inclinations began to call the government 'illegitimate', Pinochet was promoted to deputy head of the army. In 1973, as the capital seethed and divided into armed camps, he was frequently seen at drinks parties – ambition perhaps overcoming inhibition – with government ministers. In late August, as power lines were blown up by right-wing terrorists and Prats was forced to resign by his fellow officers for being too loyal to Allende, Pinochet was appointed by the beleaguered president as army commander-in-chief.

For the rest of the month and into September, support for a coup spread among, and was cajoled from, officers in all three services. The navy, historically conservative, had never liked the Allende regime. The air force held similar views. The army, split like Chile between democratic and more coercive traditions, was the pivotal body. What probably convinced a majority of officers to act, or at least not to oppose any action, was alarm: at the rising demands from the far left of Allende's coalition for 'popular militias' to replace traditional, hierarchical military units, and at the state of the country in general. That potential political interference in military matters could be seen as justifying actual military interference in political matters showed just how self-important the army – never defeated, the conqueror of the north, but without a war for decades – had become.

Pinochet remained in an ambiguous position until barely a few days from the chosen date. The coup was set for six o'clock in the morning on Tuesday, 11 September: close enough to the date of the traditional annual military parades in Santiago to give a reason for moving extra troops to the capital during the days beforehand. Over the final weekend of preparations, Pinochet was visited at home by a succession of the most senior plotters. To his reported surprise and anxiety, they told him of their intentions. He hesitated when they asked if he would join them. Finally, they presented him with a short, hastily written document to sign, committing him 'to carry out [your] phase with all the forces you control in Santiago'. On the back had been scribbled, 'Augusto: if you don't put all the strength of Santiago [to use] from the first moment, we won't be alive to see the future.'

The evening before the coup, Dick Barbor-Might and Pat Stocker were hitch-hiking back to Santiago from Valparaíso. Their visit to the coast had been cut short. He had been sick in a café: 'It was probably nerves. I was very wound up by this stage.' But they got a ride fairly easily. For two hours, they drove in the darkness along the single highway that linked the port to the capital. As they crossed the flat farming valleys, and climbed the steep intervening hills, and roared through the narrow passes and tunnels, they saw long encampments of truckers at the roadside, talking and watching.

Behind them, out to sea, the long British-built ships of the Chilean navy had suddenly just appeared on the horizon, like Cochrane's fleet before the attack on Valdivia. They had been on an annual exercise with the Americans, but between eight and nine o'clock that evening each ship's captain had received an order to return to port. They were then to carry out an 'Anti-Insurgency Plan' devised a few weeks before. Its start time, rather than its title, suggested its purpose: six o'clock the next morning. The coup had effectively started.

By the time Barbor-Might got back to Santiago, around midnight, the Communist Party had learned of the navy's unscheduled return to Valparaíso and realised its significance. The front-page headline of the next day's Party newspaper was hurriedly changed, from an announcement that Allende would make a speech at noon promising a referendum on his government to, simply, 'Everyone to His Combat Post'. But Barbor-Might sensed none of this. The wide city-centre streets round his flat were quiet. He and Pat were tired. They went straight to bed.

They woke up to the sound of gunfire. When Barbor-Might looked out of the window, he saw the concierge of their apartment block standing out on the pavement, watching something. She looked absolutely delighted. 'I knew the coup had started.' He put some clothes on, and walked down their street to where it joined the Alameda. The boulevard, usually jammed with traffic by now, was quite deserted. 'I looked along it towards La Moneda and I just saw dust.' He went back to the flat, and friends started ringing to see how he was. The centre of the fighting, from what people could tell, was very close. He and Pat got their radio out and searched the static for news. By chance, around nine-thirty, they found the only pro-government station still broadcasting, Radio Magallanes. In a thin but determined voice, Allende said:

This is certainly the last time I shall speak to you . . . History has given me a choice. I shall sacrifice my life in loyalty to my people, in the knowledge that the seeds we have planted in the noble consciousness of thousands of Chileans can never be prevented from bearing fruit. Our enemies are strong; they can enslave the people . . . But history belongs to us . . . History will judge them . . . Let me speak now to the workers, peasants and intellectuals of Chile who will now suffer persecution . . . No doubt Radio Magallanes will be silenced very soon too, and my words will no longer reach you. Yet you will continue to hear them; I shall always be with you . . . Much sooner than later, the great avenues towards a new society will open again, and the march along that road will continue . . .

Barbor-Might and Stocker listened, in his words, 'absolutely riveted'. Then, after Allende had finished, they heard something even more jolting. 'We picked up that there was going to be an aerial attack on the palace. I [Dick] said to the other people in the flat that we needed to get out of any room with windows. We got into the corridor with pillows. As we were sitting there, we heard the planes come in.'

The Hawker Hunters had been despatched out of impatience by Pinochet and his fellow plotters. Since six o'clock, they had generally suffered little resistance. Valparaíso had fallen to them in twenty minutes. They had taken 'red' Concepción by breakfast. Santiago airport and all the phone lines out of Chile were theirs soon after nine. The military radio stations had been confidently broadcasting a justification of the coup since dawn:

The government of Allende has incurred serious illegitimacy by . . . artificially fomenting class struggle . . . by its violation of the fundamental right to property . . . The agricultural, commercial, and industrial economy of the country is in stagnation and decline, and inflation is increasing at an accelerated rate . . . In the light of classical historical doctrine, we justify our intervention to depose a government which is illegitimate, immoral and unrepresentative of the overwhelming sentiment of the nation.

There was a logic beneath the pompous syntax that could support the overthrow of virtually any struggling left-wing government. In other countries, including Britain, frustrated conservatives and military men would take note. But Allende was equally convinced of his own rectitude, and he knew the power of martyrdom. Shortly after seven o'clock, he had left his home in a prosperous part of eastern Santiago (the cheek of his address alone had been enough to rouse some right-wingers to fury) and driven to La Moneda. Like his hero Balmaceda, he intended to make a famous last stand. Tubs of water were filled in the palace compound in expectation of a drawn-out siege. Thirty of his bodyguards and a few detectives arranged themselves at the upper windows with machine guns, bulletproof vests and gas masks. Government snipers took to the roofs of the neighbouring official buildings. Other employees were told to leave before the tanks arrived.

Until almost noon, as demands that he surrender came in by telephone and radio, and the tanks were grinding into position, and the snipers were firing sporadically, and the Hawker Hunters were being loaded with rockets, Allende refused to back down. After a fleeting appearance at a balcony above the deserted palace square, as if already a ghost addressing an imaginary rally, he put on a helmet and gas mask, fastened a bulletproof vest over his jacket and tie, took out a Kalashnikov Fidel Castro had given him – the theatre of it was perfect for posterity – and disappeared into La Moneda's maze of offices and cellars. At eleven o'clock, the plotters' final ultimatum to him expired. They told Allende the jets were already on their way. He and his subordinates squeezed into the remotest cellars they could find. At 11.55, the first rocket struck.

Barbor-Might hid under his pillow. For an endless quarter of an hour, the Hunters swooped and climbed and swooped again. Eighteen direct hits on La Moneda blew in its windows, caved in its roofs, set it on fire, and sent smoke worming out of its proud façade on live international television. It was the perfect symbol of democracy flattened.

But Allende and at least some of his bodyguards survived. When Pinochet's soldiers entered the palace through the smoke and blackened doorways, they had to fight for each room. Small groups of defenders surrendered, yet there was no sign of the president as they were taken prisoner and made to lie face down in the gutters outside La Moneda. The snipers were still firing from the rooftops. Elsewhere in Santiago, left-wing students were barricading themselves in the campus of the Technical University. It was rumoured that trade unionists occupying a nylon factory had shot down a helicopter.

When the tearing sound of the jets faded, and the gunfire continued, Barbor-Might suddenly felt less scared. 'Adrian and I decided to try to find the centre of armed resistance. We were angry. In my mind was the Spanish Civil War. They had not taken Madrid at the start . . .' In Spain, Franco's coup had been frustrated in the capital by improvised civilian resistance. In Santiago, the two Englishmen, a scholar and a pacifist, looked in the phone book for the nearest Socialist Party office where they could offer their services. They found one within easy walking distance, and set off.

They steered away from the Alameda, and kept to the smaller, less exposed streets that ran parallel to the south. It was a bright early spring afternoon; they tried to step quietly through the long city centre shadows. But their heads were roaring: 'You were living in the moment. It was a moral necessity to do something.' After a few minutes of passing shops with their shutters down, they came to a building with a huge door and the Socialist Party's name above it. 'It was absolutely quiet. We banged on the door. There were footsteps inside, and two or three people came to the door. They looked scared. They said, "Go away. We must all keep our heads down."' Barbor-Might pauses in his armchair, in his flat in Birmingham, and lets his big head sag forward. 'The idea of resistance died in my head at that moment.'

They walked back to the flat. After 'drinking cups of tea like fury', their sense of purpose returned. 'We were living through something historical,' Barbor-Might says. 'I saw myself as a witness. I wanted to be out in the streets.' For the rest of the early afternoon, he and combinations of flatmates made steadily riskier excursions around the fringes of the fighting. Barbor-Might took a camera. He saw the smoking hulk of La Moneda; 'little knots of soldiers crouched in corners'; a helicopter directly overhead, firing its machine gun, the sound of it 'like a physical weight'. Sometimes, he felt brave enough to take photographs. Most of Pinochet's troops, at this stage, were too preoccupied to see curious civilians as a threat or a liability. The dashing from street corner to street corner and the ducking for cover became quite addictive and emboldening, in the way that partial participation in public disorder often does. 'I got talking to a young tank commander,' says Barbor-Might. 'The lieutenant was very full of himself. He had a pearl-handled revolver. He was very keen to say he had directed his tank's shots from the command position [up in the turret, the most vulnerable location]. And he said Allende had killed himself.'

This has been disputed ever since. What is certain is that, some time between one-thirty and two-thirty, the president died from at least one gunshot wound. Beyond that all is infinitely politicised and unresolved. Supporters of Pinochet, and most historians, have favoured the suicide theory. Supporters of Allende, and members of his family, have favoured either a final gun battle, or execution. Evidence for the latter has strengthened in recent years, as it has become clear that an offer of safe passage made to Allende by the rebels during the morning was probably less than sincere. In 1998, a recording of a conversation between Pinochet and Admiral Patricio Carvajal, one of his co-conspirators, came to light in Chile. The recording shows, in what has been widely taken as authentically the general's tight, whispery voice, his response in the middle of the fighting to news that Allende might want to negotiate:

PINOCHET: Unconditional surrender! No negotiation! Unconditional surrender!
CARVAJAL: Good, understood. Unconditional surrender and he's taken prisoner. The offer is nothing more than to respect his life, shall we say.
PINOCHET: His life and his physical integrity. And he'll be immediately dispatched to another place.
CARVAJAL: Understood . . . In other words, the offer to take him out of the country is still maintained.
PINOCHET: . . . But the plane falls, old boy, when it's in flight. (*Carvajal laughs.*)

By mid-afternoon, La Moneda had been captured. The centre of Santiago had been very nearly shelled into submission. At three o'clock, a round-the-clock curfew for the whole of Chile was announced. The Englishmen went back to their flat and stayed there. Their flatmates did likewise. The phone and electricity were still connected; they had food. Barbor-Might's account blurs into the third person: 'People began to chill out, mellow out in the flat. People were probably drinking a bit.' Then it sharpens again: 'I remember the sound of tank tracks. Tanks turning. They were going south to the factories.'

The curfew stayed in place for two days. All non-military radio stations were silent. The tanks and a further aerial attack ended the resistance at the Technical University and the nylon factory. The snipers were killed or slipped away. The civil war which so many people, especially opponents of Allende, had been expecting – the talk of military advisers and arms shipments arriving from Cuba had been almost deafening in the right-wing press during 1972 and 1973 – never happened. This too would be an awkward truth for Pinochet's defenders in Britain and elsewhere over the next quarter century, with their central argument that the coup was an emergency measure to stop an imminent and violent takeover by the Left. Allende did import weapons and expertise from the Eastern Bloc, but never in great quantities. His Chile, fatally and to the last, remained a typically lightly armed democracy. It put its military faith almost entirely in professional servicemen, rather than armed civilians or political militias. Even the lawbreaking radicals of the MIR, with their semi-terrorist philosophy and their raids on armouries, had to train, Sergio Rueda remembers, just with sticks.

With the fighting quickly over, the curfew was lifted, although it remained after dark. Barbor-Might and Jansen went out in the morning to buy food. Less sensibly, they also decided to check on the welfare of the left-wing French priest Barbor-Might had met soon after he arrived, and on Mike Gatehouse, a member of the British Communist Party whom Barbor-Might knew and who had been involved in local government under Allende. Gatehouse had been well known in the shanty towns for his air of confident militancy, and his very blond hair. Neither quality, now, was exactly going to assure his anonymity.

The two Englishmen took cigarettes, a large bar of chocolate, and a radio in one of Barbor-Might's trouser pockets. They arrived outside Gatehouse's block of flats. The entrance was closed.

Adrian asked a guy in the street what was going on. The man was very edgy, trying to keep his voice down. In the gateway to the block, there were two more men, really giving us the eye. I thought, 'This is real bad stuff.' I said to Adrian, 'We've got to get out of here.' Adrian persisted with the first man for a couple of minutes.

But Jansen could not find out anything from him, so he and Barbor-Might walked off. As they turned a corner, Barbor-Might remembers, 'I heard and saw a screeching car come round the corner, and come to a halt just in front of us. Out of it jumped four *carabineros* [policemen] with rifles and machine guns . . .'

Barbor-Might stops abruptly. Then he says, 'This is the most important episode of my life.' He suggests we pause and have a look round his garden, so he can steel himself to continue.

9

In the National Stadium

Later on, I met someone else who had been in Santiago in September 1973. Barbor-Might had given me Sergio Rueda's phone number. They moved in the same small circles of anti-Pinochet activists in the Midlands. ('Dick can be very difficult to work with – he will spend two days on an anti-Pinochet leaflet.') Rueda had been living in England since the 1970s. Before that, in Chile, he had been tortured.

He met me at Coventry station in an old but immaculate Ford Fiesta. He strode across the car park, tall and in a hurry, and offered a crush of a handshake. He was middle-aged and beginning to thicken, with a moustache that suggested both confidence and sadness, and a complexion that had faded a little in the cloudiness and damp. The weather had suddenly turned hot but he did not trust it: he wore a vest under his shirt and an unzipped fleece jacket. He had pens in his shirt pocket and spectacles hanging from a cord around his neck. He looked like a factory foreman minus the clipboard.

In fact, he immediately began to explain, as we nudged through the lunchtime traffic back to his house, he worked for Marconi, the electronics conglomerate. His department was developing equipment to link telephones to the Internet. More importantly, perhaps, he was the local secretary of the MSF, the engineers' union. There were leaflets on the back seat of the car. 'I am of the old school,' he said, in his insistent, softly accented English. 'I do not believe in the new partnership between employers and unions.' He paused for a touch of rhetoric: 'You can have partnership when you are equal.'

In Chile, at least as he told it – with one strong hand on the steering wheel, eyes twinkling in his fleshy face, and the shops of inner-city Coventry creeping past – he had been a radical almost since birth. He had grown up in Arica, on the northern border with Peru. His father had died when he was very young. By the age of ten, Rueda was working on his school newspaper and sitting on political committees formed by the pupils. When I looked surprised at this, he gave me a glance that suggested that activism was the most natural thing in the world for some pre-pubescent Chileans. 'All my life I have been in a minority,' he added, with a certain bravado. By secondary school, he and his family had moved to Santiago. It was the mid-1960s; naturally, he had organised a school strike on behalf of the oppressed Vietnamese. 'Of course, I could not have placed Vietnam on a map!' In 1966, he enrolled at the capital's notoriously conservative Catholic University. Some of the people he sat next to in class went on to become right-wing terrorists for Patria y Libertad. But he was undaunted: he helped organise the left-wing minority in the undergraduate body – 'we did student reform before the students in Paris' – and he went to lectures on liberation theology, the new strand of Catholic thinking that demanded social change in favour of the poor. Becoming a priest, though, seemed too austere. 'I realised I liked girls.' Another sect beckoned instead. At this point, Rueda's story suddenly turned vaguer. 'During the late 1960s', as he put it, he joined the MIR.

By now he had parked in a street of small terraced houses. He lived on a hill above the concrete and flyovers of the city centre. His tiny front garden was the only one with any plants. In his front room, behind his armchair, a whole corner was given over to more: mostly subtropical types, their pots crammed together and their stems stretching towards the light, but all perfectly kept, like a Santiago courtyard. The rest of the room was just as precisely arranged: a small worn sofa, two mattresses stowed against a wall for guests, a mantelpiece of prints and photographs of Chile, and a set of bookshelves. There were novels by Swift and D. H. Lawrence, a Good Walks Guide, an old anthology from the *Guardian*, and a biography of Mary Queen of Scots. A print of Picasso's *Guernica* hung over the gas fire. A draught came in through the letter box.

Rueda told me to sit down, and disappeared into the kitchen to make *café con leche*. He returned with two mugs, handed me one with 'No US intervention in Nicaragua' printed across it, and continued.

At first in the MIR, he was 'on the periphery', going to political education sessions between university lectures. 'We didn't believe in the electoral process. I always thought Allende was very bourgeois. He never claimed to be a revolutionary.' But his election in 1970 was seen by the MIR as an opportunity. Rueda and other activists were sent out to the shanty towns around the capital to help dig canals and connect electricity supplies, and, in between, to spread the MIR's particular analysis of the political situation. In private, Rueda was less critical of the government's social reforms than the party line permitted. 'I buried his twenty-five basic promises [an early Allende manifesto] in a plastic bag in my garden in Santiago.' From his armchair, Rueda's gaze took on a faraway look: 'School milk every day . . . Until then, children had been *murdered* from an early age, their brain cells completely starved of nutrition . . .'

Shortly before the coup, he achieved full membership of the MIR. In public, the party permitted him to continue behaving as a left-winger, but his specific loyalty to the MIR was to be kept secret. During Allende's final months, the organisation was 'on high alert' for a military uprising. 'We built up our network: safe houses, training camps. Started to contact doctors, to see if they were sympathetic.' Rueda shaved off his beard and cut his hair in anticipation of a crackdown on radicals.

As soon as he learned of the start of the coup, he went to his post. 'My one-year-old daughter was asleep. I said to my wife, "Don't go to work. This is going to be serious."' He put on the most conventional clothes he could find, and left home on foot, heading for the offices of the state telecommunications firm ENTEL, where he had been working part time as a training officer when his MIR duties permitted.

Like Barbor-Might's apartment block, the ENTEL building was close to La Moneda. The MIR's plan, in as much as there was one, was for the employees of such strategically positioned institutions to go to their workplaces in the event of a coup, and defend them. Unlike Barbor-Might, Rueda could not avoid crossing the Alameda to reach his destination. 'I could see soldiers running, and shooting from balconies. In the arcades, there were pieces of brain on the arches.' But he reached the ENTEL headquarters. He found thirty other left-wingers inside. They locked the doors, pulled down the shutters, and waited for the guns they had been promised.

The telephones were still working, and they had radios. 'We got messages that there were army units that were staying loyal to Allende.' For a while, Rueda and the others hid on the fifth floor unnoticed, and watched the fighting – and worse – through gaps in the shutters. 'I saw a firing squad outside the gates of a building the soldiers were emptying, a block away.' Gradually, the soldiers captured the buildings between there and ENTEL. Then, 'I saw an officer pointing at my window with his binoculars. I ducked down, and the shot hit below the window sill.' A bazooka shell demolished the next-door office block. When mortar fire began to shake the walls as well, the decision was taken to retreat to the cellars. The defenders of ENTEL were still without a single gun. 'I would recommend anyone in that situation to use brown trousers!' Rueda said, holding his mug of coffee and laughing without much mirth.

Down in the cellars, with no orders coming from the MIR hierarchy – its central committee was itself engaged in a gun battle – the ENTEL workers had to decide whether to resist. Rueda was not keen. 'I am no hero. I wanted to see how my family were. I told my colleagues that we needed to retreat, to hide ourselves completely until we properly understood the situation.' The others agreed. They waited until the curfew ended, then split off in different directions. Rueda walked home unmolested. 'I felt angry. But I thought, "This is not going to last long."' On the way, though, he ran into a friend who worked in the casualty department of a local hospital. 'I asked him what the situation was. He said, "Very bad. We are lifting bodies everywhere."'

The number of people killed or wounded during the coup has been as contested since as the precise manner of Allende's death. Supporters of Pinochet, when they mention casualties at all, talk in hundreds. Opponents of the dictator speak of tens of thousands. What is certain, though, is that the human cost of the actual fighting was much smaller than what came afterwards.

Arrests were made across the country of anyone considered an enemy, or a potential enemy, of the military conspirators. Some people were shot immediately; more commonly, people were taken to improvised jails and interrogated. There was simply not enough space in the police stations and prisons used under civilian rule. The radical French priest who had so inspired Barbor-Might before the coup was bundled onto a warship in Valparaíso harbour and never emerged. Victor Jara was taken to an indoor basketball arena in Santiago and had his hands broken before being machine-gunned to death. But the most notorious and symbolic of these places of terrifying confinement, torture and murder, at least in the early days of the Pinochet regime, was the National Stadium.

It was a vast oval of outdoor seating in the southern suburbs of the capital, isolated from the surrounding streets by car parks and out-buildings. Around its long curving tiers of benches, fenced off to pre-vent pitch invasions, great crowds had been accommodated for football matches and political rallies. And beneath the seating was a labyrinth of corridors, entrances and exits, windowless changing rooms, concrete culs-de-sac – a whole architecture for controlling groups of people, already in place. Just as Chile was about to demon-strate to the world how easily a modern democracy could be turned into a police state, so the stadium, long associated with the noise and passions of a liberal society, was given a new, authoritarian purpose overnight. The first coaches full of political prisoners began arriving within hours of the start of the coup. Dick Barbor-Might was one of them.

He had been lucky not to be shot already. When the *carabineros* had challenged him and Adrian Jansen in the street, they had thought the radio in Barbor-Might's pocket was a weapon.

They came rushing towards us, shouting and pointing their guns. They pulled my trousers down. They were particularly keen on the bulky thing they could see in my pocket. I shouted 'Radio! A radio!' and they calmed down a little. I stammered 'British embassy', but they marched us at gunpoint to a police sta-tion, with our hands behind our backs.

The two Britons were led into a courtyard.

We were told to sit down opposite each other. There were twenty or thirty other prisoners – all men. A single *carabinero* was guarding us. He refused to answer any questions. After an hour or two, they brought coaches for us. We were told to get in. There was no need to use force. Everyone was very sub-dued.

Barbor-Might gives one of his piercingly honest looks: 'If the police had handed out rifles, we'd probably have asked, "What d'you want us to do?"'

They were driven south across the city centre. 'Everywhere there were Chilean flags – a "patriotic" directive had been issued by the mil-itary. But then we drove into a different neighbourhood, with large barrack-like blocks – workers' flats – and there were no flags. I felt a moment of hope. And then we turned towards the National Stadium.'

The coach stopped outside, dwarfed by the bulk of the multi-storey arena. They were ordered to disembark; Barbor-Might was too dazed by the procession of events to take in any wider details. The next thing he knew, they were being led down a broad concrete corridor, with other corridors leading off to the left and right. He could not tell which floor of the stadium's interior he was on, but guessed he was 'near ground level'. A sudden small anxiety struck him: he needed to stay close to Jansen, who spoke Spanish. Then came a larger fear. As they were walking, he noticed another group of prisoners: 'They were lying there, trussed.' Barbor-Might pauses, and raises his voice. We are sitting back at the small table in his living room. He is staring past my head. 'They were alive, I think. And they seemed wet. As I turned to look, I felt a finger on the side of my head, that pushed my head away thus . . .' He demonstrates. The finger he uses is stiff as a gun barrel.

'We were taken to a changing room. There were eight or ten of us in there, and some urinals.' Barbor-Might gets out a pad of paper, and neatly sketches the room, taking refuge in its neutral details: the bench they sat on, the toilet cubicles, the position of the lights in the ceiling. For a time, he and the others were left alone in their windowless cell. Under the bright lights, afternoon edged into evening. Nervous conversations were initiated.

I met an English businessman called Frank. He worked in textiles. He said he had been in favour of the coup, but had been detained by mistake. Before the coup, he had been to dinner parties held by the wives of army officers. The women would say how terrible the political situation was. Why would their husbands not save the country? And then Frank would get out his samples of cloth.

Barbor-Might and the others did not go to sleep on their first night in the stadium. When their conversations faded, they would watch the door. It was a shock when it opened: 'Some *carabineros* came in. They seemed very relaxed. They brought some men in to urinate, one by one. The men were wearing ordinary clothes – they looked like workers. They were holding themselves as if in some kind of pain.' Barbor-Might speaks with great deliberation now:

After they had urinated, they were hit very heavily with the butts of rifles. With each man, the tempo and the heaviness of the blows increased. The last ones were terrible blows. None of the men screamed or flinched. The last man to be led in had a bandage round his head. Where his eyes were was just blood. They didn't hit him at all.

The next morning, Barbor-Might and the others drank water from the changing-room basins for breakfast. They were brought nothing to eat or drink, but he still had his bar of chocolate: 'I think it was fruit-and-nut,' he says, smiling. 'I had a weakness for fruit-and-nut . . .' They shared it. Then the *carabineros* returned. They handed out brooms, and told the prisoners to sweep the room. 'Frank decided he was not going to be ordered about by this low-class *carabinero* . . . The police-man slammed his rifle into Frank's solar plexus. It took him hours to begin to recover.' The other Englishmen did what they were told.

Later that morning, they were taken to another, larger changing room. Frank was released. But the new room was crowded and very tense. There were Chileans, Brazilians, a Paraguayan Baptist priest – the scared remnants of the Allende coalition – just pacing and avoiding each other's glances.

I realised that sooner or later we were going to get interrogated. I was by this stage in a high state of anxiety. I had some scribbled notes on me that I had taken [before the coup] for an article I had been planning to write about the MIR. I thought, 'I had better get rid of this.' I would go into one of the toilet cubicles, tear up the notes and flush them away. But when I tried, they didn't go down.

Barbor-Might looks aghast even now. 'They didn't go down. They floated.' Then he heard someone enter the next cubicle. 'I scooped the notes out. Put them into my pocket. Sauntered out. The man from the next cubicle ran into the one I had been using.' Barbor-Might immedi-ately concluded he was an informer: 'I had a really good look at him. He was a youngish guy, Chilean, different from the others, with a smart leather jacket like no one else was wearing.' Barbor-Might sat down on the bench by the door and tried not to panic. He had left no trace in the toilet; if he could get rid of his notes some other way, he might be OK. His opportunity came quickly. The door opened, some prisoners were summoned, and in the blur of movement that followed, 'I gave the Paraguayan guy the wodge of paper. I said, "Can you take these?"' The priest agreed without a word.

Barbor-Might sinks back in his chair, and gives a devastated sigh. 'This is my shame. The man's compassion, his goodness . . . It feels shameful to me, telling you now.' For a moment, his big, kind face seems completely taken up with pain. 'I never found out his name.'

Soon after the Paraguayan accepted his incriminating notes, Barbor-

Might and Jansen were called for interrogation. Jansen told the Chileans his father was the British ambassador to Moscow. This was true. He was offered an apology, and released. Barbor-Might was questioned in more detail.

Three men sat behind a table in the interrogation room:

There was a very neat man wearing a tailored naval uniform. Slim, a small build. His name was Lieutenant Yunis, I subsequently discovered. There was an enormous man, like in a B-movie horror film. And there was an *investigacione* [detective] with a cigarette literally hanging out of the side of his mouth.

Barbor-Might was unshaven and sleep-deprived. He had started to come out in boils because of the stress. He was made to stand.

He took out his passport. 'Lieutenant Yunis, to my relief, spoke extremely good English. He asked what I was doing in Chile. I said I was writing for the *New Statesman*. I very quickly realised from his attitude that I was no longer being treated as suspicious.' A touch of remembered defiance enters Barbor-Might's voice: 'I decided to assert myself. I said I wasn't well, that I needed to sit down. The B-movie thug got me a seat.' Yunis, it turned out, had worked in London for the equipment-buying department of the Chilean navy. Since Cochrane's day, the South Americans had never stopped acquiring second-hand British warships, or commissioning new ones from British shipyards. Yunis appeared to know London well. And now he was embarrassed at what had happened to Barbor-Might. 'He apologised. He said I must understand the nature of the situation. Before he got up to leave the room, he said, very emphatically, "If you've seen bad things in this stadium, please don't blame the Chilean navy."'

Barbor-Might was not let go immediately. But he was given a packet of biscuits. The off-duty *carabineros*, he noticed, were not fed much better: 'They looked miserable, rigid, forking their meals down.' He was kept in the stadium for another night – he could sleep this time – and then taken upstairs to the open-air seating the following morning. He was still spooked: other prisoners continued to tell him terrible stories, and he had been able to listen, no longer concerned for his own safety, 'ears wide open'. But the sun on the terraces was warm. Foreign journalists had been allowed onto the pitch, to watch favoured prisoners like him, smoking and talking and wandering about up in the stands, apparently unharmed. He was already working out how he would get out of Chile and tell the world.

Then a military helicopter came throbbing dirtily against the blue sky and the pristine Andes.

Things were pouring out of its belly, and fluttering down. Some of them landed in the stands. I picked one up. It was about the size of a credit card. It said in capitals on cheap paper: 'Denounce to your police station the foreigners who have come to undermine Chile.'

The bad times were only just starting.

10

A Story on the Radio

The new government of Chile had formally announced itself within hours of the death of Allende. The make-up of the regime was a surprise, even to those who had long supported or expected a military takeover. There was a ruling junta of four: Pinochet, the head of the navy, Admiral José Merino, the head of the air force, General Gustavo Leigh, and the head of the *carabineros*, General Cesar Mendoza. All four of them had been relatively obscure figures until the last days of the Allende administration when, thanks to support from fellow right-wing officers and a panicking government, they had manoeuvred their way to the top of their respective services. Until they appeared together on television on the evening after the coup, their names had not featured in reports of the uprising.

Pinochet, in particular, had spent much of the day well away from the fighting, at the army telecommunications centre on the eastern outskirts of Santiago. He had sent his wife Lucia to a military base even further out – and even closer to the border with Argentina. Some Chilean historians have suggested since that Pinochet wanted an escape route if the coup failed; and even – more damaging still to his own heroic version of events – that his distance from the action was intended to be as much political as physical. If necessary, he could disown the uprising. He could even lead its suppression. The commander of the base where Lucia was sheltered, it has since been noted, was a known supporter of Allende. Conveniently for Pinochet, the officer in question 'committed suicide' in custody shortly after the coup.

In the junta's first broadcast, Pinochet spoke first, as the head of Chile's biggest and oldest armed service. But he sought to sound modest: 'I have no pretension to direct the junta,' he said. 'What we will do is rotate. Now it is me, tomorrow it will be Admiral Merino, then General Leigh . . .' The military takeover, he and the others went on to imply, was an emergency measure that would not be permanent. But two days later, Pinochet declared himself president. He appointed a Cabinet containing virtually no civilians. It immediately closed Congress. Decrees banning all left-wing political parties, and indefinitely suspending all others, quickly followed. The following month, Pinochet went on television to declare that his 'fundamental mission' was 'to make a prosperous nation out of a country in ruins'.

He was fifty-seven. Like Franco and Stalin, he had risen quietly and without charisma. He had been due to retire in 1974, having served the maximum thirty-seven years as an officer that the Chilean army allowed. But now, as he sensed his opportunity, his bureaucratic anonymity, his peacetime soldier's frustrations, gave way to an enormous self-assurance. You can see it in the stiff, supposedly menacing photographs the junta had taken of themselves soon after seizing power. Merino, Mendoza and Leigh are standing, in slightly vainglorious ceremonial uniforms – a century and a half of military self-regard personified – yet all their gold braid does not quite distract from the hints of nervousness in their eyes. A disorganised crowd of soldiers holding rifles in the background suggests how easily the three officer-politicians might be replaced by others. But Pinochet shows none of this: he alone is seated, his arms are confidently folded, allowing his tunic to crease, and his big head is perfectly level, hair showily greased back, expressionless face pointing straight ahead, apparently immovable as a figure from Easter Island. And he is wearing his sunglasses. In the version of the picture used in almost every British newspaper in the autumn of 1973, they hide his eyes. In the sharper print used by American magazines, however, his pupils are clearly discernible through the lenses. They are calm and emotionless as those of a fish.

In Britain, the coup coincided with an IRA bombing campaign in the Midlands, security at airports being nervously tightened, and another bomb being thrown into the booking hall at King's Cross station in London. Nevertheless, the response to events in Chile was substantial and revealing. Ron Hayward, the General Secretary of the Labour Party, spoke of 'the crushing of the hopes of millions'. Len Murray, the General Secretary of the TUC, wrote publicly to Edward Heath's Conservative government demanding that it put pressure on Chile to restore democracy. Yet a leading article in *The Times* saw the junta's initiative very differently. Under Allende, there had been 'hopeless mismanagement of the economy leading to a breakdown in public order'. The paper of the British conservative establishment continued, 'There is a limit to the ruin a country can be expected to tolerate . . . The circumstances were such that a reasonable military man could in good faith have thought it his constitutional duty to intervene.'

This was an exact echo, intentional or not, of the argument used by the Chilean junta, and by advocates of Allende's overthrow by various undemocratic means throughout the three years he had been in power. Tony Banks, then an abrasive young left-winger on the Greater London Council, was swift to spot the logical British conclusion to this kind of thinking. In September 1973, the Heath government was sinking beneath waves of industrial unrest; Labour, with the unions and the Left in general at perhaps the peak of their influence within the party, looked likely soon to return to office. 'It must now be acknowledged,' Banks wrote, grandly, 'that the election of a truly Socialist government in Britain is more likely than ever before. And therefore the question arises whether or not such a government would face the same sort of extra-parliamentary opposition encountered by Dr Allende.' In Britain in the next few years, improbably, this would become more than a rhetorical question.

In Chile, Barbor-Might quickly learned that his country's response to the coup would be an ambiguous one. When he was finally allowed to leave the stadium, he went straight to the British embassy. The ambassador, Reginald Seconde, agreed to see him but was 'cold'. The embassy gave Barbor-Might a diplomatic letter for his protection, but he sensed that they did not want to hear about the stadium. Some of the diplomatic personnel, including Seconde, had been appointed shortly before Allende's overthrow. Given the pro-military sympathies of the Anglo-Chilean community in Santiago at the time, and the right-wing government back in London, Barbor-Might has been alleging ever since – he mentioned it every time we met, and almost every time he phoned – that the British embassy had deliberately been filled with people sympathetic to a coup and the sort of regime that would follow. There is at least circumstantial evidence for this. On the first anniversary of Allende's overthrow, for example, a large advertisement appeared in the conservative Chilean newspaper *El Mercurio*, congratulating 'the honourable junta' on completing their opening year in power. The formal notice had been placed by the British Chamber of Commerce. Seconde was chairman.

Either way, Barbor-Might did not feel safe any longer in Santiago. He went back to his flat, and was reunited with Pat and the others. He fixed his letter of immunity to the front door. He introduced himself to every journalist he could find. On 21 September, the *Daily Express* published an interview with him, under the headline 'A Stadium of Terror'. Already realising how to market his experiences, Barbor-Might compared himself to James Bond and played down his political sympathies. 'Provided I had things to do, and it was daylight, I was fine,' he says. 'But at night terrors came.'

He tried to find reassurance by interviewing local people. He hoped to come across the first signs of resistance. 'Everyone said, "This will come to an end. But it will take a long time."' By the end of the month, he was still scared, and felt he had run out of reasons to be in Chile. He decided he would go back to England and raise money to help the people still being hunted by Pinochet to escape from Chile. At Santiago airport, Barbor-Might had a final brush with the new police state when a customs officer opened his suitcase, and confiscated the Victor Jara tapes he was taking back to London: 'I lost my temper.' He gave an interview about the Chilean situation as he changed planes at Buenos Aires. Amnesty International arranged a press conference for his arrival back in Britain. He was the first Briton to return from the stadium.

Other survivors of the coup had to keep much quieter. When Sergio Rueda got home from the battlefield, he took out his wedding suit and started to wear it for everything. 'Left-wing people wore jeans.' He went back to work at ENTEL until the end of the month, when his contract ended. He was unemployed for several months, and stayed at home while his wife worked instead. Then, in 1974, he got a new job in the telecommunications department of the state railways. Because he had been to a right-wing university, he was thought to be trustworthy. But when he turned up for work, his new colleagues found the fierceness of his apparent orthodoxy alarming: 'I was labelled as an army supporter. They gave me a desk by myself in a cellar. They thought I was an army spy.'

In fact, he had been back in touch with his old MIR comrades within a fortnight of the coup. 'We believed that we were going to be able to build up an opposition to defeat the military government. I thought it was going to take two or three years.' The safe houses were still there, and many activists had not fled abroad or been captured; they were joined by other left-wingers, who had dismissed the MIR as extremists under Allende, but now saw the organisation's paranoia and aggression as quite justified. During 1974, a cautious trade in contact names, useful information and false identity papers was established. New members were secretly recruited through sports clubs. Rueda assembled and distributed home-made radios, so morale could be maintained by news of support from the outside world. For May Day, the MIR decided it should make a small public gesture of defiance to mark the traditional left-wing festival. Every member was told to place ten stickers carrying party slogans where people would see them. Rueda's consignment did not arrive. 'I had to make them. Write them by hand on glue-covered paper.'

But really it was a cottage industry against a dictator, with all the advantages of a cramped, closely administered country at his disposal. A month after May Day, Pinochet appointed himself 'Supreme Chief of the Nation', effectively demoting the three other junta members to mere advisers. He had used his control of the army, and his greater political cunning, to outflank his rival officers. Every time there was a dispute over policy between them, he simply did as he wished anyway, knowing that the junta would not dare show itself to be divided in public. Once this had happened a few times, he was assumed by the population at large to be in sole charge. By June 1974, he was. As Pinochet liked to put it, 'A blade of grass does not move in Chile without my ordering it.'

The same month that his dictatorship was made official, so were his secret police. The Directorate of National Intelligence, or DINA, had been set up under his direct control within weeks of the coup. It grew to employ up to 10,000 people, and use three times that number of informers. It had interrogation centres throughout the country – one in Santiago was called the London Clinic, an appropriate prefiguring of the place where Pinochet would be arrested. It even had a foreign subsidiary for the arrest and assassination of his opponents abroad. During 1975, the DINA began to focus on the MIR.

'People around me started to be arrested,' said Rueda. He shifted in his chair. 'There was a woman they took round who shook, notoriously, when she saw a MIR member.' The DINA also used more orthodox methods of identification: 'The MIR was a kind of tree, and they would put together the branches, who would report to who.' Each arrest would yield further detentions. Rueda's organisation usually did not have the resources to hide its operatives or spirit them away to friendly countries. In the mid-1970s, it did not even have enough weapons for them to resist capture. 'We had a factory secretly making replicas of Israeli guns, but they were not very good. They got hot very quickly when you were firing.'

One day in late 1975, he heard that someone in the MIR who knew him had been detained. 'He managed to give me one day [of warning], so I took everything from my house that connected me to the organisation. My colleague said, "There's nothing to connect you. They will interrogate you and release you."' Rueda took on several false names. He slept at friends' houses: the DINA – for maximum psychological impact – usually favoured arresting people at home and at night. He carried on going to work as if nothing had happened. On 12 December, a Friday, just after eight o'clock in the morning, his manager telephoned him at his desk. Rueda was to report to him immediately. 'At that moment, I realised, because the manager never spoke to me directly. I rang a friend of mine. I said, "Look. Something is going on. I might be arrested."'

We had moved from the living room into the kitchen. It was early evening now, and Rueda had insisted on cooking me dinner. He moved lightly for his size between the squeezed-in cooker, fridge and microwave. The room was slightly damp, but everything in it was perfectly arranged. He took a very sharp knife and began to chop tomatoes.

'I thought, "Well, they are going to interrogate me, torture me,"' he continued, without drama in his voice, as if in a kind of trance, '"And if I can bear it, I will be let go after a couple of days." The most terrifying thing was the possibility that I was going to cry.' So he left his desk straight away in the basement of the railway headquarters and went upstairs to his manager's office. There were three plain-clothes DINA officials in the room. They were armed.

'They said they needed to ask me some questions, and then they'd bring me back immediately. They had a car waiting. I saw a friend of mine already in it.' Rueda's soft voice dropped further. 'And he was in a very poor condition.' There were more DINA agents loitering in the background in case Rueda tried to escape. Once he got in the car, he was handcuffed, and tape was put over his eyes. He remembered the time this happened: eight-thirty a.m.

They drove fast across Santiago – in the clogged capital, this was another habitual demonstration of the DINA's power – to the eastern outskirts near the airport. Like Pinochet in Wentworth twenty-five years later, Rueda could hear the planes departing but he was not going to be leaving for some time. They stopped at a large, detached nineteenth-century house with high garden walls that had recently been a smart restaurant. It was called Villa Grimaldi, and it was now the biggest torture centre in the country. Still blindfolded, Rueda was taken to the office of a Captain Miguel. There was no physical force involved. Very politely and formally, Rueda was informed that his wife, who was three months pregnant, and his daughter, who was now three years old, had also been arrested. Two names were read out to him, and he was asked their whereabouts. If he satisfied his interrogators, he would be released. 'We know,' said the Captain, 'that you have to sit your viva [Rueda was finishing an engineering degree] this week.' If Rueda was uncooperative, the Captain continued, 'You have to understand, I have all powers from my General Pinochet to do whatever I want with you and your family.'

Rueda knew the two people the DINA were after very slightly: he had seen them walking around the Catholic University campus. He agreed to make a phone call to their hall of residence. They were not there. The DINA drove him to the campus, and sat with him in a car, waiting for him to identify them. They did not appear; but someone from the MIR whom Rueda knew much better strolled past the windscreen. 'He blanked me.' Rueda said nothing to his escorts.

The DINA took him to their targets' workplace. There was no sign of them. The DINA made him wait for them in the Santiago streets they favoured. Nothing. Late on his first day of captivity, the DINA drove him back to Villa Grimaldi. 'The next day they started to torture me.'

Early in the morning, they came to his cell. 'The first thing they did was punch my jaw.' Rueda stopped chopping tomatoes, and opened his mouth wide. Then he moved his upper and lower sets of teeth sideways in opposite directions. The movement had an unnatural looseness about it. There was a loud click. The expression on his immobile fleshy face remained matter of fact but satisfied, like a lawyer presenting telling evidence. 'They hit me and kicked me some more,' he continued neutrally, 'And then they took me to another room.' It contained a bunk bed with a metal frame and its mattress removed, a small electricity generator, and several buckets of water.

Rueda was stripped naked. He was ordered to lie on the bed frame. His handcuffs were attached to it, and straps were also pulled taut around his arms and legs. Electrical leads were clipped to the straps – the DINA also sometimes attached the cables directly to skin, but they tended, when in use, to jump off – and then he was blindfolded once more. At the last minute, a bucket of water was thrown over him to improve his ability to absorb electricity. Finally, someone across the room began to turn a dial.

'I cannot describe it,' said Rueda. 'I have fractured an arm, had toothache, but this was all over my body.' The current was so great it cracked his teeth. 'I was thinking, "I cannot take this. I must find a way of finishing myself."' Then the current stopped. A set of questions was read out. 'I thought, "Either I die speaking, or I die not speaking." I didn't know the answers – well, I didn't know some of them – so I decided to mislead them, make them spend time and resources.' Rueda got through the first hour: 'I thought I was very convincing, that they were not sure any more that I was part of the MIR.' In the National Stadium, it had been reported, each torture session never lasted more than an hour; any minute now, he would be taken back to his cell. But the interrogation went on. The questions spat and foamed with swear words – all the earlier pretence of politeness, and rational inquiry was now forgotten. The next day, it all started again: the early-morning swing of the door, the beating, the shocks, the twenty questions. 'By the afternoon, they didn't have one answer. Captain Miguel came in and said, "How are we doing?" They said, "Not one answer." They began torturing me at night as well.'

He was kept constantly blindfolded. He was moved without explanation from cell to cell, from tiny shared rooms to solitary cupboards. He was forbidden to speak to the other prisoners. He was not permitted to wash, and was only allowed to use the toilet once a day. His health began to fray: his back weakened with the beatings; his ears and eyelids, his mouth and testicles, were all damaged by the electrodes. 'I had blackouts where I would lose the feeling in my legs.' To the DINA, such developments were not always welcome: in Pinochet's Chile, the point of torture was more often to extract information and spread terror than simply to kill slowly. Doctors were present at the Villa Grimaldi and elsewhere to ensure that prisoners could be revived, when necessary, for the next session. Broken dissidents were deliberately released to act as walking advertisements for the power of the secret police.

Rueda hid from all this inside his head. 'Every day I changed what "Sir" [the way he had to address his captors] meant. Sometimes it meant "bastard", sometimes another swear word . . .' When the DINA tried to hypnotise him, he would silently work through mathematical equations. He learned to communicate with his fellow inmates by hand signals. And whenever he was left unattended for a few minutes, usually in the yard outside the main guard house, where prisoners were deposited between torture sessions, he would try to sneak a listen to the guards' radio through the window. 'They would usually switch it off when the news came on.'

We were sitting in the dining room now. Rather, it was the room where he ate: a table against a wall, a couple of chairs and, behind them, occupying more than half the space, a large filing cabinet and rucksacks full of paper – the furnishings of a life taken up by causes. Rueda picked at his place mat as he talked. He paused frequently, as if slightly struggling for breath. The loud ticking of a clock measured his silences.

We finished eating: beef stew and rice, and salad with chopped egg and salt, Chilean-style. He said I could stay the night if I wanted to continue talking. But I was not sure I wanted to right then, so he drove me to the station. He went on with his story as we buzzed round the empty flyover. He described how, after a week, the torture suddenly stopped. How, as a special privilege, he and the other prisoners were allowed out of their cells, blindfolds lifted a little, to pluck the villa's lawns with their fingers. How his wife and daughter were released, and he was left unharmed for a few days over Christmas. How on New Year's Day the torture started again; and the long waits in his cell listening to other people being taken away to the bed frames; and the car trips in leg chains to the Santiago addresses he had 'revealed', where the supposed MIRistas always happened to be absent.

Rueda kept talking as he parked at the station. We were early. He switched off the engine, and began to tell me about his transfer from the Villa Grimaldi to a concentration camp in early 1976. Midlands commuters brushed oblivious past the car windows. When it was time for me to go to my platform, he insisted on coming too. As the train approached, and young executives gathered up their briefcases around us, he was still in full flow, recounting an escape attempt he had made from a DINA car. He had worked himself free of his leg chains, but could not get his handcuffs off . . . The door of the train carriage opened. We carried on talking through the window for as long as we could. Then the train started to move. He walked off with his hands in his pockets and a faraway look.

For most of 1976, he was kept at Tres Alamos, a detention camp in an old monastery near Santiago. Like thousands of others held in an improvised prison system that extended from the desert to icy Dawson Island in the far south, from shop stewards to Allende-era cabinet ministers, he had been defined as 'dangerous for the internal security of the state'. He had never had a trial.

Tres Alamos was slightly more bearable. Prisoners were locked indoors day and night, and slept ten to a room, but they were generally left alone. They were allowed an element of independence: cooking and cleaning for themselves, putting on plays and making leather goods for sale, the proceeds going to their families. On each national holiday, an amnesty would be announced, the inmates told to line up, and the names of those to be released would be read out.

Yet Rueda was never one of them. And he was still suffering from his torture injuries: his ears bled when he lay down. One night, as he slept on his mattress on the floor next to the communal toilet, an ant crept across from a nest under his cell. It tickled its way into his ear. 'I couldn't get it out!' he remembered with sudden emphasis, miming a violent, helpless shake of his head. Tres Alamos bred other fears as well. On potentially contentious anniversaries such as the date of the coup, the guards would grow more aggressive. And those not released during the amnesties would wonder about their prospects: 'When it got down to twenty-five of us [left], I looked round and thought, "My God. They are going to 'disappear' us."'

The arrest, murder and secret burial of dissidents had not ceased with the coup and its immediate aftermath. In part, throwing bodies into unannounced mass graves, or into the Pacific from aircraft, were practices intended to protect Pinochet and his subordinates from scrutiny. At the same time, however, these 'disappearances' were designed to attract attention to the regime's capacity for violence. The ripples of anxiety would spread much further among the acquaintances and relations of someone simply removed without explanation, it was realised, than from an officially recorded execution. Similarly, the uneasy lulls of life at Tres Alamos were intended to keep prisoners cowed and nervous. Right next door was another camp, Cuatro Alamos, where conditions were much more brutal and deaths still occurred. Worse than that, they could be sent back to Villa Grimaldi.

It was during another week's torment there in early 1976 that Rueda heard something startling. He was in the yard outside the guard house, trying to gather himself between interrogations, when he realised that the radio news had accidentally been left on. He listened greedily, and found himself hearing a story about a strike at a Rolls-Royce factory in Scotland, in a town near Glasgow called East Kilbride. The workers there had 'blacked', or refused to work on, a set of aircraft engines that had been sent there from Chile for maintenance. The engines belonged to Hawker Hunters, the very aircraft that had been used to attack La Moneda. The boycott, which had been going on for years, had been organised for precisely that reason. Rueda had a small epiphany: 'I sensed that I was not on my own. That the fight for democracy was not just my fight.' When he was taken back to his cell, he used the sign language the prisoners had developed to tell the others.

Over the following months he heard nothing more about strikes and East Kilbride. The idea that the employees of a defence contractor, on the other side of the world, in a country most Chileans had barely heard of (Cochrane had been and was still widely thought of as an Englishman) should care about the repression of South American communists – it all began to seem far-fetched.

Solidarity in East Kilbride

At Rolls-Royce in East Kilbride, there is an old file that has been specially kept, at the back of a filing cabinet in the union office, for over a quarter of a century. The file is only made of card, with a few equally flimsy folders inside, and its paper contents have become beige and creased. At some point, it has been left too close to the tea-making facilities: there are crystals of white sugar between the pages. But here, neatly stapled, the sense of a whole lost era lingers.

On 14 September 1973, three days after the coup in Chile, it is recorded that the regular early-morning meeting of the factory's shop stewards had reached 'any other business' when one of the union convenors, Bob Somerville, raised an unusual matter. He wanted the union to send telegrams to the Foreign Office and the Chilean embassy in London, protesting 'against the junta takeover of the democratically elected Chilean Government'. The motion was unanimously passed. At some point soon afterwards, eight Avon 207 jet engines belonging to Chilean Hawker Hunters arrived at East Kilbride for maintenance. On 22 March 1974, the union committee spread the word across the shop floor that work on them was to cease. For the next four and a half years, despite threats from Rolls-Royce and fury from Chile, court rulings, and interventions by successive Prime Ministers, half the engines (the other half were sent to another factory and then back to Chile) slowly rusted in their crates in a small yard towards the back of the East Kilbride plant. On 26 August 1978, by now useless, they were removed in mysterious circumstances early one Sunday morning and not seen again. They ended up back in Chile, it was said at the time, with covert British government assistance.

Reading the file's closely typed pages – minutes from union committee meetings, cuttings from half-amused newspapers, handfuls of impatient official correspondence – the episode seems like a forgotten early rehearsal for Pinochet's British arrest and what followed. But just as striking as the story of the industrial action itself is the recorded response of the public to the 'blacking' of the engines. The file is also fat with letters received at the factory, for and against. Their sentiments show a Britain revealingly divided. 'Get on with the job and stop this organised laziness,' writes D. A. S. Fraser in a neat typed letter from Inverness. 'Nobody minds you being communists, but they do mind you damaging this country.' Robert Leckie from Grangemouth, in a shakier handwritten note, is less tolerant: 'This is typical of trade unionists all over Britain . . . It is trade unions that have brought this country to its knees . . . The trade unions will be coming to an end sooner than you think.' An anonymous scribble on a small scrap of paper is more aggressive still: 'We are now taking steps to shut you up about Chillie. Also your talk about the IRA. We will be getting your black spectacles off you, so that you will not be able to see your way to work. So a warning . . .'

There is just as much melodrama in the letters of support. 'You are showing the way ahead,' says a telegram from 'Ken, Maggie, Rosie and John' in Oxford. 'Stand firm we support you,' says another from Liverpool. There are stirring messages from the Devon and Somerset Students' Association, the Kent Chile Solidarity Campaign, the Pollokshields Communist Party, the Chile Committee of Norwich, the Democratic Armed Forces Of Chile In Exile – here, in action, is the whole network of Chile activists and exiles that had established itself in Britain by the mid-1970s. Nothing, though, quite reveals the fervour then aroused by the Chilean question like the following, signed by Jimmie Quinn, Vice-President of the Warwick University student union, and Linda Pentz, 'Student Member Responsible for Chilean Affairs':

This beacon which has been lit by the workers at Rolls-Royce is burning brightly enough to illuminate the darkness of doubts and uncertainty in Chile and will be the torch to lead the masses back on to the path of freedom and happiness . . . We here at Warwick salute you as among the praetorian guard of the working class.

The manager of my bed and breakfast in Glasgow still remembered the boycott, even though East Kilbride was twenty miles away. 'It was a trauma for the town,' he said, getting me my keys. 'Rolls-Royce was a much bigger employer then. Lots of other businesses depended on it.' He gave me a meaningful look: 'Things got quite nasty in the factory.'

East Kilbride no longer looked like the sort of place where political confrontations took place. It looked like Milton Keynes: new brick starter homes on the outskirts, then car dealerships and a ring road, then a centre of clean concrete and flower beds, with everything low-rise and well spaced and little life on the pavements. The shops were aspirational – a pine showroom, a tanning salon, a boutique called 'The Village' – with a hint of financial anxiety underneath. A pub advertised 'Great meals from £1.49'.

Rolls-Royce were on the edge of town. I walked from the station along the swishing ring road. It was October 1999, with winter already in the damp wind. I saw the thick white factory chimney, under which the Chilean engines had been stacked, a quarter of an hour before I reached the gates of the plant. At the roundabout where I turned off, a vintage claret-coloured Rolls-Royce suddenly swept past. Then, beyond the town cemetery, was the long pale sprawl of the factory. It sat in a valley surrounded by newer businesses: PC World, an out-of-town Sainsbury's. From the road, the plant looked neat and modern, but behind its freshened façade and dainty hedges there was an infinity of oily yards, worn walls and piping, internal streets and Portakabins, waiting crates. Corrugated roofs receded into the far distance like old teeth.

Bob Somerville met me at the gates. He was a middle-aged man now, in an anorak. He was stocky, with the pink skin and swept-back silver hair of lots of men that you see in East Kilbride, nearing their retire-ment in the town's remaining factories. He was the only person who had been involved in the boycott still working at Rolls-Royce. But he had promised 'to get the word out' locally, and he had brought the file; as long as we were discreet – management were still sensitive about what had happened – we could talk about Chile.

The factory's social club was just outside the perimeter fence. We sat for an hour in one of the empty bars as the glasses from lunchtime clinked in the dishwasher. The bar was brown and dark in the drizzly mid-afternoon, with 1970s-looking furniture and decor, and Somerville spoke about the boycott as if it had happened the day before. He began: 'The actual blacking of the engines started when this lad saw the record card for one of them.' These gave details of the work to be done and the name of the customer. 'He noticed it said

Chile, and came over to the union office. We didn't need any persuading. We called a shop-floor meeting.'

Somerville was a member of the Communist Party then, and was familiar with the business of international political gestures. But he found himself 'surprised at how much people did know of the basics about Chile. A lot of the time when you do something like this, you have to keep going back to people and asking for their support. This time we never had to.' Three days into the protest, the management declared itself 'more than concerned . . . We are unable to establish any grounds on which work should be stopped.' But the boycott continued, and news of it spread rapidly. It was early 1974; there was a new Labour government, with a larger left-wing component than ever before. To ministers such as Tony Benn, Eric Heffer, and Judith Hart, Allende's fate and Pinochet's dictatorship were both issues in themselves and extensions of British politics. By late spring, there were frequent debates in the House of Commons about whether Britain should continue to lend money or sell arms to Chile. Such questions became a test of the Wilson government's wider intentions. Rolls-Royce, as a famous, struggling and recently nationalised company, with a reputation for militancy among its employees, was the perfect symbolic arena for a battle between socialist ideals and more profit-driven notions. On 21 May 1974, the Prime Minister was compelled to give Parliament his views on events in East Kilbride.

His evasive language made obvious his feelings about the boycott: 'For some considerable time, workers engaged on the work – a total of sixteen, I think, which is 1 per cent of the total employed at East Kilbride – have refused to do it. If the Right Honourable gentleman [Edward Heath, the Conservative leader] can suggest how they can be made to . . . perhaps he will help the House.' Heath replied, with unusual aggression, and to Conservative cheers, that Wilson's equivocation was a 'further capitulation to his left wing'. Wilson spat back: Heath had 'a lickspittle attitude' to the Pinochet regime. Another Labour MP joined in: 'It is in the true traditions of the Conservative Party that they do so rabidly support the fascist Chilean junta.'

By July, Rolls-Royce were worried enough about the 'adverse publicity' of it all to threaten the union in East Kilbride with predictions of a reduction in orders placed at the factory and in 'the future level of employment among your members'. Repair work was grudgingly done on the engines that winter, and four were removed to a less squeamish plant in Paisley. But Somerville and the others would compromise no further. The four remaining engines, which weighed a ton and a half each, were put back in their long crates, lightly wrapped in packing material without any moisture absorbers, and left to the Scottish weather. The workers watched them in shifts, day and night. The Chilean air force stencils faded from the containers. Journalists from right-wing British newspapers came to peer through the perimeter fence and write articles about the dangerous passivity of the Labour government and the management. Here in an ordinary Scottish town, it seemed, a tiny group of radical workers could effectively hold a whole factory hostage for their own political ends. Nobody could force them to resume work for fear of provoking a larger disruptive action – this, to Conservatives at least, was the state of British industrial relations epitomised.

In April 1977, it was noticed that the corrosion detectors in the crates were registering high levels. The same year, a Scottish court declared that the engines should be returned to their owners. Yet nothing moved from the yard at the back of the factory. 'They couldn't even lift them with helicopters,' one of Somerville's younger comrades told the *Daily Express* as he stood proudly on guard in his overalls at the main gates, like an Allende-era worker announcing a factory occupation. The expression beneath his faintly Victor Jara haircut was cheeky but satisfied. He leaned proprietorially on the barrier. 'They're too heavy.'

When the factory management asked the workers to take the engines out of their containers so they could be sprayed with preserving fluids, they refused. Some of Rolls-Royce's directors came up from company headquarters in Derby to add weight to the request. The workers refused again. Somerville, who looked from certain angles a little like Derek Hatton, the famous Liverpool militant from the 1980s, remembered the sense of escalation with fondness: 'It became a natural progression for us all.' In the centre of East Kilbride, people would stop the Rolls-Royce workers in the street and ask how 'it' was going. 'We went down to the Conway Hall in London for a Chile rally. We were mobbed. It was unbelievable.' On another demonstration, they learned that news of the boycott had crossed the Andes.

But at the start of 1978, a sheriff in Hamilton granted the Chilean government the right to come and retrieve the engines. Nothing happened for a while. In June, General Leigh of the junta in Santiago gave an exasperated interview to the *Daily Telegraph* about the unhelpful-ness of British officialdom. 'I am astonished at this disrespect by the Government in England towards a decision by the independent judi-ciary,' said Leigh, who was not known in South America as a backer of judicial independence. He continued: 'It is the sort of thing that hap-pened in Chile under Allende.' The *Telegraph* article was sympathetic, noting that the general was 'of partly British descent'. With a general election thought to be nearing in Britain, the East Kilbride boycott swelled again as a political embarrassment: after pressure from the Conservatives in the House of Lords and the House of Commons, and anxious that legal action might be forthcoming from Chile, the gov-ernment finally agreed in mid-July that the engines should be released.

It was the month that the Rolls-Royce plant closed for its annual summer holiday. With the compound almost deserted, and manage-ment having already given the Chileans 'or those authorised on their behalf' permission 'to enter its premises to take possession themselves', rumours spread in Scottish union circles of an imminent 'raid' to seize the engines. A private transport company had been hired, it was said, and bailiffs had been arranged to escort the trucks. 'We are prepared to exhaust all legal possibilities,' warned the Chilean government, omi-nously.

Some sort of confrontation seemed likely. 'There is no way any of our members will get those damned engines out of Britain,' promised the General Secretary of the Scottish TUC, Jimmy Milne. 'If scab labour is brought in, they will not get past the door.' A plan was estab-lished to rush pickets to the factory. The Road Haulage Association said it feared the sabotage of any lorries used by the Chileans and assaults on their drivers. Almost half the Labour MPs in the Commons signed a motion against the engines' release. James Callaghan, now Prime Minister, appealed to Chile not to turn to 'subterfuge'. Rolls-Royce, it was reported, were advising against the use of troops. Dennis Canavan, another Labour MP, predicted that 'the Chilean government might use force.'

But July passed without incident. So did most of August. Then, at four o'clock in the morning on the twenty-sixth, a Saturday, the only day the plant was silent, three trucks marked 'Harvey Haulage' arrived at the gates. The names of their drivers and their number plates were recorded by the security guard, in the usual fashion, and the trucks were allowed in. For the next two hours, the engine crates were carefully loaded on board. The yard where they had stood was swept clean. And, again without challenge, the trucks left.

'We were caught completely by surprise,' said Somerville, sitting slightly rigidly on his bar stool and looking straight ahead. 'If they'd come in during working hours, there would have been a massive picket. We would have lied down in front of the trucks.'

The crates were 'sighted' over the next few days at several Scottish dockyards, the RAF base at Brize Norton in Oxfordshire, and at a shipping agent in Hayes in Middlesex, near Heathrow airport. Unions across Britain threatened to track them down and prevent their export to Chile. But the 'moonlight smuggling' at East Kilbride, as the newspapers called it, had succeeded: the engines disappeared. 'Harvey Haulage' was found not to exist. The lorries' number plates were discovered to be false. The local police, who had allegedly been seen with a bailiff accompanying the trucks into the Rolls-Royce plant, denied any knowledge of the entire episode. Almost two months later, on 7 October, an international press agency reported that the engines were back in Chile and 'in service', according to the head of the Chilean Air Force Supply Command.

There were consolations for the protesters. In August, a letter had arrived for the Rolls-Royce workers from the Chilean TUC, which was in temporary exile near King's Cross station in London, thanking them for their 'magnificent solidarity'. The following autumn, Allende's widow Hortense came to Glasgow to give thanks in person. Somerville and the others took the train to meet her at a union office in the city centre. 'Here was a person that we'd only heard of,' he remembers. 'But there were no airs and graces about her. We shook hands.' A reverence has entered his quick voice. 'I believe she used the words, "This was a symbol to my people."' The workers walked with her in the rain down the hill to the River Clyde, and formed an improvised guard of honour. Then they escorted her across one of the footbridges. The cold water was grey beneath them, the dripping northern city rose on all sides of them, and Somerville's head was full of the drama and strangeness he sensed in the situation. 'There had been threats on her life. We were her protection . . .'

He let the anecdote fade. He got up from his bar stool: he needed to go back to work. Rolls-Royce had been privatised in 1987, and the spikiness of its workforce had been eroded; nowadays employees did not spend their working hours worrying about politics. We walked back to the factory gates. The barrier that the Chile protesters had leaned on was still there, I noticed. But it was getting cold now. I headed back into town, towards the pine shop and the tanning salon.

Crossing the ring road, the first set of houses I came to was a bleak grey curve of pebble-dashed terraces, with sickly green graffiti on the street sign. Somerville had suggested I stop off here: another veteran of the protest was living out his retirement at number thirty-seven. I was not ringing the doorbell with great enthusiasm when a short man in slippers with startlingly blue eyes appeared in the hallway. Dugald Gillies gave a wiry handshake and directed me into his spotless living room. There were cookery books on the coffee table, and not a single political volume anywhere to be seen. Before I could get him on to Chile, Gillies told me that he had lived here as a council tenant for over thirty years, but that when he had retired from Rolls-Royce in 1985, he had bought the property with his send-off payment – in the manner encouraged by Margaret Thatcher. 'I was never a member of the Communist Party,' he made sure to mention when we started to discuss the boycott.

His memory of the episode was slightly different from Somerville's. In the factory, before the coup in Chile, 'We knew about the Allende government,' he said, 'although we didn't pay it that much attention.' Gillies was a union official, but more junior than Somerville. 'When the coup happened, we saw it on TV. The nearest comparison I could make was to Spain in 1936.' Yet he and some of the other workers also noticed something contemporary about what was happening in Santiago: 'We knew it was Hawker Hunters that had bombed the palace, and we knew there were Rolls-Royce engines in them.'

Gillies gave a lopsided grin in his armchair as he thought about what followed. 'We got someone to paint "Chile" on the side of the engine crates.' He pointed to the glass doors which led on to his back garden. Beyond his hedge was the factory chimney. 'I could almost see them sitting in the yard from here.' During the blacking, the workers would not even agree to read the care instructions on the engine containers. Gillies took a sip of tea. 'We were maybe getting a bit cocksure in those days.'

What did he think happened to the engines in the end? He shrugged: 'They probably dumped them in the Atlantic or something. But we played a wee part against Pinochet, the old swine.' Gillies abruptly stopped grinning. He leaned right forward in his chair and raised his voice. 'When I see that old bastard Thatcher saying he brought democracy back to Chile, I shout at the television. He took it away!' Gillies sat back again. He offered to fetch some cuttings he had about the boycott. As he shuffled out of the room to get them, he added, 'Of course what made the blacking all worthwhile was that there was this guy in jail in Chile, and he heard about it on the radio.'

Sergio Rueda was kept at Tres Alamos until November 1976. In the end, criticism from foreign governments, and Britain and America in particular, led to the camp being closed down altogether. But this apparent relaxation was deceptive: just as important to the Pinochet regime as a more benign image abroad, now that the 'national emergency' of the coup and its aftermath were over, was the need to maintain an anxious population at home. Very soon after his release, Rueda realised he was being followed.

'I used to take the train to work. Mine was the first station on the route. Usually there would be a handful of passengers, but this chap used to stand next to me, when he had the whole of the rest of the carriage to sit down in.' He tried to maintain his privacy at home by having an ex-directory phone number. But the DINA rang his mother, and pretended to be friends of his who needed help with a forthcoming exam paper. 'Then they called me,' Rueda says. 'They said, "Hello. How are you?" And then they hung up.'

Seeing friends became impossible: unmarked cars would always materialise outside their houses. His physical and mental health were still fragile from his months under arrest, and he was not getting the treatment he needed. Like many former political detainees, he wanted to stay in Chile and wait for better times – even to work towards them, very discreetly – but temporary exile came to seem unavoidable. He already had a contingency plan. While he had been in Tres Alamos, his wife had written to the World University Service, an international organisation that placed refugees in foreign countries to study. She had applied for a grant for the whole family to come to Britain. Why did she choose Britain? Rueda – he and his wife have long separated – spreads his hands: 'There was no reason . . . There were other countries: France, Canada. But there was good health care in Britain. There were Chilean doctors in Britain.'

The application was accepted. Rueda would be permitted to study at

Loughborough University in the Midlands. He would learn the necessary English when he got there. He had no idea where Loughborough was. In May 1977, he and his wife and daughter flew from Santiago airport, then still small and ominously quiet – departing dissidents were sometimes re-arrested at the last minute – to the incomprehensible noise and muddle of Gatwick.

During the mid-1970s, over 2,000 Chilean refugees settled in Britain. Almost five times that number sought residential status. These totals were not the highest internationally: Latin American countries such as Argentina and Mexico, predictably, were more popular destinations, as were traditionally liberal states such as Sweden and Canada. But the movement of Chileans to Britain was surprisingly large given the distance, and the initial hostility of Heath's Conservative administration to fleeing supporters of Allende when the coup took place.

The British embassy in Santiago, unlike many others, did not open its gates in September 1973 to Chileans seeking sanctuary. The Home Office's Immigration and Nationality Department refused to treat Chileans differently from other immigrants. By the end of July 1974, months after detailed accounts had reached London of events in the National Stadium and elsewhere in Chile, only eighty-seven Chilean refugees had been accepted – compared to 806 in Sweden, for example. But by then Labour were in power, with their strong pro-Allende faction. One of the first acts of this new government was to announce in Parliament that requests from Chileans would be considered 'sympathetically'. Haltingly and then more rapidly, during the second half of 1974 and over the next five years, a South American diaspora was allowed to crystallise in British cities.

New arrivals would usually stay in London for their first few weeks. There was a frayed stucco hostel for Chilean refugees in Notting Hill, an area then renowned for its squatters and would-be radicals rather than its merchant bankers. The offices of the various Chile-connected charities, support groups and exiled political parties were relatively close at hand – the MIR in Ladbroke Grove up the road, the Chile Committee for Human Rights down in Pimlico, the World University Service over in Islington. Their addresses changed frequently but their premises were always the same: a few high-ceilinged rooms in some grand but gone-to-seed terrace, defiant posters on the walls, busy typewriters and kettles, political struggles carried on by box files and rationed phone calls.

Inner-city London in the mid-1970s was shabby and cheap and full of possibilities; it was not unlike Santiago under Allende, or Valdivia and Valparaíso now, with their avenues of neglected mansions, just waiting for the next generation of militant students to turn them into headquarters. In present-day London, though, little trace remains of the offices of the Chile campaigns. The MIR's base has become the Kensington Eye Centre, with net-curtained flats above whose buzzers show the presence of other nationalities. Only the still-flaking stucco and the old cars parked in the street – gentrification has not quite got this far – give a hint of the world that Rueda's exiled comrades once occupied. In Islington, the links to this past are fainter still. The former premises of the World University Service have been polished and refurbished into an enormous terraced house, with brass on the front door and restored Georgian decor. As I stared at the façade from the pavement, the door opened, and two young boys in hooded tops rollerskated out. They clattered past, talking in the same carefully downmarket vowels as the Prime Minister.

Once the Chileans were considered acclimatised to Britain, they were often dispersed away from the capital. The left-wing Labour councils in cities such as Sheffield, Coventry and Glasgow were keen to house them, citing the need for international justice and solidarity in a manner that seems almost unworldly now. In East Kilbride, after the Rolls-Royce affair had died down, Somerville got involved in finding flats and furniture for the refugees. Local people took them in while accommodation was sorted out. 'People were more aware of political things then,' Somerville says. He is still in touch with a couple of Chilean families who have stayed in Scotland: 'I talk in pidgin English, and they talk broad Scots.'

But the meeting of the two cultures was not a fairy tale. Within months of the first mass arrivals from Santiago, there were reports in British right-wing newspapers that Chilean 'students, political activists, and intellectuals', as the *Daily Mail* disapprovingly described them, were 'jumping the queue' for council housing. The inference was the same as during the Rolls-Royce boycott. British left-wingers cared more about making gestures for Chile than about their own country's well-being. There appeared to be local councillors and disgruntled Britons on waiting lists for flats who would back this up. 'The Labour Party is suffering once more,' commented the *Mail*, 'from what [the former Labour foreign minister] Nye Bevan described as "an emotional spasm". The subject this time is not Spain or South Africa but Chile.' The *Daily Express* went further. There was, it claimed, an 'Allende Marxist' group within the government: 'a new kind of socialism' was 'quietly being substituted for that old-fashioned, semi-virtuous British sort'. The Prime Minister 'now has to doff hats in the direction of . . . [this] Marxist Group.' In the photographs of Benn and Hart and other alleged members of this group that the paper published to accompany its investigation, the portrait of Eric Heffer – swept-back hair, square face, thick black glasses – made him look almost exactly like Salvador Allende.

In truth, though, all these speculations and accusations, while revealing much about Britain's wider political anxieties, told newspaper readers little about the actual experience of arriving Chileans. Even the *Guardian*'s much more friendly coverage often said more about the South Americans' heroic symbolism than the awkward reality of their new existence. (The paper frequently featured photogenic exiled actors and musicians: the mini-craze among British liberals for Chilean performers was substantial enough for a tribute concert to Victor Jara to fill the Albert Hall.) When Sergio Rueda and his family emerged from the terminal at Gatwick, their eyes adjusting to the grey English light, with 200 American dollars for emergencies and five pounds sterling in cash, the first thing he realised was that it was Sunday. And that the next day was a bank holiday.

They took the train into London. He had the address of a bed-and-breakfast in Notting Hill for which the World University Service would pay. But the taxi from Victoria station deliberately drove them round in circles; by the time they pulled up outside, almost all their English money was gone. The next day was an obstacle course. A contact from the WUS was supposed to come and see them and give them a cash allowance, but no one turned up. Breakfast was unfathomable: 'My wife and daughter were not used to tea and a bit of milk.' When they all went for a walk to test the area, they got lost, expecting the streets to follow an orderly grid like most of Santiago, and had to approach passers-by with their address on a piece of paper. When Rueda went out again, to meet some Chilean friends who were already established in London, he couldn't find the street they had agreed on. When he got back to the bed-and-breakfast this time, all he could think to do was buy milk: 'I knew if we had milk we would survive.'

For the next few days, London remained bewildering. Rueda had been advised by other Chileans to buy fish and chips, and take it back to his room to eat. 'In the chip shop they said, "Wrapped or unwrapped?" I thought: "What?" It didn't mean anything.' He bought baked beans, and rinsed them to get rid of the weird-tasting sweetness. He managed to find Hyde Park, but then his daughter asked for an ice cream. 'I saw "Flake 99" on the side of the van and thought, "I'm not paying that." It took me months to realise . . .' At their bed-and-breakfast, their landlady could not understand why they wanted to take daily showers. At bus stops, Rueda could not understand why he and his family were not allowed on buses if there were already standing passengers. 'The man would say "full". I thought it was racism.' Sitting comfortably in his front room in Coventry, Rueda suddenly screwed up his eyes and laughed. 'The concept of "full"! In Chile, if the bumper is free . . .'

But in truth, he had more serious things to worry about than England's unfamiliarity. He was still a member of the MIR. His ordeal in Chile had not dissuaded him, merely made his involvement more cautious. He had come to London 'carrying information' – Rueda frowned and went quiet when I asked for more details – and with instructions to get in touch with the organisation in the British capital. Yet the DINA, too, was conducting operations in foreign cities. London, as in the early days of the Chilean independence movement, and in the period leading up to Cochrane's recruitment, and during the opening stages of the Chilean Civil War of 1891, and in the controversy over Pinochet's extradition to come, was the external arena in which Chile's competing political groups had chosen to manoeuvre.

Exactly a year before Rueda arrived at Gatwick, the *London Programme*, a respected local current affairs show, had broadcast an investigation into the harassment, and worse, of Chilean exiles in Britain by the Pinochet government. The report opened with someone from the Chilean embassy taking photographs at the demonstration held in Trafalgar Square on the anniversary of the coup. This was not as minor an intrusion as it sounded. Every September during the mid-1970s, a large crowd would collect around Nelson's Column, and swing the red banners of the Chilean Left against the glowering stone buildings in the background, as they once had in Allende's Santiago. Many of those chanting and clapping against the junta still had relations, like Rueda did, back in Chile.

The programme also included an interview with an Englishman calling himself John Cooper, who said he had been hired by the Chilean government. Cooper, who was 'well-known in Conservative and right-wing circles', had been attending a meeting of the Monday Club, the Conservative Party pressure group then much concerned with more authoritarian alternatives to the messy British status quo, when he had been approached by an official from the Chilean embassy. Cooper had been offered a salary; in return, at first, all he had to do was collect the literature of the anti-Pinochet groups in London. Then he was instructed to find out the times of their meetings and what would be discussed. He was supplied with a camera and tape recorder. Soon he was entering darker waters. He was told to print pro-Pinochet leaflets and drive with them to marches organised by his dissident 'targets'. He parked near the routes of the demonstrations, piled the pamphlets up on his bonnet, and let them blow into the path of the marchers, hoping – unsuccessfully – to provoke disorder. Further missions similarly combined farce and nastiness: he probed Judith Hart's marriage for blackmail potential; he was given her home phone number by the Chileans to ring anonymously at night; he sent a death threat to a left-wing Chilean student at Edinburgh University.

Cooper told the *London Programme* that he had begun to feel uneasy. After he organised a pro-Pinochet demonstration outside a technology college near London, which ended as planned in a confrontation with Chilean left-wingers and a grapple with the police, the embassy supplied him with the names of Scottish dock workers who were running a Rolls-Royce-style boycott of frigates belonging to Chile. These trade unionists were to be 'roughed up'. Cooper refused. He was told to come to an address in Hendon in north London. A man from the DINA was waiting inside the detached, mock-Tudor house. He wanted Cooper to break into and vandalise the various British headquarters of the anti-Pinochet activists. 'Do you have a gun?' Cooper remembered the man asking. He quit his Chilean employment soon afterwards.

Rueda, given all this, was almost as jittery in London as he had been in Santiago. 'I continued to look over my shoulder. If a car parked outside the bed-and-breakfast, I wouldn't enter. I would walk around the corner and wait until the situation was clear.' When Chileans from a neighbouring bed-and-breakfast came round, he treated them as complete strangers. He could not wait to get out of London.

It took two weeks to arrange his move to Loughborough, where he was due to take up his place to study in the autumn. 'I knew some people in the Midlands, people from my university in Chile.' In the mean time, he lived a subsistence existence in London. He began receiving his student grant (many of his fellow exiles were living just on benefits). He found a Chilean doctor for his injuries. He struggled across to Islington to see the World University Service caseworker who had been assigned to him. But his mentor spoke no better Spanish than Rueda did English.

Then his new life was ready: a school in Loughborough for his daughter, a psychiatrist for himself, a share of a house near the university with another Chilean family. The MIR gave him permission to leave London. 'They said to me, "There are enough people here."' The Ruedas set out for Middle England. What they found was like a clean slate. The campus was modern and spread out, set in flat countryside north of Coventry, seemingly in the middle of nowhere. It was very different from a Chilean university. It specialised in uncontentious courses like physical education. Rueda soon noticed a young man called Sebastian Coe running round the houses for practice in the evenings.

Rueda studied and saw doctors. He began, very slowly, to think and talk about what had happened to him at the Villa Grimaldi. But his mind was still in Chile. 'I lived with my cases packed. I didn't decorate the house. I never bought anything permanent.' At Christmas and New Year, other Chilean refugees came to stay, bringing well-fingered copies of Santiago newspapers and fresh rumours. There would be thirty people sleeping on the floor – it was like his cell in Tres Alamos. 'We would have arguments as members of different political parties. The majority of us were MIR. There was a communist family, and a socialist family. There were a lot of people still fighting unfinished battles.'

A decade later, in 1986, a World University Service survey of its Chilean initiative still found 'an attitude of aloofness towards British society and culture', and 'a ghetto mentality' among some exiles. Rueda agrees: 'It was only 1983 or 1984 when I realised I was not going back soon.' Even now, he buys rice in ten-kilo sacks, as if living under siege from British cuisine.

There remains an air of self-sufficiency about Chilean gatherings in Britain. When I went to the London commemoration of the twenty-seventh anniversary of the coup, only a few months after Pinochet had gone back to Santiago, I spotted at most two other Britons in the large, crammed room. Everyone else was waving to each other. All the adults were talking in Spanish as they waited for the evening to formally begin. Tupperware containers were conjured from rucksacks, and sandwiches and paper plates laid out on a side table. Victor Jara tapes were passed between the rows of seats. The haircuts and the way people wore their clothes seemed little affected by decades in London. A skinny teenage boy with a video camera, far too young to have experienced even the aftermath of the events being remembered, was conscientiously filming the whole evening for some future showing.

There were readings and film screenings and more readings. The young children at the back of the room were kept quiet. Their older brothers and sisters went to the front, stood and faced the audience, and told stories about shootings and disappearances. They spoke in English, with London accents, but you could see the realisation dawning on them about where they really came from. After three hours, I slipped away – it was a weekday, and well past ten o'clock. The faces I passed on the way out were all still rapt.

A month later, the same Chilean activists hired the Conway Hall, a famous London venue for political meetings, for another commemoration. This time, it was the second anniversary of Pinochet's British arrest. A whole new calendar of significant dates had opened up for perpetuating the cause.

It was a soaking evening, but again the faces I had seen on the protests came crowding in. The austere tiled lobby of the Conway Hall, with its noticeboard advertising an 'Ethical Thinker Lecture Series', was steaming with drying umbrellas and the mince-and-pastry smells of baking *empanadas*. People were already queuing to buy tickets for drinks and food, and queuing again to present them, the way everyone did in small shops and restaurants in Santiago. In the main auditorium, the back wall had become a single long collage of photographs celebrating the anti-Pinochet protests in Surrey and London. Here, in well-composed colour snaps, were the white crosses for the disappeared being planted in Parliament Square; a banner being waved outside the Home Office reading 'Pinochet Trained Dogs to Rape Women'; endless crowds of smiling but determined faces; caricatures being paraded like carnival floats; and, most striking of all, another banner, with painstakingly neat letters, in action on the pavement out-

163

side the London Clinic. It read 'London Picket 17 Oct 1998'. Pinochet was arrested late on the sixteenth; the banner must have been stitched overnight.

I got talking to a middle-aged man in Allende glasses, who was pressing a petition on people in the lobby. Did he think Pinochet would ever go on trial in Chile? 'No.' The man gave a small world-weary smile. 'The military still control Chile.' Then his smile widened into a full, gap-toothed grin: 'The Pinochet who is in Chile now is not the same Pinochet who came here in 1998.'

I left the man still smiling. In the auditorium the dancing was starting. People were getting the banners out, again. I found myself wondering whether Pinochet's arrest was the best thing or the worst thing that could have happened to expatriate Chileans.

By October 1998, Rueda had almost become an Englishman. He had worked hard at it. He had struggled with his course at Loughborough, but had to drop out because of language difficulties. So he volunteered for community work, visiting old people's homes, helping out the blind, delivering for Meals-on-Wheels. Again his English was too poor. Finally, unemployed and without a phone – 'the level of frustration that I had was extraordinary!' – he applied to 'about a hundred places' to study once more, did an English course, and got a place at Imperial College in London. During 1979 and 1980, he endured the capital and earned a diploma in electronic telecommunications. The following year, he was offered a job at Marconi in Coventry.

He bought his terraced house and thought of buying a bigger one. He made enough friends to hoot his car horn at people in the street. He learned to small-talk about council tax and the weather. He had a regular prescription from the local surgery. He even went out 'for a balti'.

Coventry was a good place, even better than Loughborough, to get over the past. The concrete city centre and the new bypasses had been built on the ruins left by German bombers. Rueda was involved for a time with the city's Centre for Christian Reconciliation, which was housed in the shell of the original cathedral. One evening, before I caught my train back to London, he insisted on showing me the scorched and preserved church compound. We walked on the wine-red flagstones while Rueda gave a short lecture on firebombs. Then he pointed out his favourite parts of the 'extraordinary' new cathedral next door. I asked him if he liked Coventry in general now. Rueda shrugged: 'Kind of.' Then he looked more definite. 'I know people. This is my home.'

Visits back to Santiago had changed his view of Chile. His mother and brother were still there, and starting in 1990, Pinochet's last year in power, Rueda had flown over every year or two, taking English scarves with him as presents. Yet increasingly he found it difficult to gain a mental foothold in his former homeland: 'There are some raw materials there from the past, but people have changed. There is an entrepreneur kind of mentality. You will find people that you know will say, "Oh, you are abroad. We can do business. I am selling doors."'

His MIR connections, likewise, had become something from another era. He admitted them only rarely and discreetly. 'I am still loyal to my old organisation,' he told me once, but not before we had been talking for many hours. He took on a grave look, small eyes narrowing above his drooping moustache. 'There are some levels of my activities I am not ready to talk about for some years.' He paused, breathing slightly heavily. 'It is not for me to release the information.' Another pause. 'I completely disagree, for example, with those ex-IRA people who write about their organisation. You never know when things could turn around. If someone tried to kill Pinochet, there would be reprisals. I would have to take precautions.'

But such speculations were far from his mind in October 1998. He was driving into the car park at the supermarket with the radio on as usual when he heard about the arrest at the London Clinic. 'I stopped the car. A queue built up behind me. I didn't care. I started clapping. I couldn't believe it. I knew people were doing things against Pinochet in Spain. But not here . . .' After the shock, Rueda's old instincts came back to him. He drew up a petition demanding the general's extradition to Spain, and went to Coventry city centre. Then he stood in the wind in the concrete shopping precinct and collected signatures. 'It was very easy,' he told me. 'I got over a thousand.'

Yet one thing about the events in London puzzled him. The Chilean military had its own elaborate hospital system. Pinochet, because of his status as a retired general alone, was entitled to use it. Instead he had flown to Britain with his ailments, just as Rueda did. There was a justice in this, of course. The ex-dictator was beginning to repeat the experiences of his victims: the midnight arrest, the confinement, the undignified search abroad for the right medical treatment. But as Rueda travelled down to the London Clinic a few days later to join the picket, he was still thinking to himself: 'Pinochet didn't even need to come here.' So why had he?

12

'Thatcherite before Thatcher'

In August 1990, before I knew anything much about Chile, I was staying with my parents for part of the university holidays and trying, as usual, to extend breakfast deep into the morning by reading every page of their copy of *The Times*, when I came across what seemed a slightly shocking article. For months, ever since the breaching of the Berlin Wall, British newspapers had been full of uncharacteristic political optimism. Oppressive governments everywhere were falling; capitalism, it was widely reckoned, was making liberal democracy inevitable. But here, on one of *The Times*'s grandly self-assured comment pages, someone begged to differ. 'It is a comforting thought that the most benign form of governance provides the appropriate system for material advance,' the article began. 'Comforting. But quite wrong.' Several dusty paragraphs of economic and political philosophy followed. Then came the writer's evidence: 'Pinochet's Chile . . . was not a democracy. There was much bloodshed and numerous political prisoners were taken. But [while] Pinochet limited political freedom . . . he massively expanded the freedoms of the individual, giving him access to foreign goods . . . low tariffs . . . a free labour market, and prices [that] were unregulated and unsubsidised. These freedoms,' the article concluded, 'were the basis for vigorous economic recovery, the wonder of the rest of Latin America.'

The cold frankness of this argument stayed with me. And so did the name of its author: Alan Walters. He had recently been the chief economic adviser to Margaret Thatcher.

When Pinochet was arrested in London eight years later, Walters was still a working economist with an international reputation. He had a knighthood. He was based in the British capital. Yet despite his familiarity with Chile, which included decades of visits, personal meetings and even collaborations with Pinochet and his subordinates, Walters' opinions on the general's treatment were conspicuous by their absence during the protracted controversy that followed. While Anglo-Chilean businessmen, right-wing newspaper columnists, Conservative politicians with or without Chilean connections, and most notably Thatcher herself all noisily joined the campaign to free Pinochet, Walters, by reputation politically indiscreet and keen to see his views in print, did not. 'I thought I ought not to intervene,' he said when I met him. 'I talked to Margaret and she said, "Best to stay on the sidelines."'

With discussion of the ex-dictator's brutalities on the news almost nightly, it would not have been wise, perhaps, to celebrate the close connection between his prison camps and his privatisations. But there was more to Walters' silence than that. Following Pinochet's social and economic policies had not just been a side interest of his, a bit of free-lance work for a restless Prime Ministerial adviser. Walters was a potential liability because he had acted as a link, officially and other-wise, between the Thatcher and Pinochet administrations. And through this link many ideas about how to change Britain had quietly flowed from South America.

Only fleetingly was this acknowledged, in public at least, by the Britons who lobbied against Pinochet's captivity between 1998 and 2000. Not in Thatcher's speeches and letters to newspapers, which were hoarse with outrage but also careful to mention Pinochet's assistance to Britain only in connection the Falklands. Not in the elaborate events staged by Chilean Supporters Abroad, as the general's allies in Britain neutrally called themselves, where battalions of guest speakers kept strictly to patriotic and Cold War generalities. Nor in most of the literature Pinochet's advocates published on expensive paper and distributed in ambitious print runs to British 'opinion formers'. The admission that Chile had been the model for modern Britain came buried in the middle of a paragraph on page fifty-eight of a pamphlet justifying the coup against Allende: 'This is not the place to describe the details of Chile's new prosperity under Pinochet. Suffice to say that it was Thatcherite before Thatcher, though with a tougher stance towards the trade unions and a more consistent commitment to monetarism and markets.' Once Pinochet had flown back to Chile, and British feelings about him had had several months to cool, it seemed wise to talk to Walters about this.

He was working still, at the age of seventy-four, as vice-chairman of a company called AIG International. His voice was small and probing on the phone. But he agreed to see me; and on the morning of our appointment, as soon as his office building came into view, it was obvious where his confidence came from.

The company's London branch was in Wapping, the part of the capital most completely transformed by Thatcherism. Everything around AIG International suggested the triumph of market values: the ostentatious balconies of the nearby bankers' apartments, the neighbouring bulk of Rupert Murdoch's News International headquarters, grey-brown and unrepentant in its ugliness, the shabbiness of the older East End buildings cold-shouldered by the property speculators. The AIG premises themselves were in a thick glass tower, jostling for height in a scrum of other hard, shiny structures. High Victorian walls, left over from the area's time as docks and warehouses, shielded Walters' compound from the Wapping traffic. Raw capitalism and its enthusiasts, I reflected as a BMW almost ran me over outside the gates, had been a British export for centuries.

Inside the AIG tower, there was near silence. It was mid-morning on a weekday; only the air conditioning and a lone café waitress, waiting for customers in her slightly humiliating apron, stirred in the vast lobby. I took the lift to the top floor as instructed. At the entrance to AIG, there was a metal plate on the wall with the outline of a hand on it. There was no one in reception behind the locked glass doors. I waited for a few minutes. Then someone appeared and pressed their palm to the metal, and I was let in. Walters, I was told, had not yet arrived, and I was left in the deserted reception. There was nothing to indicate what the company did, just generic black-and-white photographs of New York on the walls and a sterilised sunlight coming through the tinted windows. I waited for another few minutes, until Walters was properly late for our appointment, and then decided to explore. A glass-walled corridor led towards his office, with the London skyline on one side and a great plunge down to the floor of the main lobby on the other. His office was small but strategically positioned, like a foreman's, across from a large open-plan room with banks of computer screens and telephones. This was full of young men in shirtsleeves, shouting into their receivers in the manner of financial traders. Some of them had London accents, others sounded American, others Middle

Eastern; I spotted a sign that said that AIG had another office in Hong Kong. Yet a clearer signal of the status of the business came in the next room. Even the toilets had their own palm-reading security.

Walters finally arrived from his home in Mayfair an hour late. He did not offer a handshake. He gave a half-excuse – the traffic had been bad and his diary had been confused – in his small, dispassionate voice. Despite a suntan and a smart pale suit, he looked much older than I remembered him from newspaper photographs during the Thatcher era. His long, thin face had tightened and his limbs looked frail as he shuffled to his office. But then, in the doorway, he turned, and I saw that his eyes were startlingly blue and mischievous. 'Would you like coffee?' he said. 'Caffeine-free or *caffeine-loaded*?'

As he shuffled off to fetch it, I took in the biographies of Thatcher and Ronald Reagan on his bookshelves, next to a volume of Machiavelli and something entitled *Why Wages Don't Fall during a Recession*. A fax from the Bank of Malaysia lay on his desk. A miniature flag of St George stood on top of his computer monitor. Then Walters returned, lowered himself into his chair, and began to reminisce about his days in Chile.

'I didn't visit during the Allende period,' he said. 'I had a passing interest in Allende but the first time I visited, I think, was in 1975.' Walters was working for the World Bank, although not exclusively. The bank had been increasingly reluctant to lend money to Allende but was now increasingly keen to lend money to Pinochet. 'We got involved in a housing project. It was a very good project: private housing with a state subsidy.' Walters pursed his small lips with approval: 'Very good. Very efficient. Because they had competitive tendering.' On that first trip, he also met Chilean civil servants and Pinochet's finance minister. 'I liked the Chileans – engaging people. The civil servants were very good, very honest. I can't say I positively liked Pinochet at that time. Later I came to like him.'

In 1975, Walters already had a reputation as a right-wing economist of some fierceness. He had been born, as he described it in the biographical summary he sometimes included in his pamphlets, 'of working-class parents in a Leicester slum'. His father was an 'ultra-left-wing Socialist' of unshakeable convictions. 'So,' said Walters with a cheeky look, 'I went the other way.' During the 1950s and 1960s, he became a disciple and then a peer of the American economist Milton Friedman, who rejected the socially conscious economics that had dominated the thinking of democratic governments since the Great Depression of the 1930s. Friedman and Walters called themselves monetarists: they believed that inflation, not recession, was the great enemy, and that governments should restrict the amount of money circulating in the economy at all costs, rather than print more of it to help those struggling when times were hard. During the early 1970s, Walters became involved in a concerted and successful campaign to convince the Conservative Party of this new philosophy. And beneath the dry surface of his careful economist's prose, and the seminars he attended at bland-sounding think tanks such as the Institute for Economic Affairs and the Centre for Policy Studies, daring political thoughts began to crystallise.

The idea that 'a government could do no good', in the words of a Walters pamphlet, if it interfered with the rough business of the free market, had unpleasant implications for the trade unions, the poor, and the other left-wing or vulnerable interest groups to whom British politicians had been paying increasing attention since the Second World War. What Walters and his allies were proposing was a return, you could say, to the brand of Victorian capitalism that had produced people like the Nitrate King. At the same time the monetarists viewed the status quo of the mid-1970s – in particular, the messy inclusiveness of British politics – in the same way that Chilean right-wingers had regarded Allende's rule: as a time of unprecedented danger. Walters still does. 'You can have democracy and no freedom, as we've had in Britain at various times including the 1970s,' he said, suddenly stern behind his desk. 'In those days it was said widely that the Anglo-Saxon economic model was finished.'

But the sheer instability of the period was also an opportunity. Radical, even extreme notions, like monetarism (or military coups) had more appeal in a crisis. The problem was finding a suitable country to test them in. Then came the coup in Chile. Here was a small economy and society, already quite modern, urbanised, and used to receiving economic prescriptions from abroad. Its new ruler was right-wing but without much of an existing ideology. He faced no elections where bold policies might get him ejected. And he had the authority derived from a complete apparatus of state security. Finally, his predecessor had been overthrown against a backdrop of strikes, shortages and corrosive inflation. Almost any subsequent 'reforms' could be made to look like progress. When Walters first flew to Santiago in 1975, what he was really doing was going to measure it.

He would not be disappointed. In Chile, even before Pinochet seized power, a new school of right-wing economists had begun to emerge. Like Walters, they had started as followers of Friedman in the 1950s. After the failure of American advisers in 1955 to persuade Chile to run its economy according to a rough early version of monetarism, the United States government had set up a system of scholarships for Chilean students to attend the University of Chicago, where Friedman was teaching and developing his ideas. When these students returned to Chile, many of them began teaching at the University of Chicago's equivalent in Santiago, the conservative Catholic University. With American money, its campus was moved to the foothills of the Andes, east of the city, the habitual preserve of the Santiago rich, where the smog and the bustle of the slightly shabby capital would not disturb the students' ambitious thoughts. Over time, as the Chilean version of the counter-revolution also brewing in Chicago and London began to receive local attention, its young male participants were given a name: the Chicago Boys.

With the election of Allende, their thinking took on a greater urgency. Just as the new president saw himself as part of a long left-wing tradition in Chile, going back to Balmaceda and the striking nitrate miners of the 1890s and all those who had opposed foreign exploitation of the country; so the Chicago Boys, for all their modern theory and training, were also the latest hopes of the other Chile, equally old: the Chile of the right-wing and wealthy, with their terror of social reform and inflation, and their enthusiasm for opening up the country to international capitalism. As Allende struggled against this opposition in public, the Chicago Boys met privately with the military and the other groups who were turning in favour of a coup, and drew up a plan for a new Chile, to be implemented when the gun-smoke had cleared.

At first, after Allende had been overthrown, it was not obvious that the Chicago Boys' blueprint would be chosen. Introducing competition into every area of Chilean life, as they proposed, was almost as alarming a prospect to some conservatives as it was to the left. During the first unsettled weeks of junta rule, with factions of all kinds jockeying for power, rival schemes were proposed that were closer to old-fashioned fascism, of the kind still practised by Franco in Spain, with a repressive state giving orders to business rather than collaborating with it. But then, in Santiago, the political weather abruptly changed in the Chicago Boys' favour. Pinochet became dictator.

By early 1974 he had outmanoeuvred the other junta members and established a national headquarters in the Diego Portales convention centre in Santiago. The symbolism of the location was strong. The convention centre was named after a hero of conservative Chileans. It was modern and brutal-looking: a long hangar of a building, blank and secretive, that loomed just to the east of the centre of the capital. Its distance and difference from the old official Santiago around La Moneda, with its debating chambers and democratic public spaces, was a kind of warning. Even nowadays, if you walk the narrow streets around Pinochet's former headquarters, which have become gentrified and attractive with arts cinemas and restaurants full of chattering academics and late-opening bookshops selling rival political volumes – on a warm evening, it feels like an advertisement for the freedoms of post-Pinochet Chile – you only have to look up, and there, at the end of the street or above the cute rooftop apartments, will be the gloomy, rust-tinged cliff face of the general's old eyrie. On my very first afternoon in Chile, when I went for a wander around the nearby hotel I had chosen by chance, I instinctively knew what it was.

In April 1974, Pinochet made a speech to copper miners in the north of the country. The experience Chile was about to undergo, he promised, would involve 'scrubbing our minds clean'. The idea of the country starting afresh appealed to him for several reasons. First, like many in the Chilean military, he had a strong sense, derived from the country's nineteenth-century history, that men in uniform were the natural saviours of the nation. The frustrations of decades of peacetime service – suffering cuts in military spending, watching politicians fall short – had only strengthened it. Secondly, he knew very little about how to run the country. His previous experience of administering civilians had been confined to running prison camps. And Chile in 1974 was a mess, in part an ongoing consequence of the sabotage of the economy by Allende's opponents: inflation after the coup, for example, rose far beyond the levels considered unacceptable under his administration. Thirdly and finally, Pinochet came to realise that the upheavals the Chicago Boys promised would consolidate his own position. Only a single strong leader, most likely, could force the population to endure what Friedman, without a trace of irony – or sensitivity to the general's law and order policies – called 'shock treatment'.

Between 1974 and 1976, a few dozen fresh-faced and bespectacled young graduates were permitted to gut the Chilean economy. From their comfortable new government offices, the Chicago Boys ordered state spending to be cut by over a quarter. Overnight, industries previously subsidised or shielded from competition were exposed to the full strength of market forces. Tariffs on imports and price controls on local products were removed simultaneously, making foreign goods vastly cheaper and Chilean ones vastly more expensive. Wages were allowed to collapse to half their 1970 level, while VAT was increased, and interest rates too, to a suffocating 178 per cent in mid-1975. The social consequences of all this were dramatic. Unemployment leapt, by the official measure, to almost a fifth of the national workforce. (If you included those on a temporary work scheme set up by the government, it was closer to a third.) The welfare state established by Allende and his predecessors fell apart: so many companies were going bankrupt that the government stopped receiving enough social security insurance payments from employers to enable them to pay unemployment benefit. Only soup kitchens run by the church kept people from starving. By mid-1976, there were over 200 of them in Santiago alone.

The chaos and entropy of it all may possibly have been greater than the Chicago Boys intended. As in Britain, where 'shock treatment' would be tried next, under Thatcher in the late 1970s and early 1980s, the ideas of Friedman and Walters and their intellectual allies proved very blunt instruments in practice. But much of the damage done to the structures of everyday life in Chile was, like the cruelties inflicted at Villa Grimaldi and elsewhere, quite deliberate. It was a prelude to the making of a new society.

At its crudest, the Chicago programme was class vengeance. It reversed the creep towards a more egalitarian country that had been occurring under Allende and Frei. The Chilean rich were restored to their traditional position of dominance over everyone else. More ambitiously, the increased likelihood of poverty, unemployment and insecurity for the majority of the population under Pinochet was intended to change their politics: people without work were less likely to join trade unions; people suddenly abandoned by the state were more likely, it was thought, to become entrepreneurial in outlook; people struggling to make ends meet were more likely, in general, to put themselves first. This logic, in slightly diluted form, would be thoroughly absorbed by Margaret Thatcher.

Starting in 1978, the Chicago Boys imposed what they called the 'seven modernisations'. Each sought to reform an aspect of society irreversibly, by setting up new institutions and instilling new habits in Chileans, with their own – occasional – rewards. When Walters went to Santiago for the World Bank again, 'in 1978 or 1979', he met Pinochet. 'He wasn't an economist,' Walters remembered thinking, 'but like Margaret Thatcher, he liked good housekeeping arguments.' The general told him, 'Chile will be safe from communism when every Chilean has their own car and house.'

Privatisation, a new and untried notion, was at the centre of this strategy. First, the firms that had been nationalised by Allende were returned to commercial ownership. Then older state enterprises were sold off: the airline Lan Chile, the national telephone company, the electricity-generating network and the remaining nitrate mines. In many cases, the prices paid for these businesses were questionably low. The beneficiaries of these hurried auctions were often the same old money-making families that had dominated Chilean commercial life since the nineteenth century. Tacit official admission of this came in the mid-1980s, with an attempt to rebrand the privatisation programme as 'popular capitalism': less wealthy Chileans were encouraged to buy shares, and employees of state enterprises that were about to be sold were sometimes offered small stakes in them at a discount. By the late 1980s, the *Financial Times* estimated that Chile had a greater proportion of shareholders than any other Latin American country. As with the other economic benefits that would be claimed for Pinochet's rule, however, the actual distribution of this new wealth was less impressive than the general's advocates, both inside and outside Chile, liked to insist. Only one working person in nine owned shares, admitted one of the heads of the privatisation programme, Major José Martinez, in 1986.

More relevant to most of the population were the changes to the institutions that had previously offered them a degree of social protection. Trade unions were weakened: their powers to bargain for their members were reduced and strikes in support of other workers were outlawed. The national health service had its budget reduced, while private health care was encouraged: Chileans who used it were offered half-price treatment vouchers by the government. The state pension system, one of the oldest in the world, was replaced by private funds into which people paid compulsory contributions. State schools and universities substantially lost funding, and had their syllabuses purged of courses considered to have been 'infiltrated' by subversive ideas, such as sociology and political science. Business conglomerates bought up chains of campuses, and were given tax breaks to run them. The benefits system in general was reformed, in the approving words of a special report on Chile in *The Economist* in 1980, 'to reward the thrifty, while providing a safety net about an inch from the floor for the less virtuous'.

The British business magazine was hardly alone in its enthusiasm. During the late 1970s, the Chilean economy had begun to recover and then prosper after the near-collapse of the coup and 'shock treatment' periods – at least according to the measures preferred by foreign bankers and investors, which did not count the soup kitchens. Inflation fell. Productivity rose. Overall growth reached levels far higher than those being achieved in the stuttering economies of America and Europe. To the parts of the British press that were influenced by Walters and Friedman, here was evidence that monetarism worked and, by implication, that it should be applied in Britain. The *Spectator* praised 'the Chilean economic miracle'. The *Daily Telegraph* described the Chicago Boys as 'honest, idealistic and admired'. The *Financial Times* said Pinochet was 'presiding over Latin America's best-managed economy'.

In a repetition of the Allende era, foreign observers sympathetic to what was happening in Chile flew out to Santiago. And in the same clean Andean light, they saw what they wanted to.

Associations from the coup were still there in the city-centre streets, in the straight dark boulevards down which the tanks had come, in the heavy stone government buildings the snipers had occupied, in the sun-struck squares where civilians had run for cover, in the shrapnel holes, not quite smoothed away, on the thick columns of La Moneda. But high up in the new foreign-owned skyscraper hotels that were rising around the Diego Portales convention centre, with their spotless lobbies and brisk, international ambience, it was easy not to notice. And immediately to the east, towards the mountains, another version of the capital, less obviously burdened by history, was asserting itself.

In this part of Santiago, the land rises steadily upwards. The air freshens. There are fewer Latin-American-looking palm trees and more European-looking firs. And behind them stand rank upon rank of pale new office blocks and apartments, lawn sprinklers swishing between them, new dual carriageways humming below. Every second car seems to be a Mercedes, every pavement seems swept and hosed. There are whole streets of restaurants, pristine and international as the ones in Canary Wharf. There are golf courses, electric gates, maids with downward gazes doing the shopping in the midday heat. Up here in Las Condes, La Dehesa, Vitacura and the other spreading suburbs of the Santiago rich, the beneficiaries of the Pinochet dictatorship are pretty plain to see. Only an enormous army base, with plush accommodation and men with machine guns patrolling among the topiary, acts as a reminder of how this new Chile was underwritten by the military.

This was the country Walters saw as he visited with increasing frequency during the 1980s. 'It was very exciting. I was an honorary Chicago Boy.' He gave a small, proud laugh. 'Which I quite enjoyed. It was the great experiment in liberal economics. The reform of the social security . . .' There was a lift now in his voice. 'That was a pure Chicago leap! A great thing!'

Walters remembered the names of the important Chilean economists and ministers of the time as if he had just met them for lunch. 'The Chicago Boys,' he said, 'were undoubtedly very able.' His blue eyes gleamed at the memory of it: 'There was miracle growth, yes . . . And there has been since. I'll give you the actual numbers.' He picked up a glossy pamphlet from his desk. 'Yes, average annual real growth per capita in Chile . . .' He ran a bony finger down a column of figures. 'For 1990 to 1997, it was 6.5 per cent.'

Did he worry at all about the torture? Walters' eyes cooled. He spoke slowly and carefully: 'I knew that with revolutions of that kind you are going to get casualties. Obviously, nasty things went on.' He did not seem keen to pursue the connection between Pinochet's repression and his reforms any further. Instead, he continued more cheerfully, 'I took my wife with me in 1979. She was expecting a police state. The only police she saw were a riot squad, of about twenty people, playing football.'

Nevertheless, outside Chile at least, Walters thought he had to be discreet about his Santiago trips. During the 1970s, his job at the World Bank gave him a cover ('I got away with murder!'). During the 1980s, when he was working for Thatcher, his visits were officially 'private'. In Britain even then, a decade after the coup, Walters felt, 'Everyone hated Chile – except Margaret. I'd probably talked to her about it for the first time some time in the 1970s. She knew I'd been there, and she asked me about it . . . She admired Pinochet for putting Allende out of office.' From then on, 'I let her know if I was going. She said, "Keep quiet about it. Don't advertise it."'

Margaret Thatcher had become Conservative Party leader in 1975. At this point, the coup in Chile and the question of Pinochet were matters of mainstream concern in Britain, as much for the Right as for the Left. But the right-wing interpretation of what had happened and was happening across the Andes was starkly different from that held in East Kilbride. It took a few months to emerge, as the rubble and obvious casualties of the coup were tidied away, and then appeared in all the main Tory papers almost simultaneously in the spring of 1974.

The argument went as follows. The idealism and liberalism of the Allende regime were 'a myth'. In fact, he had been 'preparing a full 1917-style revolution' along Russian lines, in order to 'set up a Marxist dictatorship'. The military had overthrown him purely to prevent it. This version of events was identical to that presented by the junta days after the coup, in the form of a pamphlet entitled *The White Book of the Change of Government in Chile*.

This publication was based around a document, supposedly discovered among the papers of the Allende government, called 'Plan Z'. It detailed, in suspiciously lurid language, the 'Organization of a Coup D'Etat in order to conquer *Total Power* and to impose a *Proletarian Dictatorship*'.The plan included 'street riots' and the 'beheading' of military officers. Its authenticity has been widely questioned ever since it so conveniently appeared in the hands of the junta, shortly after they had taken power. Yet among Pinochet's apologists, 'Plan Z' remains a sacred text. During the general's British confinement, it formed the unspoken basis for many of the pleas for his release. In 1999, it was included as an appendix in a pro-Pinochet booklet published in London by Chilean Supporters Abroad. The writer of the rest of that polemic was someone called Robin Harris. Like Walters', his name had a certain resonance for followers of British right-wing politics. The author biography at the back of the booklet summarised his career as follows: 'Dr Robin Harris served during the Thatcher Government as special adviser at the Treasury and at the Home Office, as Director of the Conservative Research Department and as a member of the Prime Minister's Policy Unit. He continues to advise Baroness Thatcher.'

When I phoned her London office and left a message for him, he quickly called me back. His tone was brisk, but helpful. 'The coup took place when I was at Oxford,' he began. 'Like for other people, it was a polarising thing. I was on the Right, and I thought it was a bloody good thing it had happened.' His confident voice grew more thoughtful. 'I came to it as part of . . . what was really happening to the world in the 1970s. The advance of Soviet power, both directly and indirectly . . .' What did he mean exactly? 'Well, quite clearly Britain was not poised on the brink of revolution, but from 1973 until about 1977, there were symptoms in common with Allende's Chile: hyperinflation, trade-union activism . . . There were certainly elements in the Labour Party who wanted Allende-style solutions. I was following things very closely. There was a feeling on the Right that there was a crisis – the whole Chilean issue was part of that.' He paused. 'Mrs Thatcher came to the Conservative leadership in the same period.' Then he added: 'I would want to interview her.'

He gave me the address of her office. 'By all means, drop us a line,' he said. It was July 2000; Pinochet had been back in Chile for a few months; perhaps Thatcher would welcome the chance to discuss her part in the successful campaign for his release. A few days after I wrote to her, a letter arrived on thick cream headed paper: 'Lady Thatcher was very interested to read about your project as the relationship between the two countries is both intricate and fascinating. However . . . she has had to restrict herself to [contributing to] those books being written by either close personal friends or former colleagues.'

I read her memoirs instead. In the acknowledgements to the first volume, *The Downing Street Years*, she emphatically thanked Harris, 'my indispensable sherpa'. In the text, she also praised Walters, 'upon whose judgement I came more and more to rely'. She continued: 'He knew that he could always have access to me more or less when he wished.' And strikingly, in her account of her formative political years during the 1970s, which took up a substantial part of the book and its companion volume, *The Path To Power*, the perspectives of Walters and Harris about the state of Britain and the world, at that time, seemed almost exactly the same as her own. More strikingly still, her analysis of what was to be done then, in its political concepts and its rhetoric, carried distinct echoes of the thoughts of their favourite dictator.

Britain in the mid-1970s, she wrote, required 'a fundamental change of attitudes . . . to wrench [it] out of decline.' Her picture of British life under Heath and Wilson was close to apocalyptic: 'Mass infringement of the law, as in the miners' strike of 1972 . . . the subversion of moral values . . . fraternal relations between trade-union leaders and the Soviet bloc . . . militants clearly out to bring down the Government . . . fundamental liberties under threat . . . inflation threatening to destroy our society . . . the FT Ordinary Share Index down to the lowest level for twenty years . . .' In 1974, the Conservative Party lost power, and such anxieties reached their peak in British right-wing circles. 'I renewed my reading of the seminal works of liberal economics and conservative thought,' Thatcher wrote. 'I also regularly attended lunches at the Institute of Economic Affairs where Alan Walters and others were busy marking out a new non-socialist economic and social path for Britain.'

Since the late 1960s, she had been one of a small group of ambitious Conservatives, including Enoch Powell and Keith Joseph, who wanted the party to adopt more free-market policies. Their hopes had been briefly raised by the Conservative general election victory of 1970: here was a chance, it seemed, to put their new ideas about 'denationalisation' (as Thatcher then tentatively called privatisation) and a more competitive society into practice. But the only state-owned enterprises the Heath government actually sold off were the travel agent Thomas Cook and, bizarrely, the pubs of Carlisle, which had been left under state control since the First World War. Within a year, faced with strikes and economic difficulties, Heath had abandoned any further gestures towards right-wing radicalism. Yet Thatcher and her intellectual and political allies were not discouraged – quite the opposite in fact, as Heath's more pragmatic approach failed, and the British 'crisis' deepened.

During 1974 and 1975, Thatcher manoeuvred her way to the party leadership. Joseph, whom she had originally wanted to assume it, ruined his prospects with a speech apparently in favour of eugenics – a measure of the reckless thinking going on among the monetarists, and on the British Right in general – so she mounted a coup against Heath, of the bloodless, party-political variety. All the while, her programme for governing Britain moved closer and closer to Chilean-style 'shock treatment'. A future Conservative government should 'risk some increase in unemployment'. If inflation was to be reduced, 'monetary growth had to be curbed'. Then Walters began making his trips to Santiago, and Thatcher began to hear encouraging news from South America. 'Chile was on our side,' as she put it in her memoirs. 'A dramatic demonstration of how liberal economics makes the difference.'

Within eighteen months of winning the 1979 general election, she sent her Minister of Trade to Santiago, the first British official visit to Chile for over a decade. Cecil Parkinson gave an interview to the Pinochet-supporting newspaper *El Mercurio*. 'There's a good deal of similarity between the economic policies of Chile and those of Great Britain,' Parkinson said. 'And what would you see,' his interviewer asked, 'as the chief differences between the two experiences?' Parkinson replied: 'The basic difference is that our experience takes place in a democratic context, and that of Chile was undertaken by an authoritarian regime. So Chile could impose a policy and a speed of application in that policy which just isn't possible in this country. Here we have to work with the consent of the majority.'

Parkinson may not have known it, but not everyone on the Right back in Britain had always welcomed that restriction. During the 1970s, running in parallel with Thatcher and her allies' response to Pinochet, and sometimes intersecting with it, there had been another, even more sympathetic school of thought. In this case, however, the British calls to imitate the general did not limit themselves to his monetarism.

13

A British Pinochet?

In Britain, as in Chile before Pinochet, it had long been a conventional wisdom that coups and military rule simply did not happen. Moments in the country's history that challenged this assumption, such as Cromwell's army government during the 1650s or the flirtations of the *Daily Mail* and the conservative establishment with Oswald Mosley's British Union of Fascists during the 1930s, were not dwelt on.

Yet the decade leading up to the coup in Chile had, in fact, seen a revival of interest on the fringes of British politics in schemes to replace modern parliamentary democracy with something more rigid. As in Santiago, the roots of these schemes lay in a feeling among some right-wingers that the country was changing in unacceptable ways, and in particular in the frustrations of soldiers.

The first real hint came over Rhodesia. In 1965, the British colony had effectively rebelled against a new Labour government in London, which wanted Rhodesia's black citizens to have more political rights, by issuing a Unilateral Declaration of Independence. Yet when the prospect arose of British military action in response, perhaps even an invasion of Rhodesia to restore London's authority, rumours spread in Whitehall that British soldiers would refuse to act against the colony, which had a substantial population of white settlers with British military connections. Denis Healey, the Labour Minister of Defence, 'heard there had been some mutinous mutterings among senior army officers'. The invasion never happened – Labour had a tiny parliamentary majority and more pressing domestic tasks – but exotic allegations surfaced for years afterwards that a mutiny over Rhodesia would have had dramatic political consequences in Britain itself. In 1977, a former MI6 officer called Anthony Eaton claimed that several Scottish peers with assets in the colony, together with 'a small band of top-ranking officers', had in 1965 or 1966 'actually approached the Queen Mother with their plan for a coup' in Britain. She supposedly rejected their proposal, which also involved a general revival of the British empire in Africa. In 1981, another version of this story appeared in the *Sunday Times*. Lady Falkender, the private secretary and confidante of Harold Wilson, the Prime Minister at the time of the Rhodesian crisis, 'had gained the impression that . . . meetings had taken place in the mid-1960s' at the Ministry of Defence in London, where 'there was a map of the United Kingdom and people present went over the movements for a coup with a pointer'.

During the late 1960s, as the Wilson administration struggled with a collapsing pound, anti-Vietnam militancy and an increase in strike activity – a taste of the greater instability to come in the following decade – there was talk in British newspapers of further plots. Some of these sounded relatively harmless. Cecil King, the owner of the *Daily Mirror*, spoke up publicly for a 'National Government' of all the main parties, as there had been during the 1930s, the last time that economic troubles and broad political unease had coincided. But he and other prominent British company executives then went on to argue that this government should have 'a large business element'. From there, proposals for replacing the Wilson administration grew wilder. Lord Mountbatten, the Queen's uncle and the recently retired head of the British armed forces, was approached by King and others – most likely senior bankers from the City of London – and asked to lead an 'Emergency Government' and even, according to some accounts, a military coup. It was rumoured in 1968 that army intelligence had chosen the Shetland Islands as a centre for holding political prisoners (just as Pinochet was to use Chile's extremities), if or when the need arose.

Behind all these strategies, fantastical or otherwise, lay an undeniable change in how the British army was beginning to regard the society around it. Since the end of the Second World War, the army had been engaged in a series of small but brutal wars against guerrillas in British colonies such as Malaya and Kenya. By the mid-1960s, these conflicts were mostly over and much of the Empire had been dismantled. But the lessons which the British army felt it had learned – that communist 'subversion' was a global threat; that this enemy would sometimes hide within legitimate-seeming protest organisations – came home with the soldiers. In 1969, the updated British Army Land Manual included domestic 'subversives' in its list of potential enemies. These were defined very widely as 'people who take action to undermine the military, economic or psychological morale, or political strength of a nation and the loyalty of its subjects'. Two years later, a rising young brigadier called Frank Kitson took this notion of a politicised military further in a book, published with army approval, entitled *Low Intensity Operations.*

'The reader will not find in these pages a purely academic theoretical exercise,' he began. Kitson went on to describe, in the carefully bloodless language of army planning, how soldiers might be used to counter 'strikes, protest marches . . . pickets and street-corner meetings . . . sit-ins and various forms of obstruction' of a subversive nature. Using dry-looking diagrams, he demonstrated how a joint military-civilian emergency government might be structured. He recommended that soldiers be specially trained to run 'essential services', informers be recruited, and that, if necessary, 'The Law should be used as just another weapon.' He went on: 'In this case, it becomes little more than a propaganda cover for the disposal of unwanted members of the public.'

By the time his book came out, Kitson had been sent to Belfast with a brigade of infantry, to test out his theories in a situation that seemed to justify them. From the early 1970s onwards, the accelerating disorder in Ulster, and the official British response to it – the internment of suspects without trial, the suspension of the local parliament – acted as a daily, high-profile example of how military rule might arrive one day in the rest of the United Kingdom.

The other example was Chile. During 1974 and 1975, with Pinochet securely established, the support for his coup in the British right-wing press began to turn bolder. Crude attacks on Allende and rehashings of the junta's self-justifying pamphlets were replaced by a more positive line of argument: approval of how Pinochet was actually governing. In March 1974, the *Sunday Telegraph* sent Peregrine Worsthorne, one of the stars of British conservative journalism, to Chile for ten days. His impressions were published at great length two weekends running. They began:

What is happening in Chile today unquestionably deserves a more open-minded, possibly even a more sympathetic, effort at understanding from this country . . . I was in Chile [as a] guest of the junta, invited presumably because of my Right-wing sympathies. They paid for my trip and provided me with much hospitality.

Worsthorne went to Santiago and Valparaíso, and even the far south. 'The junta,' he concluded, 'enjoys very widespread popularity among all classes.' The Chilean army were:

Everywhere to be seen, just as in Northern Ireland . . . But they appear relaxed and friendly, and there is certainly no air of tension in the towns; still less in the country . . . In talking to senior officers, including members of the junta, there is no hint of that kind of fanatical ideological commitment out of which true horror springs. Their language is painfully reminiscent, not of Hitler, but of Field-Marshal Montgomery.

As the climax to his trip, Worsthorne was granted a visit to a detention camp. He was flown to Dawson Island, a windswept former missionary outpost down towards the Antarctic, where the surviving senior members of Allende's administration were being held. The description Worsthorne gave of life in the compound was not one that Sergio Rueda, or the many Chileans being tortured or worse at that moment, would have recognised:

The commandant of the camp was there to meet me, a young Chilean army officer aged about twenty-four, with apple cheeks and a meltingly sweet and humorous smile . . . His jeep led the way, and I followed in another driven by a tallish civilian in dungarees, who looked like a Cheltenham colonel down on his luck . . . I was surprised to hear a voice, speaking in a strong West Country accent – just like Ralph Wightman of *Any Questions?* – asking me in perfect English where I came from. His grandfather, he said, had come from Devonshire after the first war and set up a prosperous sheep farm on the [Chilean] mainland.

Worsthorne was given a tour of the prison. Conditions among the cold low huts and wire, he judged, 'were hard but not harsh'. He was permitted to speak to the detainees with the commandant present. 'There had, they said, been no brutality, either physical or mental.' When a former ambassador of Allende's asked him what he was going to write about the camp, Worsthorne recorded, 'I did not know what to reply. If I had been coldly truthful, I should have said that they were lucky to be alive, since it is very doubtful whether a communist Chile, which they wanted to set up, would have treated its political prisoners as humanely . . .'

At the end of his final article, Worsthorne expanded this point into a passage of pure rhetoric:

All right, a military dictatorship is ugly and repressive. But if a minority British

Socialist Government ever sought, by cunning, duplicity, corruption, terror and foreign arms, to turn this country into a Communist State, I hope and pray our armed forces would intervene to prevent such a calamity as efficiently as the armed forces did in Chile.

In the mid-1970s, as in the previous period of speculation about coups in Britain, there was a Labour government in office led by Harold Wilson. His pragmatic, slightly directionless style of governing could not easily be mistaken for socialism, let alone pro-Soviet communism. Yet some members of the British security services, as Peter Wright's book *Spycatcher* would subsequently confirm, had managed to convince themselves that Wilson was a Russian agent. This was absurd, if revealing of the paranoia and ideological assumptions then current in MI5 and the right-wing milieu it drew on. However, there *were* small signs, in 1974 in particular, that the new Wilson administration might be more radical than past Labour governments. Within weeks of its election in February, it had increased corporation tax to pay for more generous welfare benefits. It also set up a National Enterprise Board to take over private companies that were perceived to be failing. The most vocal advocates of this new, more aggressive programme of nationalisation were Tony Benn, the Secretary of State for Industry and the public face of the Labour Party's large and growing minority of left-wing MPs, and Judith Hart, still strongly associated with Allende's Chile.

There were other alarming developments for right-wing Britons of an apocalyptic disposition. There were all the strikes and economic anxieties. There was the disarray of the Conservative Party – not yet rescued by monetarism and Margaret Thatcher – which had just completed a chaotic four years in government, lost a general election, and was about to lose another in October 1974. There was the fact that two elections in a single year had been necessary at all, that the electorate was seemingly too alienated to give either main party a practical majority. There were the IRA bombs. And there were other, more general fears about national decline: the British population fell for five successive years between 1975 and 1979. Even a sober contemporary textbook about the October election could conclude, 'Fears of impending national disaster which had taken root in the early 1970s grew substantially in the course of 1974.'

A common right-wing response to all this was to declare that British democracy was doomed. In September 1974, Samuel Brittan, the most prominent columnist on the *Financial Times*, gave a public lecture on

'The Economic Contradictions Of Democracy', and predicted that the British parliamentary system would collapse within people's lifetimes. *The Times* published a leader the same month warning of a 'last chance Parliament'. The following year, Robert Moss, the director of the *Economist* Intelligence Unit, a kind of think tank attached to the magazine, which briefed companies on the political situation, published a book called *The Collapse of Democracy*.

Its text was predictably melodramatic – inflation was being 'used to destroy the middle class'; 'Trotskyist schoolteachers' were distributing 'propaganda' in 'schools in north London' – but more striking was the way recent happenings in South America found their way into almost every chapter. Britain, Moss predicted, would fall to 'the next Allende' without drastic countermeasures. As in the coup in Chile, these should include middle-class strikes, 'counter-violence', the ending of trade-union militancy 'by whatever means are necessary', and the emergence of a strong new national leader. The precise source of such thinking became clear from the book's acknowledgements: Moss thanked two prominent Chilean supporters of Pinochet, two British generals, and Peregrine Worsthorne and Alan Walters.

It would probably be wrong to call this a conspiracy. It was more that, by the mid-1970s, the feelings of parts of the British army and British business, of certain economists and journalists, of some intelligence personnel and politicians, were all beginning to lead in a similar direction: the status quo was unsustainable; political change of an unprecedented nature was required; and that change was going to be influenced, one way or another, by what was happening in Chile.

Moss's own background and connections demonstrated how intertwined support for Pinochet and advocacy of a right-wing rescue of Britain were becoming. He was a young Australian academic who had begun working for the *Economist* in the early 1970s. In 1972, he had gone to Chile to write a book about Allende for a series called 'World Realities' published by Forum World Features, later shown to be a company funded by the CIA. Whether Moss knew this or not was never proved; but the volume he produced, written 'a few days after the coup', perfectly fitted the anti-Allende, pro-junta line. Ten thousand copies were bought by the new Chilean military government, and distributed to the country's embassies in Washington and London. The books were then proffered to anyone proposing to visit Chile. My uncle, who was a Latin American correspondent for *The Times*, was slightly puzzled to be given a copy before a trip to Santiago in the late 1970s.

By then Moss had switched his attention to British politics. Besides working on *The Collapse of Democracy*, he helped establish a new right-wing pressure group called the National Association For Freedom (NAFF). From its beginnings in 1975, it would be most publicly associated with campaigning against trade unions, yet it was also the first formal gathering point for those with more general, Moss-style anxieties about the state of the country. *Free Nation*, its polemical magazine, discussed, among other topics, whether the British army should 'intervene'. Worsthorne became a NAFF member. So did six Conservative MPs. Margaret Thatcher spoke at the organisation's first fundraising dinner.

The Collapse of Democracy was NAFF's first official publication. Thatcher was sufficiently impressed by Moss and his analysis that she hired him as a speechwriter soon after she became Conservative leader. In 1976, he drafted the famous attack on worldwide communism which caused her to be christened 'the Iron Lady'. Moss might still enjoy the fact that this phrase is the first thing most Chileans say to you when you mention her name.

From that peak of influence, however, he gradually slipped back down. Once Thatcher became Prime Minister in 1979, she had dozens of speechwriters and advisers. Moss turned to writing thrillers, where his increasingly lurid speculations about left-wing plots were assured of an audience. The books did well, and he moved to America. He married, and bought a farm in upstate New York. His politics softened. 'He opted out of the whole problem,' says an old NAFF colleague. 'He came to London once and looked me up. I asked him why he'd pulled out. He said, "I couldn't stand the stress."' In 1996, Moss published his most recent book, *Conscious Dreaming: A Unique Nine-Step Approach to Understanding Dreams*.

Moss, I was advised, would be unlikely to grant me an interview. However, there was another equally representative figure from his unsettling mid-1970s circle who might. The man in question had been Moss's mentor, and was said to be have been close to Thatcher, Pinochet, and certain dissatisfied members of the British army. He still lived in London. In October 2000, I obtained a phone number. The person who gave it to me said that if I got through I would probably be asked about my politics. I should say I was 'for freedom'.

The number had been disconnected. I also had an address for a flat near Victoria station in central London. I took the Underground there one lunchtime. The flat was in a quiet street behind the station, made up of smart, faintly military cream-and-grey mansion blocks. I found the right number, a basement flat with mirrored glass, and waited for a few moments as the odd pedestrian passed and platform announcements crackled in the distance, then rang the doorbell. There was no answer for perhaps half a minute. I rang again. I was about to walk off when the door swung open and a middle-aged woman in white stockings and thick make-up appeared. The man I was looking for had moved out, she said in a slightly upper-class voice, but she had been forwarding his post. She had his address somewhere. Would I like to come in?

Her flat was across a tiny hallway from his. The living room was like a junk shop: there were books and pieces of paper piled on every surface, warped old business cards, a worn and dusty set of volumes of *Burke's Peerage*. Although it was a warm day, she had her heating on and a small television was blaring. She slowly started sifting through the sediment. 'He was a very nice man,' she said as she looked. 'Moved out a year or two ago. Must be well into his eighties now. He used the flat as an office. He used to sleep there overnight occasionally.' She scrabbled around in silence for a minute, then added, 'Years ago you used to see him on the box quite a lot.'

After a quarter of an hour, she gave up. As a last resort, she had a look in the phone book. There were a couple of entries with his surname; it felt rude not to write them down. On my way back to the station, I went to a phone box and called the first, just to make sure. A voice answered, disarmingly smooth, but clipped as a palace lawn. Within a few sentences, Moss's old boss had established my intentions, my background ('My God, I'm twice your age!') and arranged to meet me for lunch at his club. A few days later, he phoned to change the venue. His club guaranteed privacy for its members, he said. 'And I assume you'd like to take notes.'

The restaurant he had chosen was in a half-hidden side street in Piccadilly, around the corner from Fortnum's and Pinochet's other favourite London shops. It served fish, as it had done since 1916. There were model ships in the window. The staff directed me towards his usual table with the formality of a bygone era. Outside, there was a lunchtime cloudburst in progress and the street had turned black, but in here all was bright white tablecloths, clinkings and murmurings. He was sitting on his own at a large table, reading *The Times*. He glanced up immediately. He was wearing a blazer, a waistcoat, a pin with his tie and a blue striped shirt, but he looked younger than eighty-two. His hair was swept back in the Pinochet style. He was still quite trim, and his eyes were watchful. 'I had an interview with Allende in 1964,' he began. 'I found him rather pompous.'

Brian Crozier, like Moss, was an Anglicised Australian. He had joined *The Economist* in the early 1950s to write about south-east Asia, in particular the wars in that region between communist-influenced guerrilla movements and the colonial powers. Crozier had once been left-wing himself – 'when the Spanish Civil War started I had just joined the Left Book Club' – but had exchanged that faith for a dogmatic anticommunism. In the early 1960s, his attention shifted from south-east Asia to South America: 'I was very interested in Chile, because I knew the Soviets were very busy there.' He visited during the Frei and Allende periods, saw what he wanted to see ('a Soviet colony . . . descending into chaos'), and came back to London convinced that 'the Santiago Model' was the latest, most dangerous manifestation of global left-wing subversion.

Crozier responded with a flurry of counter-measures. He set up the Institute for the Study of Conflict, a right-wing think tank that examined, and relentlessly talked up, the communist threat. He became a director of NAFF. He helped the CIA run Forum World Features. Pausing over his dressed crab, he added importantly, 'I was the person who sent Robert Moss to Chile.' Crozier also tried to contribute more directly to Allende's overthrow by befriending, and publicising the views of, a conservative Chilean businessman called Hernán Cubillos, who, in Crozier's words, 'masterminded' the truckers' strike that prepared the country for the coup.

All these achievements were proudly summarised in an autobiography that Crozier published in 1993. Its breezy veteran's tone – 'the next move from my CIA friends was to suggest that there was a need for a book on Chile . . .' – conveniently blurred the fact that Crozier, at least some of the time, had been fishing in some very dark political waters. In 1974, he wrote a book that included a justification of torture. The practice, he said, could 'appreciably reduce the duration of [a] conflict' and avoid 'wasted money and resources, fear and the disruption of people's lives'. In another book in 1979, Crozier argued openly for an 'authoritarian interlude' in Britain. 'Party democracy,' he wrote, 'has no moral content . . . If party democracy ceases to deliver freedom . . . party democracy must be replaced by something else.'

In the restaurant, as we ate our delicate starters, and Crozier charmed the foreign waiters ('I'm trilingual!') and made witty little remarks about his increasing age and forgetfulness, there were moments when the chill of his past associations completely faded. But only moments; his enthusiasm for dictators had not diminished. Crozier had gone to Chile to meet Pinochet twice after the coup. 'He was a statesman,' Crozier said with slow emphasis. Then, lightening: 'I liked his sense of humour. He would talk seriously to his cabinet and then would crack jokes – some of which I even understood.' Crozier's second visit, he said, was at the dictator's instigation: 'Pinochet invited me back to Chile. He was working on a new constitution, and he asked me to draft it. I took a rough draft with me to Chile that I had done here. I was with his cabinet for a week. Very interesting.' Crozier said he also had a private, one-to-one meeting with the general. 'We spent about an hour together.'

As with Walters and Moss, Crozier's ability to shuttle between Santiago and London, between international and British issues, between apparently respectable right-wing circles and much more extreme ones, drew him to the attention of Britain's conservative saviour-in-waiting, Margaret Thatcher. In the mid-1970s, her understanding of world affairs was limited. She found Crozier's tireless warnings about the Soviet Union and its supposed allies in the international Left very persuasive. From 1976 to 1979, he acted as her adviser on this and his other pet subjects. Crozier would go round to her house in Flood Street in Chelsea, an immaculate little street near the Thames where the chaos of the rest of London and the world could be discussed at leisure. Crozier talked and, as he put it in *Free Agent*, 'The lady took notes.' In the restaurant, sitting very upright in his waistcoat, he took on the expression of a wise but patient counsellor. 'I tried to explain to her what had happened in Chile and why.' Was she interested? 'Yes, she was.'

Yet as long as Thatcher was only Conservative leader and not Prime Minister, Crozier was not ready to throw his lot in with her entirely. In his autobiography, he makes it clear that, like other people on the

British Right, he was also prepared to explore more radical options. 'During this critical period of 1975–78,' he writes, 'I was invited several times, by different Army establishments, to lecture on current problems.' One of these lectures took place in Harrogate in north Yorkshire, before an audience of 200 officers. Crozier gave his standard speech about subversion and the importance of the British army in helping combat it. Then, sensing approval in the crowd, he followed his argument through to its logical conclusion. 'I went so far as to suggest that the army would have to take over.' The response was immediate: 'There was this sort of storm of clapping.' Crozier put down his fish-knife and fork and shakily mimed the applause. He looked faintly nostalgic. According to his autobiography, his standing ovation in Harrogate went on for five minutes.

'I don't want to exaggerate,' he continued, 'But at one stage the army was seriously wondering whether it would have to take over. I was in touch with General Sir Walter Walker. I got the impression that if there had been a crisis, he might have been the man to take over.'

Walter Walker was born on a tea plantation in India in 1912. A sense of duty and vigorous self-importance ran in the family. His grandfather had won military medals for storming rebel forts during the Indian Mutiny. His father, besides running the plantation, rode as an officer with the Assam Valley Light Horse, played polo to national standard, and had a hospital wing named after him. At the end of the First World War, the family moved back to Britain. Walker, one of four sons, was sent to boarding school in the West Country.

Many of his teachers were former soldiers. They too played polo and talked about India and gave orders as if Queen Victoria were still on the throne. Walker, who when very young had enjoyed 'larking', now fell in love with discipline. 'When I became head of the school's day boys,' he wrote in his autobiography, *Fighting On*, 'I found them to be a motley bunch of idle, unpatriotic, unkempt, and "couldn't care less" type of youths. I decided to straighten them out.' Still barely a teenager, he formed the boys into his own private army: 'We could show the school what smartness on the parade ground meant.' Then he imposed his version of law and order on the school as a whole: 'Bullies received a straight left to the nose or an uppercut to the jaw if they insulted me.' Eventually, the teachers became alarmed. 'The headmaster summoned me to his study and explained the difference between driving and leading. While being grateful to me for what I was achieving, he wrote in my term's report: "He must not allow his zeal to outrun discretion."'

The episode and its conclusion were his career to come in microcosm. He joined his grandfather's regiment, the 1/8th Gurkha Rifles, at the age of twenty-one. During the 1930s, he conducted 'punitive operations' as a young officer against local tribesmen on the North-West Frontier of India. Watching the hot dry mountainsides – like the young Pinochet guarding Chile's desert borders with Peru and Bolivia – he acquired an early suspicion of the Soviet Union to the north. 'Were the Frontier tribesmen,' he speculated in his autobiography with perhaps a note of excitement, 'in the pay of would-be invaders, preparing his way?'

Walker fought in Burma during the Second World War. The jungle made him thin and periodically ill, but the difficulty and remoteness of the campaigns suited his way of doing things. Discipline could be feudal. Supervision by superiors was limited in the close, sweaty spaces and sudden, small-scale battles. He was promoted to colonel and acquired a reputation for intensity and restless tactics. In 1948, he was sent to Malaya, where communist guerrillas had started attacking British rubber plantations. It was a situation that perfectly fitted his emerging world view: 'I had been studying the internal security situation in Malaya in the light of the violent labour and industrial unrest in the mines and rubber plantations and the frequency of rioting, all of which had been stirred up by the Chinese communists, who had wormed their way into key positions in the trade unions.' Walker blamed the Labour government in London for not banning the Malayan Communist Party. He was less inhibited in his methods. He formed the plantation owners into a civilian volunteer force. He set ambushes for the guerrillas where every last one of them would be killed. He used informers and double agents. By 1958, he was a brigadier and a Commander of the British Empire.

Next, Walker learned how to take over a city. In 1959, he was ordered to police the first post-colonial elections in Singapore. Faced with 'screeching mobs' of voters, he ordered his soldiers 'to achieve an intimate knowledge of every road, alleyway, footpath, [and] traffic light . . . peaceful crowd dispersal was to be rehearsed . . . liaison with every helicopter pilot was to be so close that soldiers could be winched on and off flat roofs with the minimum of delay . . . each battalion was to be trained to such a pitch that it could completely dominate its slice of the city.' Walker made sure that these preparations were as public as possible. The strategy worked: the elections went ahead peacefully. Walker left Singapore with a clear sense of how soldiers could overawe civilians.

He went back into the jungle for much of the 1960s. This time it was Brunei and Borneo, to the east of Malaya, but the situation, in Walker's view at least, was essentially the same. A foreign power, in this case Indonesia (of which Borneo was a part), was using a left-wing revolt, this time in Brunei, to infiltrate and possibly capture a territory with close links to Britain. Walker was now a major-general and even more impatient with any restrictions on his military activities. He told his superiors that the only way to defeat the Indonesian-led rebellion was to launch secret raids from Brunei into Borneo itself. He was quietly permitted to do so; his Gurkhas and helicopters did the rest.

In Walker's view, this was a spectacular success – the Vietnam War as it should have been fought. Back in London, however, the general's risk-taking and abrasiveness had acquired him a reputation as a brilliant liability, a sort of latter-day Cochrane. And with most of the British empire now shed, there were few remaining colonial emergencies in which Walker's talents could be used. In 1965, he was recalled to Britain. From then until his retirement seven years later, he was given no further active service. Instead, he was promoted to a series of largely desk-bound positions: Deputy Chief of Staff in charge of Plans, Operations and Intelligence at a NATO complex in France ('I was appalled by the peace-time tempo'); Commander-in-Chief of the army in northern Britain ('the physical and educational standard of recruits left much to be desired'); and head of the NATO forces in northern Europe, based in liberal Oslo in Norway ('dealing with a bunch of ministers and politicians who were stark afraid of upsetting the Russians').

Walker developed a complex of interlocking frustrations. Yet the more the 'ungrateful army hierarchy' denied him the decorations, postings and hearings for his ideas that he felt he deserved, the more he began – following Cochrane again – to conceive of himself as a public figure of wider significance. He began giving television interviews, and quickly realised the appeal of his 'outspokenness' to producers. He agreed to take part in a television documentary called *A Day in the Life of a General*, which he planned to use as a platform for his undiplomatic opinions about the Russian threat and NATO's readiness to combat it. When the film was banned on security grounds, Walker only grew more convinced that he was 'revealing the true state of affairs which the politicians are hiding from the public'. By the time he retired in 1972, he saw official decadence all around him: 'ceasefire soldiers, old men of Vichy . . . fat cats of the Establishment . . . sanctimonious creeps.' Before long, he would see Britain as a whole in the same terms, and want to do something about it.

His vehicle would be an organisation called the Unison Committee for Action. It was set up independently of Walker in early 1973 by a group of anonymous British bankers, ex-intelligence and military personnel, lawyers and businessmen, and was led by a Conservative parliamentary candidate. Its original purpose, in line with the thinking of Kitson, Crozier, Moss and all the country's other prophets of chaos, was to create a 'vigilante group to help protect the nation against a Communist takeover'. For its first year of existence, its membership remained secret; with all the other activity on the right-wing fringes of British politics, Unison received little publicity.

Walker, meanwhile, was living in a small village in Somerset and trying to keep himself occupied. He had a long, thatched farmhouse with thick walls and tiny windows. He had the seventeenth-century stonework and a lot of lawn to look after. He had converted a stable into rooms for guests. His study was a small library of military and intelligence publications. His daily life, as he later described it to several newspapers, was as follows:

6.45 a.m.: Get up, give dogs a drop of milk warmed with tea. Then a cup of tea in bed for my wife.
7 a.m.: Collect the paper.
9 a.m.: Bath and shave.
10.10 a.m.: Collect part-time secretary from the next village for dictation.
Noon: Run secretary back, then lunch.
1.30 p.m.: Back to study until three o'clock when I take the dogs for a walk.
6.30 p.m.: More work in study.
7 p.m.: My wife brings me a flask of whisky. It's the time the sun went down in the Far East. I never drink in the day.
9 p.m.: An evening meal.
10 p.m.: Watch the news on TV.
1 a.m.: Lights out.

Walker was only just into his sixties. He looked a little older: he had lost most of his hair in the jungle, and his face was lean and slightly drawn. But he still wore his moustache straight as a parade baton, and his eyes were like drills. By the summer of 1974, he had grown 'so shocked at the appalling state of the country', and in particular 'the power of the militant trade unions', that he wrote to the *Daily Telegraph*:

Sir . . . What is lacking is dynamic, invigorating, uplifting leadership. A true leader who inspires trust and confidence; who puts love and country before all else . . . who puts country before career; the national interest before party politics; who has the moral courage to expose and root out those who try to rot us from within and hold us to ransom by anarchy, blackmail and brute force. The Communist Trojan horse is in our midst with its fellow-travellers wriggling their maggoty way way inside its belly . . . The patience of some of us is beginning to wear thin . . . The country yearns for a leader . . . It is inconceivable that we should not be able to produce such a man – before it is too late.

The letter was published in early July. Walker immediately began receiving sacks of replies, many of them enclosing money, 'and urging me to give a lead'. Among those who contacted him, according to Walker, were 'Admiral of the Fleet Sir Varyl Begg, Marshal of the Royal Air Force Sir John Slessor, a number of British generals, ex-MPs, the popular Goon comedian, Michael Bentine, and the shipping magnate Lord Cayzer'. Letters also came from estate agents and doctors, solicitors and rectors, pensioners, small businessmen and the National Association of Ratepayers' Action Groups, a pressure group recently formed by the owner of a sportswear factory in Sussex called David Petri. He had set up his organisation to protest against rate increases, and claimed an improbable thirteen million members; now Petri announced he was abandoning the rates issue to campaign instead for a new British leader. By that, he hinted strongly, he meant Walker. As in Chile in the countdown to the coup, the frustrations of sections of the middle class, which had been accumulating through the 1960s and 1970s, seemed suddenly to have found a channel. It did not lead towards any of the usual political solutions.

In the second week of July, Walker gave a front-page interview to the *London Evening News*. 'Does General Sir Walter Walker visualise the day,' the reporter asked, 'when the Army might take over Britain, as the Army has taken over so many South American republics?' Walker responded: 'Perhaps the country might choose rule by the gun in preference to anarchy.' The interviewer narrowed his focus. 'Would the general accept office if . . . he were drafted in?' Walker replied: 'Well, I have a [military] Reserve capacity of five years, of which I have served two . . . I shall be sixty-two in November, but I hope to have some years of activity ahead . . . I think it is the duty of all of us who care about Britain to . . . try to waken the country from this awful sleeping sickness.'

By early August, Walker had joined Unison and effectively become its leader. His farmhouse became its public headquarters, busy with well-wishers and phone calls and visiting reporters. He posed for photographs against the pale old stone, looking grave but purposeful in his regimental tie and blazer. He gave varying descriptions of what he and Unison intended. Sometimes, he talked about 'volunteers [who] would act if there was a collapse of essential services . . . in the event of a breakdown of law and order'. At other times, he spoke less speculatively: 'The first priority of Unison is to select local controllers, whose immediate task will be to compile a register of trustworthy citizens.'

Walker also announced that several owners of light aircraft had promised to fly him around Britain on a nationwide recruiting campaign. This did not materialise, but during the rest of August – otherwise a strange political limbo, with Parliament in recess and the year's second general election approaching – the outline of Walker's organisation became clearer. It changed its name to Civil Assistance. Its tasks 'when the crunch came', as the general liked to put it, would include everything from protecting property to driving lorries, providing emergency accommodation to keeping the country's lines of communications open. Members of this supposed administration-in-waiting began to declare themselves. Many of them were old soldiers and Royal Air Force veterans. A colonel from Hampshire called Robert Butler emerged as a spokesman for Walker and 'chief executive'. Butler told *The Times*, ominously, that any British government 'that has not secretly decided to capitulate quietly and over a period to the communists will welcome the knowledge that such numerous, powerful and technically skilled support is available [from Civil Assistance].' Butler's next sentence made the threat more explicit. 'It would indeed be extremely sinister for a Government . . . to say it did not welcome it.'

Civil Assistance began appointing its 'controllers' for each region, county and locality. A circular letter from Walker was sent out to his subordinates, specifying how further recruits should be vetted. Anyone with 'character defects', a drug or alcohol dependency, or who had 'indulged in conduct that might leave them open to blackmail', was forbidden to join. Despite these restrictions, Walker claimed at the end of August that the Civil Assistance membership 'has already reached the figure of at least 100,000'. He continued, 'At this rate, and it is accelerating each day, our supporters could well amount to several millions by this time next month . . . Nothing shall stand in the way of this revival of patriotism.'

Just how much of this was letters-page bluster was unclear. But the Wilson government was worried enough for the Defence Secretary, Roy Mason, to interrupt his holiday and put out a statement warning of a 'near fascist groundswell'. In early September, a private memo was leaked to the press from Colonel David Stirling, the former founder of the SAS and general military adventurer, who was attempting to set up a British volunteer organisation of his own called GB 75. Stirling had been in touch with Walker. Their motivations – hostility to the unions and the political status quo – seemed similar. Yet Stirling, whose beliefs were more eclectic, wrote that he was 'uneasy about the apparently highly militaristic and *very* Right-wing nature of Unison's management and, therefore, of that management's long-term intentions'. In a creepy echo of what had just happened in Chile, a *Times* letter-writer wondered whether Britain would 'see Lord's cricket ground crammed with political prisoners'.

Then Walker went quiet for a while. With the general election set for October, he issued a single statement saying every candidate should indicate 'how [they] intended to defeat industrial disruption and blackmail', then stopped giving interviews. It was reported that Civil Assistance were training people to take over power stations. October came, and Labour were re-elected with a small majority. To some British right-wingers, this was a matter for relief: an Allende-style regime was pretty unlikely when Wilson had only three more MPs than the Opposition. But to others, the result was further proof that British democracy was fatally stalled. Walker, unsurprisingly, was of the latter opinion. In early 1975, he began to tour boardrooms in the City of London seeking money and support. He met executives from what were then some of its most prestigious firms: Lazard Brothers, Cazanove, M and G Unit Trusts. Also present at these lunches with the general was Nicholas Ridley, a Conservative MP, soon to be a minister under Margaret Thatcher. Walker later remembered him 'talking in riddles . . . It seemed to me that what he was trying to convey, but hadn't the guts to say openly, was that the only hope for this country would be a military coup.' Another person who came to listen to Walker was Sir Berkeley Gage, the former chairman of the British National Exports Council for South America.

In late February, Walker's City contacts secured him an opportunity to address a public meeting inside the Square Mile. It would take place in the lunch hour, so as many people as possible could attend, in a church called St Lawrence Jewry.

St Lawrence Jewry is a golden-brown building with a squat tower and very high windows, five minutes' walk from the Bank of England. It was designed by Sir Christopher Wren, destroyed by the Luftwaffe, and faithfully rebuilt. It offers services to City workers twice a week, and lunchtime music recitals: piano on Monday, organ on Tuesday. A fountain trickles outside; the church's flower beds are typically immaculate for the area. The only noteworthy thing about St Lawrence Jewry, you might think if you walked past, is the fact that the Guildhall, the ceremonial headquarters of the Corporation that runs the Square Mile, is right next door. This is not, in fact, a coincidence. The church is the City's official place of worship.

Inside, away from the local traffic noise, it soon becomes clear that St Lawrence Jewry has another significance. Its high white-and-gold interior is full of old military and colonial banners. They hang frayed and still above the main door. They stand in corners in the side chapel. They are even picked out in stained glass in the windows. Names catch the light that seem to come from a vanished era: the Burma Star Association, the Federation of Malaya, the Royal Naval Comrades Association, London Central Branch.

Walker's audience on 25 February 1975 was middle-aged but large. There were bank managers, conservative churchmen, men with hearing aids and City dignitaries, and, above all, retired servicemen. The British communist newspaper, the *Morning Star*, which infiltrated the gathering, counted twenty-three former officers, including a general, six brigadiers and nine colonels. Walker, dressed in his most austere pinstripe suit, raised his eyes to the crowd and spoke: 'There is no room for don't-knows. Which side are you on?' He called the British Left a 'cancer' and the 'worm in the apple'. He called organisers of political strikes 'traitors'. He warned of 'Burgesses and Macleans in every branch of the state'. He accused Labour MPs of being subversives. Civil Assistance was ready to act against these forces, Walker promised. Its controllers had 'excellent relationships with chief consta-bles'. Bank managers would be used to detect 'extremists'. When the general had finished speaking, to great applause, a clergyman present said that Walker had expressed 'all the thoughts that had been lurking in the back of our minds'.

As the public meeting dispersed, the hundred or so Civil Assistance members present were ushered into the side chapel. Walker then walked slowly along the pews, under the Empire flags, shaking every single person by the hand.

The planned coup – if that was what it was – never came, of course. Walker's 'private army', as Civil Assistance had become widely known, melted away. Its national council spent much of 1975 and 1976 argu-ing about whether to join forces with Moss and Crozier and the rest at the more respectable National Association for Freedom. More impor-tantly, now that Margaret Thatcher was Conservative leader, and was clearly open to ideas from Britain's radical Right, democracy slowly came back into fashion among the soldiers and City gentlemen who had been so keen to support Walker.

The general himself faded from the newspapers. On his rare re-appearances during the rest of the 1970s, he seemed caught between his old belligerence and an awareness that he had nearly gone too far. 'It is obvious to me that I am the stumbling block,' he told the *Guardian*, of all newspapers, during the merger negotiations between Civil Assistance and NAFF, 'mainly because of the risk of NAFF being smeared with the "private army" image.'

Perhaps, in the end, Walker was too much of a dutiful soldier to overthrow the established order. Or at least not without the kind of right-wing coalition behind him that the Chilean junta enjoyed in 1973 – and which the Labour government of the mid-1970s was never left-wing enough to provoke. So the general went back to Somerset, and confined his energies to ink and paper. He published a twice-monthly newsletter about 'the enemy within and without', and wrote ferocious books about the same subject. He travelled abroad – twice to Rhode-sia, almost annually to apartheid South Africa – for further confirma-tion of his world view. He was also encouraged by the British army to take up charitable work on behalf of the Gurkhas. Until memories receded of the early 1970s, and of the political restiveness of many offi-cers at that time, Walker was perhaps best kept out of the way.

During the 1980s, his health collapsed. Two blundering hip opera-tions in military hospitals left him 'chronically disabled' and in 'excru-ciating pain'. In 1990, Walker sued the Ministry of Defence. He won a settlement out of court. The same year, his wife died. Walker became largely housebound, except for attending memorial services for old comrades from Burma and Malaya. He watched television and read and wrote alarmist letters of diminishing length to newspapers. His name could be found on far-right websites alongside speculation about UFOs.

In October 2000, a few days after my lunch with Crozier, I decided to visit Walker. His address was in *Who's Who* (alongside his recreations: 'normal'). He had moved to Dorset, somewhere near Sherborne. I had the name of a farmhouse, but no telephone number. I got the train from London anyway. It was a bright autumn morning with rain forecast, coming up from the direction of Dorset.

The fields were already bare and wintry when the train reached the West Country. This was the England that soldiers had long favoured: grey garrison towns like Warminster and Andover, the chalky empti-ness of Salisbury Plain for manoeuvres, isolated stone houses for a retirement watching the hills. At Sherborne, the other passengers get-ting off wore tweed and waxed shooting jackets. I walked into the town centre, past a bandstand and a Morris Minor. A billboard for the local paper said: 'Row Over Sherborne Taxi Rank Plan'. There was a shop called 'Forever England', and 'senior citizens' specials' in all the pubs. I went into a second-hand bookshop, looking for a local map. They did not sell them, but there was a whole long wall of military his-tory.

At the Post Office, after I had asked three people, they found some-one who had heard of Walker's address. 'It's just a collection of houses,' said the man, nodding towards the hills above the town. I took a taxi. For a few minutes, it climbed; then the road levelled out and steadily began to narrow. The taxi juddered over patches of dried mud. The hedgerows rose on either side. Then we raced into a hamlet and, at its far end, with a track leading up to it, in its own valley of sheep and rusting chestnut trees, there was a cream farmhouse.

The taxi dropped me in its driveway. I walked up to the front door, past a conservatory with a large empty armchair, facing down the val-ley across the lawn. No one came to the door. I circled round the back of the house and discovered that there was a small stone cottage attached to it. Laundry was flapping in the cottage's front yard, so I knocked. The man who answered was wearing tracksuit bottoms and a T-shirt, despite the rain in the breeze. He was also a Gurkha.

When I had explained what I was doing, he politely told me to follow him into the main house. Even in his slippers, he walked with a certain menace. We paused in the kitchen. It was as warm as a hothouse. Ready-laid trays with egg cups and silver cutlery sat on the counters. The general, the Gurkha explained, was upstairs, but he was very ill. I should wait in the living room while my request for an interview was considered. The Gurkha led me through the hall, which was hung with *kukris*, the curving knives his regiment favoured for decapitations. Then he left me and padded silently up the stairs.

The living room was like a museum. A clock ticked heavily. Military books were laid out on the tables in undisturbed, perfectly parallel piles. The walls were lined with photographs of people in uniform. There was one of Walker, in his younger days, walking beside the Queen across some rainswept parade ground. He loomed over her, slim and tall, upright as Pinochet in his ceremonial uniform. He was talking. Her head was turned towards him, and she was looking up at his eyes. I thought she looked deferential.

The Gurkha reappeared in the doorway. He wanted me to speak to the general's secretary. She was on the phone now. 'Of course he won't see you,' she said sharply when I picked up the receiver. 'Because of his severe disability.' Was there any chance he might see me in the future? 'It depends how he's feeling. He's not too clever at the moment.' The Gurkha showed me out. The general's secretary lived just up the road; she would give me a lift back to Sherborne. 'Have a nice day,' the Gurkha said neutrally as I stepped out into the cold.

The secretary was waiting for me outside her house with the engine running. She drove briskly to the station, without saying much. When we got there, she made sure there was a train to London soon. I could write with questions if I liked, she offered before she drove off. I did, a few weeks later, but there was no reply. The following summer, I read Walker's obituary in the *Daily Telegraph*. They gave him a whole page, but Civil Assistance got barely a paragraph.

14

Quite Helpful to Us in the Falklands

If Walker ultimately proved a disappointment to what you might call the Pinochet tendency in British politics in the 1970s, then Margaret Thatcher would provide substantial consolation. Her election as Prime Minister in May 1979 would introduce Britain, most obviously, to the harsh Chilean formula of economic 'shock treatment', cuts in the welfare state, privatisation and anti-trade-union legislation. Less obviously perhaps, her way of governing would also involve the domestic use of force and men in uniform. While never remotely on a Chilean scale, or even on the scale Walker may have intended, soldiers *were* frequently deployed to run essential services during industrial disputes in the early 1980s, and policemen *were* used in a paramilitary fashion during the miners' strike of 1984. Pinochet himself was particularly impressed by Thatcher's lack of squeamishness in defeating the latter.

But it was in foreign policy that the connections between the two regimes were at their most quietly intricate. When Thatcher took office, six years after the coup in Chile, the Pinochet dictatorship was still seen by most of the world as a brutal, barely legitimate administration. Its law and order policies were condemned annually by the United Nations. Yet one of the first acts of the new British Prime Minister was to begin the restoration of diplomatic relations with Chile, which had been formally cut off by the Labour government in the mid-1970s. In September 1979, Crozier's old friend Hernán Cubillos, now Pinochet's Foreign Minister, was invited to London to discuss a renewed exchange of ambassadors with his British counterpart, Lord Carrington. In January the following year, the respective embassies in London and Santiago were reopened.

In February, one of Carrington's junior ministers, Nicholas Ridley –

General Sir Walter Walker's former lunching companion, and an alleged enthusiast then for a British military coup – began to question the actual extent of torture under Pinochet. Ridley had a meeting with a delegation of Labour and trade union figures who opposed the new friendliness between Britain and Chile. In particular, they cited the case of Sheila Cassidy, a British doctor who had been imprisoned and tortured in Santiago in 1975. She had written a convincingly raw book about her experiences, complete with diagrams of the instruments used to electrocute her, and had briefly become a celebrity on her return to Britain. Ridley, however, appeared not to believe her: 'I cannot know for sure what happened,' he said. Or, as the Labour delegation remembered his words: 'Maybe she was wrong.'

Cassidy's treatment had been one of the reasons why, during the 1970s, Labour had banned the sale of arms to Pinochet, and ended the system of Export Credit Guarantees easing the path of British exports to Chile. In the aftermath of Ridley's intervention, both these trade links were reopened. A year later, in 1981, a defence attaché was despatched from London to Santiago, specifically to boost local sales of British arms. That autumn, the British government announced that Chile would be buying a destroyer and an oil tanker from the Royal Navy.

Such transactions had been going on since Cochrane's day, but this time Chile's need for warships was particularly urgent. For the first time for a century, it had recently been thinking about going to war.

At the very southern tip of Chile, where the land narrows to almost nothing and then shatters into tiny islands, like the tip of a bent and broken sword, the country's border with Argentina had been disputed for decades. One section was contentious in particular: the Beagle Channel. Charles Darwin had discovered this cold east–west waterway in the 1830s and named it after his ship. The channel's practical use as a sea route was limited – it was too narrow and shallow for large vessels – but it had an obvious symbolic value. Since it cut right across the bottom of the continent, whichever country controlled the Beagle Channel would be able to claim both an Atlantic and a Pacific coastline, a dream of Chile and Argentina since independence.

When both countries had been Spanish colonies, the bare and mountainous area around the channel had never been properly divided or controlled by the imperial government. The issue was left unresolved for years after the Spanish departed, while Argentina and Chile established rival trading posts and settler populations. In 1881, a treaty was finally agreed that drew the border right down the middle of the Beagle Channel, giving Chile – in theory – every island south of this line. But Argentina refused to give up its claims to the three easternmost ones. Until the late 1970s, the small wooded outcrops of Isla Nueva, Isla Picton, and Isla Lennox – the names were an indication of long British influence – were sporadically argued over. Like another territory in the region claimed by Buenos Aires, the Falkland Islands, the three green fragments in question remained out of Argentinian hands. Unlike Britain, Chile took the trouble to fortify its disputed possessions and garrison them with convincing numbers of soldiers. In 1978, after a British-administered international panel again awarded the islands to Chile, Argentina sent twenty-three warships to the Beagle Channel for 'operational exercises'.

For the whole of that year, the two countries edged around the brink of war. Both moved over half their fleets to the region. Opposing ships sailed directly at each other, only to turn away at the last moment. Chilean troops strung barbed wire along the controversial beaches. Argentinian aircraft deliberately bombed the empty interior of the islands in sight of the Chilean positions. Just before Christmas, with a real Argentinian attack reportedly hours away, the Vatican negotiated a flimsy truce. It held through 1979 and 1980, but the border was not settled and neither side reduced its military presence. The prestige of two authoritarian regimes was at stake (like Chile, Argentina was dominated by a strongly nationalist dictator, General Galtieri); perhaps just as importantly, it was now believed in both countries that territorial supremacy in the far south would bring more concrete benefits. Argentina and Chile had land and ambitions in the Antarctic, only a few hundred miles away. There were also thought to be valuable oil and mineral deposits under the region's seabed. By 1982, the Beagle Channel dispute still had not been resolved. The Vatican negotiators, however, were slowly leaning towards Chile. So the Argentinian government decided to seek an easier strategic and psychological triumph. In April, they invaded the Falklands.

The detail of the collaboration between Britain and Chile that followed, and which was quite probably decisive in the recapture of the islands, has remained conveniently vague ever since. In November 1982, a few months after the Argentinians had been defeated, the

British Foreign Secretary Francis Pym told the House of Commons that 'Chile was quite helpful to us in the conflict.' Sixteen years later, Margaret Thatcher offered a slightly more concrete summary of Santiago's contribution. Visiting Pinochet at Wentworth, she publicly thanked him for 'the information you gave us, the communications, and also the refuge you gave to any of our armed forces'. But these words concealed as much as they revealed, and she gave no further details.

There are plenty of reasons why British and Chilean politicians might not want to dwell on their joint military and intelligence operations during the early 1980s. Chile was officially neutral during the Falklands War. Diplomatic relations with Argentina have improved considerably since, and would be unlikely to benefit from a revisiting of past tensions. In Britain meanwhile, the popular memory of the conflict is still of the country acting alone, for good or ill. The idea that the sailing of the task force, and the terrible sinking of British ships, and the eventual, photogenic march to victory across the treeless islands, was made possible in large part by the torturer of Santiago, is still not very palatable.

Chileans who are not government officials, however, tend to be less sensitive about it all, perhaps because they have become used to uncomfortable revelations. In Santiago in November 2000, the lunchtime before my interview with Professor Miguel Benado at the University of Chile, I was sitting on a bench in one of the spotless parks in the middle of the capital, reading a memoir about the Pinochet years, when two untidy men approached me, and they were passing a large beer bottle between them. They were probably in their early twenties. One of them had a mischievous-looking goatee beard, the other had a lot of tattoos; they were both a little drunk. We began a brittle conversation. There was mockery in their glazed eyes; I wondered whether they were sizing me up for a robbery. Then I mentioned I was English. They both took a few seconds to register the information, before the one with the tattoos smiled broadly and said, in very deliberate English: 'Falklands.' The one with the goatee grinned too, and added, 'Good friend against Argentina.' They offered me a swig of their beer, and we settled into a discussion of which English rock bands they liked.

Afterwards, up in the professor's austere office, once we had finished talking about Cochrane and North and their role in Chilean history, Benado too was keen to mention the Falklands. 'It was the crucial point in Margaret Thatcher's career,' he said with certainty. 'And she gives Pinochet . . . the neutralisation of the Argentinians. Wonderful!' Benado theatrically tucked his long legs under his chair. 'According to Chilean mythology, we lost land in the south to Argentina. In the Chilean consciousness still is the view that Argentina robbed us of Patagonia [an area north of the Beagle Channel], and that they will continue to push towards the Pacific.' For a moment, Benado's sceptical politics seemed to leave him. Straight-faced, he continued: 'Old European maps show Chile with both sides of Patagonia.'

Did he think it had made any difference during the Falklands War that Pinochet had been the Chilean leader? Benado smiled. 'I would have supported the British myself if I had been in power.' Even Margaret Thatcher? His look of amused detachment returned. 'People who are over thirty-five in Chile think of Thatcher, "Even if she was a bastard, she was our bastard."'

In April 1982, even more than it usually did, Thatcher's administration felt exactly the same way about Pinochet. The long-established and tiny British garrison in the Falklands – recently reduced even further by Conservative defence cuts – had surrendered to the Argentinians after a few minutes' resistance. An occupying force of several thousand, with armoured cars and artillery, was entrenching itself in the islands. Within a day of the invasion, the British Prime Minister had announced her intention to send a fleet 8,000 miles south to retake them. Yet there were no British colonial remnants or overseas bases within useful military distance of the Falklands, nor, apparently, any close British allies. According to the newly appointed British ambassador to Chile at the time, John Hickman, who was preparing to fly to Santiago when the Argentinian invasion occurred, there was then only a single British intelligence agent in all of South America. The agent was expelled from Buenos Aires immediately after the Argentinian landings.

And while this foreign policy crisis developed, Margaret Thatcher's government was also facing domestic collapse. The 'shock treatment' and monetarist miracle cures that Walters had seen at work in Chile, and had persuaded Thatcher to adopt, were all very well in a dictatorship – no election would ever test their effectiveness. But in Britain in the early 1980s, when unemployment swelled monstrously and industrial production shrivelled, just as the stern monetarist physicians had predicted and indeed recommended they would, the result was riots, strikes and a revolt in the opinion polls. During the winter of 1981, Thatcher's personal approval rating dropped to 23 per cent, the lowest that had ever been recorded for a Prime Minister. The British experiment with Chilean economic and social policies looked doomed. A few months later, it was appropriate, then, that the duty of helping salvage it fell to General Pinochet.

The Argentinian capture of the Falklands was not a welcome development for the Santiago government. The islands contained the best natural harbour in the South Atlantic. The tense balance of power in the region might now be upset. So within a week of the invasion, Chile agreed that the British could have unofficial use of its airfields and army bases nearest to the Falklands. It also offered to share with Britain any Argentinian signals intercepted by its extensive system of surveillance stations. After the recent confrontations over the Beagle Channel, the necessary Chilean facilities and personnel were already mobilised. In return for all this, Britain would further relax its restrictions on selling arms to Chile; provide Pinochet with another squadron of Hawker Hunters (the type of aircraft he had used to bomb La Moneda) and between three and six Canberra high-altitude spy planes (very useful for a vulnerably narrow country with a hostile neighbour); and, perhaps most appealing of all to the dictatorship, discreetly oppose the United Nations' continuing investigations and condemnations of the use of torture in Chile.

From mid-April onwards, elaborate precautions were taken to keep this deal secret. First, the Canberras flew unannounced from their base in Cambridgeshire to an airstrip in the former British colony of Belize in Central America. There they were repainted in Chilean Air Force markings. Then they continued south to Punta Arenas, the main air base at the bottom of Chile. On the way, they may have refuelled at Santiago: a British television journalist, Jon Snow, saw two Canberras in Chilean colours at the international airport while changing planes, en route for the far south himself. Once the surveillance aircraft arrived at their final destination, their British crews stayed with them. For the duration of the war, the Canberras then criss-crossed the Falklands, southern Argentina and the ocean in between, taking pictures. They could fly too high to be intercepted; the risk came, as at Santiago, when they were on the ground.

The Chilean Air Force station at Punta Arenas, then as now, is part of the same complex as a small civilian airport. The land around is flat and grey-brown. Bushes and trees, where they grow at all, grow low and at an angle in the incessant southern gale. The air is scrubbed clean by the wind, and visibility is close to perfect.

The military aircraft stand partly concealed behind banks of dry earth. There are a few hangars, a high fence, and some shallow man-made depressions. Otherwise, the Air Force base is in plain view of the passenger terminal. Chilean businessmen and oil workers, and American and European adventure tourists, with their new hiking boots and anoraks and their visions of the Patagonian wilderness to come, could, if they wished, note the specifics of each warplane as it taxied past.

In 1982, the Chileans whitewashed all the terminal windows facing the runway. Guards were stationed around the building to stop anyone peering through any sliver of glass the decorators had missed. Civilian flights landing and taking off at Punta Arenas were told to keep the blinds down on their passenger windows 'for reasons of national security'. Despite these measures, there were reportedly curious sightings at the airport during the Falklands War: Chilean Air Force planes with the wrong, European-style camouflage; aircraft with 'Fuerza Aerea de Chile' misspelt; and unusually pale pilots walking about, speaking in English accents.

Yet news of this did not spread far. There was a tradition, after all, of British military personnel making unofficial appearances in Chile at times when the country was tense or in confrontation with its neighbours. During Cochrane's campaigns, during the War of the Pacific, during the Civil War of 1891 – on all these occasions British mercenaries or regular units had been seen in Chilean ports. And then there were the regular peacetime contacts between the Chilean and Royal Navies; the frequent deliveries to Chile of British-built warships; and Santiago's habit of buying second-hand British vessels. During the Falklands, the airport at Punta Arenas would not be the only place where this ease and familiarity with the British military would prove valuable in screening the task force's errors.

There were local reasons, too, why the far south of Chile was a favourable base camp for the British. One of them was the isolation of the region. Punta Arenas and the few towns around it are separate from the rest of the country. The Pan-American Highway gives out several hundred miles to the north; between this point and Punta Arenas lies a roadless emptiness of glaciers and monkey-puzzle forests. Even flying across it, which is the only, expensive alternative to a slow and stormy boat journey, makes the remoteness of the south feel very concrete. Deep-blue gulfs and archipelagos slip slowly past below, then uninhabited headlands and mountains pressing closer and closer to the coast; as you continue southwards, more of the land turns from khaki to white; black crags spike upwards through ice fields and uncrossable valleys hang suspended between the inland ranges; then the cloud that streams across almost constantly down here, blown by the Pacific winds, begins to thicken and conceal; for the last hour or so, the land disappears. When the plane finally descends towards Punta Arenas, it is a shock to see a spindly road below, then the first building, then to remember that anyone lives here at all.

In fact, the town south of the airport is a substantial sprawl. There are dead trees in the civic flower beds on the outskirts, but there are also determined little gardens in front of bungalows, traffic jams of pick-up trucks and army vehicles beginning to form, and new executive homes going up at the roadside, in the same 1980s style that you see in Basingstoke. The centre of Punta Arenas, meanwhile, is a defiant grid of older stone buildings, the straight streets aligned as if the wind did not exist, the prestigious addresses designed with exaggerated solidity. Teenage girls sit bare-legged on the benches in the main square, eating crisps, while tourists hurry by in their zipped-up fleeces.

Casual visitors tend not to linger in Punta Arenas. The town was established on its shallow slope down to the sea in 1848, as a lonely experiment involving Chilean settlers and, shortly afterwards, as a penal colony. In 1876, sheep from the Falklands were introduced into the surrounding grassland, and Punta Arenas began to boom, as the market town and port for the bleak but profitable farms. Oil drilling and industrial fishing followed in the twentieth century, then came the military build-up during the Beagle Channel dispute. The town was still full of soldiers when I visited in December 2000. Across from my hotel, where the walls were thin enough to hear litter scraping along the pavements at night, there was a fortified rooftop with guard towers and bundled-up sentries, facing in the approximate direction of Argentina.

From the start, Britons were intimately involved in Chile's acquisition and consolidation of its southern territories. An earlier attempt at a Chilean settlement in the region, forty miles down the coast from Punta Arenas, had been led by a man from Bristol called John Williams, who was paid by Santiago to raise the national flag and some log cabins before the Argentinians or anyone else did. Punta Arenas itself was named after another English seaman's description of the local shoreline: 'Sandy Point'. When the first sheep arrived, they came from a British colony, and the first farm to graze them around Punta Arenas was British-owned. There are relics of these and later dealings with the British all over the town, for those inclined to notice. On the west side, a prim little Anglican church sits wooden and upright next to the British School, where pupils wear striped ties and gingham coats, and still sometimes show English ancestry in their faces. A lone boy was doing detention the first time I walked past, well after seven in the evening.

Down by the harbour, wrecks of old British ships sit beached, with ribs like dead whales and boys swinging from their anchors. Beside the coast road, an abandoned anti-aircraft gun made by Vickers in 1928 still points at the clouds. In the regional museum in the town centre, there are editions of the defunct *Magellan Times* and an old 'Patagonian Fortnightly' called *The Observer*, full of advertisements for 'Lawes' Sheep Dips', 'Douglas R. Lethaby, Accountant & Farm Agent', and the Hotel Royal, 'The English Hotel of Punta Arenas'. But most revealingly Anglophile of all, in a quiet street behind the docks, there is a chilly but perfectly kept set of upstairs rooms which used to belong to a British merchant and are now the local naval museum. It has so many British exhibits that their national origin is often not even mentioned. There are cabinets of maritime instruments made by Evershed's and Simpson; photographs of Pacific Steam Navigation Company vessels docking in Punta Arenas; more photographs of British explorers in the town before setting off for the Antarctic; a blackened plank from a Royal Navy ship, HMS *Dotterel*, that blew up in the harbour in 1881, killing 143 sailors (people still poke plastic flowers into the memorial in the town cemetery); a local map printed in London in 1790, with handwritten comments: 'a rocky mountainous desolate land', 'savage people here – they have boats'; and a list of even earlier British explorations of Patagonia: 'Drake 1578, Hawkins 1594, Narborough 1669, Anson 1741, Cook 1774 . . .'

In April and May 1982, the British sent another expedition to southernmost Chile: members of the Special Air Service or SAS. The plan was to use these elite soldiers, who specialised in surprise attacks inside enemy territory – among other, sometimes illicit military tasks – to infiltrate Argentina itself and destroy the airfields there, which were being used to launch raids on the task force. One Argentinian base was considered an especially important target: Rio Grande, a set of cold runways near the Atlantic coast.

On 4 May, two jets from there had sunk HMS *Sheffield*, the first British ship lost in the conflict, in a single swift assault with Exocet guided missiles. Argentina had a limited stock of these highly effective weapons and of the aircraft capable of carrying them, and both were concentrated at Rio Grande, which was the closest airstrip to the Falklands. It was also very close, however, to the Chilean border. The obvious strategy for an attack on the Argentinian base was to use this nearby friendly territory, either as a launchpad or as a refuge for the SAS afterwards, or both.

What exactly happened around Rio Grande in mid-May remains as cloudy as the region's weather. In the autobiography of the head of the SAS at the time, General Sir Peter de la Billière, while there are detailed descriptions of secret missions by his soldiers on the Falkland Islands themselves, there is no mention of any SAS activities on the South American mainland. Yet it has long been established that when dawn broke on 18 May, the burnt remains of a Royal Navy helicopter had appeared on the wind-flattened grassland a few miles from Punta Arenas. Alan Walters, for one, can testify to that. Shortly after the war ended, he went to Chile to visit Pinochet and was invited down to the far south by the Chilean government to see where all the anti-Argentinian intrigue had gone on. 'They took me to where the helicopter landed,' says Walters. 'There were lots of nods and winks and guffaws.'

The helicopter, depending on which account you believe, had taken off from either a British aircraft carrier or an unofficial SAS base in Chile. It was rumoured during the war that Dawson Island, the long empty land mass south of Punta Arenas where Peregrine Worsthorne had paid his visit to a concentration camp, was quietly in use as a British staging post. Either way, once airborne, the helicopter and its passengers – a small SAS unit – had flown towards Rio Grande, staying in Chilean airspace for as long as possible. To the north of the Argentinian airfield was an isolated country estate where, the plan went, the soldiers would be landed in darkness. They would then survey the defences around Rio Grande undetected before a full-scale assault on the airstrip. But as the helicopter was touching down, and the first SAS men were already on the ground, rocket flares burst in the distance; the officer in charge decided that the operation was in danger of being discovered, with all the consequences that an abortive attack of dubious international legality would bring. The soldiers scrambled back on board, the helicopter took off, and headed for safety.

Wherever it had originally flown from, its final destination had always been intended to be Chile. No British helicopter had the range to make it to Rio Grande and then back to the task force. So the helicopter clattered westwards, away from the Falklands and the British fleet, over the darkened lakes and vast sheep farms of southern Argentina, across the Chilean border, low over the freezing estuary that led to Punta Arenas, and towards the empty hills west of the airport. Then the helicopter began to run out of fuel. Its crew knew what to do: they landed the SAS unit in a deserted spot, where it slipped away and was eventually picked up; then they flew on a little further, landed again, and set fire to the helicopter. Some hours later, the local Chilean *carabineros*, either by chance or design, came across the wreck and the crewmen.

Several days of bad acting followed. The Chilean government made a show of being offended. The airmen were interviewed in Punta Arenas and then flown to Santiago. There, the Chileans persuaded the British embassy to present the helicopter crew at a press conference. Looking shifty in slightly ill-fitting civilian clothes, the servicemen sat in a line with their hands in their laps while their pilot read out a statement: 'We were on sea patrol when we experienced engine failure due to adverse weather. It was not possible to return to our ship in these conditions. We therefore took refuge in the nearest neutral country.'

This explanation was generally accepted at the time by the international media, if only for a lack of alternatives. Shortly after the press conference, the helicopter crew were flown back to Britain and given medals. In early June, Jon Snow was shown a photograph of Rio Grande by an officer in Chilean naval intelligence who was working with the British: there were five wrecked aircraft beside the runway. The abortive raid, it appeared, had been useful practice for another, more successful one. From June onwards, there were no further confirmed Argentinian attacks involving jets carrying Exocets.

The Chilean government's reward was fast in arriving. By the end of May, while the war was still going on, their promised Hawker Hunters had been delivered. In September, within weeks of the British victory, the Thatcher administration marked the ninth anniversary of Pinochet's seizure of power by sending another trade minister, Peter Rees, to Santiago. Rees called the general's regime 'a moderate and stabilising force'. Also that autumn, the head of the Chilean Air Force, General Matthei, was invited as a guest of the British government to the Farnborough Air Show. When the Labour Party protested, and the visit became too politically awkward, it was simply rescheduled for the following March.

For the rest of the 1980s, while remaining ostracised by most countries, Chile had regular and profitable dealings with Britain. With the Falklands War over but the question of the islands not necessarily settled, Britain had a vested interest in allowing a well-armed Chile to act, still unofficially of course, as its local ally. With an agreement over the Beagle Channel not secured until 1984, Chile had a reason to continue to want British weapons. And with American support for Pinochet beginning to weaken, as the oppressiveness of his rule failed to diminish with the passing years, the general needed a respectable ally.

In 1982 and 1983, the British argued in the United Nations that the Pinochet regime should no longer be specially scrutinised for human rights violations. In 1984, Britain gave one of its Antarctic bases to Chile. In 1985, the British government allowed a demonstration model of a new British half-track military vehicle to be shipped to Santiago. Britain also sold Chile anti-tank missiles; further deals involving helicopters, fighter aircraft, and the refurbishment of Chilean nuclear reactors only fell through because of, respectively, financial problems in Santiago and a sudden earthquake. By 1988, Britain had shipped so many weapons to Pinochet anyway that the American government complained publicly about the internal stability of South America being disrupted. There is little evidence that the reprimand made any difference. As John Hickman said of part of his time as ambassador in Santiago between 1982 and 1987, 'People spotted as British in Chile . . . were liable to find themselves unusually popular.' For the Chilean dictator, for much of the following decade, the lure of London would be similar.

15

Pinochet in Piccadilly

During the late 1980s and early 1990s, Pinochet's position in Chile went into slow decline. Part of the reason was economic. As in Britain, the 'miracle' produced by monetarism turned out to be a patchy one. Periods of wild growth, when the skyline of eastern Santiago seemed nothing but cranes, were matched by periods of plunging recession, when bankruptcies were more common than in the most chaotic days of Allende. And even in the best years, many Chileans did not benefit. In 1987, the *Financial Times* estimated that average salaries were still significantly lower, if you allowed for inflation, than they had been in 1970.

The success of the Pinochet regime in creating a docile, depoliticised population was ultimately just as limited. For ten years after the coup, the DINA's unmarked cars and the desire, widely held, for a quiet life after the national convulsions of the early 1970s, kept resistance to the dictatorship at a low level. But quite suddenly, in 1983, two strands of opposition emerged. The poor began to riot, and the old political parties began to demand a return to democracy. Pinochet's response was to send out police trucks and water cannon. While this worked as a law and order policy, the political consequences of mass arrests and tear gas on the streets of Santiago, screened on television all over Chile and the rest of the world, were less positive.

In 1988, Pinochet confidently called a referendum on whether his rule should continue. The new Chilean constitution that Brian Crozier had helped draw up in 1980 had included a provision that the general should eventually seek some sort of electoral mandate. By the late 1980s, Pinochet and his advisers had decided that a favourable result in a referendum would give the dictatorship the domestic and international credibility to continue for at least another decade. To make the decision look authentic, a brief campaign was permitted. Pinochet's opponents were allowed fifteen minutes a day on television, while the general enjoyed non-stop support from almost every newspaper and broadcaster, and tacitly from the repressive apparatus of the state. Two thousand people were arrested for political offences in the first half of 1988 alone.

Yet Pinochet lost. In October, after a turnout far exceeding that of any Chilean election, 55 per cent of voters were found to have backed the opposition. Support for Pinochet carrying on as head of state had stalled at 43 per cent – no more than the large minority the Right had traditionally won at elections in the pre-Pinochet era. According to the constitution, there would now have to be a presidential election, involving civilian candidates. With unexpected speed, the end of the dictatorship was in sight.

After the worldwide approval the referendum had received, the process could not be halted. A second coup, or some other form of military intervention to keep Pinochet in office, was simply impractical. It was not 1973 any more; and the general, who was seventy-three now, still straight-backed but rather stout in his ceremonial uniforms, had been defeated according to rules of his own devising. However, he did still have one thing in his favour. The election to replace him was not due to take place for over a year, in December 1989, and the new president would not actually take power until March 1990. This interlude could be used to fix the Chilean political system in favour of the military and the ex-dictator.

During 1989, this was exactly what happened. Pinochet appointed himself as head of the army for another nine years, and as a life member of the Senate from then on. He arranged immunity for himself from prosecution for his actions in government. He granted the military permanent control of its own budget, defence policy, and senior appointments. He made it impossible for the dictatorship's civilian bureaucrats and officials to be sacked. He ensured that the system for electing Congress had a right-wing bias by favouring rural areas, and personally appointed a fifth of the members of the Senate. He changed the make-up of the Supreme Court to his advantage. He cut the Central Bank loose from future government interference. He further cemented the Chilean free market with a last set of privatisations. Finally, he ensured it remained an offence to 'defame, injure or slander the president of the republic, ministers of the state, senators, deputies, members of the high courts, commanders-in-chief of the armed forces, or the general director of the *carabineros*.'

Pinochet's public statements were as unrepentant as his actions. In July 1989, he told a Chilean news weekly, 'I am prepared for everything. My enemies, however, shouldn't forget something: the army will always protect my back.' In October, he warned in the same publication, 'The day they touch one of my men, the rule of law will be over.' Later, when he was under arrest in Britain, such sentiments would prove awkward for those who argued for his release by casting him as the willing restorer of Chilean democracy. As Ariel Dorfman, the left-wing Argentinian writer and veteran critic of Pinochet, drily put it in 1999, 'Saying Pinochet brought democracy to Chile is like saying Margaret Thatcher brought socialism to Britain.'

Yet for all his threats and constitutional manoeuvrings, once the campaigning started for a civilian president, Chilean politics inevitably slipped a little further from Pinochet's control. The general's preferred candidate was his finance minister, Hernán Buchi, a latter-day Chicago Boy, clever and blond and young. The opposition put forward a stooping seventy-one-year-old called Patricio Aylwin, with a lifetime of deal-making for the Christian Democrats behind him. The Buchi campaign hired Margaret Thatcher's favourite public relations adviser during elections, Tim Bell, to make the contrast even starker. The Chilean electorate, by the humiliating margin of 55 to 29 per cent, chose Aylwin. For the next four years, his administration cautiously probed the brutalities of the Pinochet era and the protections the general had arranged for himself and his subordinates. An official human-rights investigation, the Rettig Commission, was set up. In 1991, it announced a figure of 2095 for those killed by the dictatorship, plus a further 1102 'disappeared'.

Intermittently, Pinochet called his troops out onto the streets to discourage further human-rights initiatives. But public opinion continued to drift away from him: at the next presidential election, in 1994, the anti-Pinochet coalition won even more heavily, by 58 to 25 per cent. With former dissidents returning from exile, and surviving victims of the dictatorship feeling steadily bolder, and relations of the dead and 'disappeared' beginning to sense their opportunity, a substantial groundswell for human-rights prosecutions began to form. In 1995, the former head of the DINA was imprisoned. In January 1998, for the very first time, a group of government politicians proposed the impeachment of Pinochet himself.

During these first slightly troubled years as an ex-dictator, Pinochet regained his old appetite for travelling abroad. He had been to America for military training in the 1960s and on state visits to eastern Europe with Allende in the early 1970s, but since the coup he had been almost completely confined to his own strip of a country. His only trip to Europe had been to Franco's funeral in 1975. Otherwise, even a visit to see Ferdinand Marcos, the tyrant of the Philippines, had to be abandoned after international protests in 1981, with Pinochet's plane circling above the runway at Manila airport, having flown all the way across the Pacific. But after 1990, the general's official status abroad appeared to become more ambiguous. The Cold War had just ended, and all sorts of pasts were being smoothed over. Besides, Pinochet was still head of the Chilean army. As such, he had a legitimate reason to travel to foreign capitals: to buy arms.

Shortly before he had handed over power to Aylwin, Pinochet had suggested to the incoming government that he should act as a kind of roving international deal-maker for the Chilean defence industry and military. During the 1970s and 1980s, the restrictions on weapons sales to Chile had caused local arms manufacturing to take off. The everyday secrecy of the dictatorship and the empty, military-controlled spaces of the northern deserts made the country ideal for private weapons projects. The Chileans also became expert at getting round international embargoes by quietly obtaining what they could from friendly governments, such as Britain, and by embarking on joint ventures with foreign arms companies. Santiago in particular became a well-known venue for the more sensitive sort of weapons trading. Both the illicit sale of arms to Iraq by British companies and Colonel Oliver North's efforts to secure military equipment for the Nicaraguan Contras involved the Chilean capital. In 1990, a British journalist, Jonathan Moyle, who had been investigating an alleged collaboration between Chilean and British firms to sell helicopter gunships to Iraq, was found hanged in a cupboard in Santiago's grandest hotel, right across from La Moneda. An inquest gave a verdict of unlawful killing.

This sort of scandal, however, was hardly likely to put off Pinochet from exploiting the good contacts he had made in the international arms trade over the previous two decades. Since the Falklands, and sometimes even earlier, many of these contacts had been with British firms such as Royal Ordnance and its parent company British Aerospace. In April 1991, barely a month after he had ceased being dictator of Chile, it was announced that the general would be coming to Britain. Royal Ordnance had issued an invitation after being approached by Pinochet's office. It was rumoured that he might see Margaret Thatcher at the same time. A spokesman from the Foreign Office in London did not anticipate any problems: 'Any Chilean can get on a plane and come here at any time. He doesn't need a visa . . . This is a private trip, by a private person invited by a private company.'

Pinochet arrived by private aircraft at nine a.m. on 18 May. It was his first visit to Britain. He landed at an airfield owned by British Aerospace in Hatfield, on the quiet northern fringe of London. Policemen in plain clothes were on hand to prevent any demonstrations. The company then flew him by helicopter to a research centre owned by Royal Ordnance near Aylesbury in Buckinghamshire. Screened by the thick spring hedgerows and the concealing hills of the Home Counties, and a ring of high fencing and private security guards, the helicopter touched down; the general and his entourage of twenty-four Chilean military officers and bodyguards got into two black limousines and disappeared into the bowels of the compound.

While protesters, unsure of Pinochet's itinerary, picketed the headquarters of British Aerospace in central London, he inspected a system for launching cluster bombs. The Rayo (Spanish for 'lightning') had been developed partly by Royal Ordnance and – this was typical of the way the Chilean military now operated under Pinochet – partly by a privatised offshoot of Famae, the weapons-manufacturing wing of the Chilean army. The Rayo worked by firing groups of rockets, as many as thirty-two at a time. Each rocket contained a Royal Ordnance engine and a cluster bomb. A single Rayo unit could fill a football pitch with screaming metal fragments. The potential and relative cheapness of this system had so enthused Royal Ordnance and Famae that they had set up a joint company to sell it around the world. The British military had obligingly allowed the Rayo to be tested on one of their firing ranges.

After Pinochet had gauged the weapon's progress, he took off again for Hatfield. He left Britain that evening, without venturing into London to see Thatcher. In addition to the demonstration outside British Aerospace, the Chile Committee for Human Rights, one of the anti-Pinochet charities still based in the capital, had recently written to

Britain's Director of Public Prosecutions demanding that the general be tried for assault, torture, conspiracy to kidnap and unlawful imprisonment. There was one further echo in Britain in 1991 of the almost forgotten Chile activism of the 1970s: a small advertisement appeared in the *Guardian* criticising Pinochet's visit, placed by the Chilean Socialist Party. 'We call upon all citizens of this country to protest,' it began. 'Show your support by calling your MP and have General Pinochet declared a morally reprehensible and unwelcome visitor.' It seemed hopelessly optimistic.

In February 1994, Pinochet came to Britain again – this time for a holiday. He and his wife Lucia stayed in London for five days, and developed a routine he would follow on future visits. He chose a hotel in Piccadilly, the bone-grey central quarter of the British capital, with its tall stone streets full of clubs for right-wing gentlemen, discreet shops for wealthy Anglophiles, and hurrying crowds of other tourists as useful camouflage. He went shopping for ties in Jermyn Street. He and Lucia took a chauffeured drive to Hampton Court, the palace west of the city associated with Henry VIII, widely considered the most dictatorial of English monarchs. They went to Windsor Castle and paid for the usual guided tour. And all the while, British policemen lingered watchfully in the background. Pinochet was impressed by the security arrangements: he was recognised once by some Chilean tourists, but there were no protests. He arranged another visit to England four months later. By then, moreover, his relationship with the country had considerably deepened. In between the two trips, he met Margaret Thatcher.

It happened a fortnight after he got back to Chile. But a first encounter between them had been coming for years. Since 1990, in particular: that year, a few months after Pinochet had been forced to give up supreme control of Chile, Thatcher had been forced to give up the Conservative Party leadership. Both of them had dominated their countries for a decade and a half. Both of them needed to find something to do in their enforced retirement. Thatcher, like Pinochet, did not leave office loved. Like Pinochet, she now looked abroad for some of the rewards she felt she had been denied at home. Plenty of right-wing politicians and businessmen outside Britain admired her achievements apparently without reservation; she began to travel and give speeches to these friendly audiences. Like Pinochet again, she organised her public persona in retirement, at least at first, like an efficient privatised company, making sure of both the political and financial benefits. Thus in early 1994, while she was promoting her recently published memoir, *The Downing Street Years*, Thatcher agreed to go on a short tour of Latin America. She started in Brazil. By mid-March, she had reached Chile.

It was her first trip to the country, but she was not short of hospitality. She stayed at the seaside home of Eliodoro Matte, one of Chile's post-coup tycoons. Her five-day visit was sponsored and arranged by the Chilean Manufacturers' Association, a right-wing Chilean think tank, and Hernán Briones, a millionaire builder with personal links to Pinochet. The itinerary was like a distillation of two decades of Anglo-Chilean connections: a dinner with some of the Chicago Boys, a day at Santiago's enormous biannual arms fair, a reception at the British embassy and an excited succession of other cocktail parties. Newspaper speculation that the general might attend some or all of these accompanied Thatcher throughout.

Midway through her stay in Chile, she was scheduled to give a speech at a Santiago hotel to several hundred local businessmen. It was a typical late-summer day in the capital, the heat thick by noon. The former Prime Minister, who was now sixty-eight, intended to give a forty-five-minute address. She was at the podium in the hotel dining room, and had reached the final page of her speech about the advantages of her brand of free-market economics, when she gasped, quite loudly, and crumpled to the ground, striking her face on a microphone. She was helped to her feet, apologised to the audience and, to applause, walked out of the room. A statement put out by the British embassy said that she was suffering from a stomach infection, possibly brought on by the hot weather and eating seafood. For the rest of the day, Thatcher was said to be resting 'flat out' in her hotel. The symbolism of the whole incident was obvious – her impregnable days had gone – and also a warning, perhaps, of the bad things that could happen to over-confident former leaders in foreign capitals. Yet she had recovered sufficiently two days later to go to the British embassy for another engagement before she left. The reason was not hard to guess. As the embassy blandly phrased it, 'General Pinochet was invited to the reception and he attended.'

Between that day in March 1994 and his arrest in London four and a half years later, the former Chilean dictator saw Thatcher 'on some ten occasions', according to friends of the ex-Prime Minister. She did not make any further visits to South America. His enthusiasm for

Britain, however, continued to grow. In June, he was back at Royal Ordnance for discussions about the Rayo. A British Aerospace spokesman was optimistic about the collaboration: 'We have the British government's support on arms sales to Chile.' In September 1995, an agreement was signed between Royal Ordnance and Famae to build the artillery system in Chile, for use by the Chilean army. The following month, Pinochet was a guest of British Aerospace again, 'seeing officials and visiting some of our facilities', according to the company, 'at his own request.'

The general now felt sufficiently at ease with the British to send Thatcher flowers and chocolates on her birthday each October. In 1995, 1997, and 1998, he chose that month for what had become his near-annual trip to London. He would see her at her white terraced house in Chester Square in Belgravia for tea or drinks. The only other person present would be her husband Denis. Afterwards, Thatcher would sometimes help Pinochet, who was beginning to walk with a stick, down her immaculate front steps to the street. She would wave to him as he was driven off.

Away from all this warmth and mutual regard, however, there were signs in Britain of a more organised hostility to Pinochet's visits – a sense, even, among his opponents, that his regular presence in London could be used against him. In June 1994, a week before the general arrived in Britain for his stay that summer, the high-profile human-rights pressure group Amnesty International instructed an equally well-known liberal lawyer, Geoffrey Bindman, to ask the British Attorney-General to prosecute Pinochet for torture.

It was a legal breakthrough of sorts. The use of torture had been condemned for decades by the United Nations, but it was not until the coup in Chile and its aftermath that this statement of principle began to solidify into an international law. In 1987 the UN Convention Against Torture finally came into effect. The following year, a version of it was accepted as law in Britain. The new legislation allowed prosecutions of public officials of any nationality, as long as they were in Britain to be arrested. Pinochet's visit to London in June 1994 was long enough and sufficiently advertised in advance for Amnesty to pass documents alleging his responsibility for torture to the Attorney-General's office. While the ex-dictator was at Royal Ordnance, being ferried around in limousines, the British police started an inquiry against him. Before it could gain enough momentum for an arrest, Pinochet had flown back to Santiago, but a precedent had been established.

In 1996, the Progressive Union of Public Prosecutors, a group of liberal lawyers in Spain, turned their attention to human-rights abuses in Chile in the 1970s. As in Britain and other countries, left-wing Spaniards had been intrigued three decades previously by Allende; some of these people had gone out to Chile; and some of them had been imprisoned, tortured and even killed. In addition, there had long been a feeling in some Spanish radical circles that Spain owed the Chilean Left a favour: in 1939, at the end of the Spanish Civil War, Allende had arranged as a young minister for 2,500 Spanish republicans, recently defeated by Franco and being held in concentration camps in France after fleeing across the border, to be released and shipped to Chile.

In early 1996, the Progressive Prosecutors in Madrid discovered a clause in Spanish law that allowed a case to be brought against any foreign government that practised genocide or torture. In June, they began proceedings against Pinochet. Chilean and Spanish witnesses were called to Madrid. Killings, disappearances and incidents of torture not properly investigated by the Chilean authorities were probed for evidence.

But legally establishing Pinochet's involvement, let alone convicting him, was an ambitious and ever-widening task. After all, few human-rights convictions had been secured in Chile itself so far, even against his more minor subordinates. After several months, during which their efforts attracted little attention outside their own country, the Spanish lawyers decided to transform their private prosecution. They recruited Baltasar Garzón.

He was perhaps the most famous investigating magistrate in Spain. He had recently helped bring down the national government by revealing the secret involvement of the Spanish state in 'death squads' used against the Basque terrorist group ETA. The law and order policies of Chile in the 1970s presented a similar but much greater edifice of official cover-up and violence. From 1996 onwards, Garzón began to learn its contours and vulnerable points.

If Pinochet realised this was going on, he did not show it. He carried on coming to Britain, although it had an extradition treaty with Spain. He did not appear to take any notice of the change of government in London in 1997. This new administration was full of people, from the Prime Minister downwards, who had been stirred by events in Chile during the 1960s and 1970s. During the months to come, news of set-backs for Pinochet in his struggle against extradition would prompt cheers in the House of Commons.

In retrospect, the trap seems to have been well baited by the time the general arrived in London in late September 1998. Then again, he had already been to Britain since the 1997 general election, without incident. Legal moves against him when he was abroad had come and gone before, after all. In mid-September 1998, the Chilean embassy had contacted the British government with the news that Pinochet intended to come to London again later that month. Although the general had stood down as commander-in-chief of the Chilean army in March, they were assured that he would get VIP treatment.

He landed at Heathrow airport on 22 September, and was guided to a reception area used by the Foreign Office for visiting dignitaries. The general, his wife Lucia and their daughter Veronica waited in the Hounslow Suite, a sort of first-class lounge with fewer facilities but more status, while some of their Foreign Office escorts disappeared to fetch their luggage and have their passports stamped. The Pinochets then set off for their favourite part of the capital. The first night, they stayed at the Athenaeum, the gentleman's club in Piccadilly. Over the next few days, they had dinner at White's, another nearby club of conservative reputation, and at the restaurant at Fortnum and Mason, where the manager was not in the least put out by the circle of bodyguards that stood around the ex-dictator's table throughout: 'He was a familiar face here.' Pinochet was eighty-two now, and he shuffled a little as he walked, but his big head and white swept-back hair and moustache were still international, if ambiguous trademarks. One day a few weeks later, he went to the small Piccadilly branch of Books Etc – the general's taste in local bookshops was quite diverse – and had a look through the biography and encyclopaedia sections. Some of the staff thought they recognised a well-known figure and crept towards him behind the shelves and piles of discounted books to make sure. A few minutes later, Pinochet left the shop with a life of Adolf Hitler.

The Chilean had never spent so long in Britain before, and his relaxed programme of activities reflected it. He did his interview with *The New Yorker*. He went to see Margaret Thatcher in the first week of October. He went to Madame Tussaud's to inspect the waxworks. In front of the likeness of Lenin, Pinochet later recalled, he stopped and said, 'You were wrong, sir! You were wrong.'

Over it all, there hung a slight air of reflectiveness, of the ex-dictator pondering his place in history. He was an old man, something that the monstrous energies of his sixties and seventies had long disguised. He wore a pacemaker for his heart these days and he suffered from diabetes. And he had a bad back. A disc had been torn in his spine for some time; while he was in London, Pinochet hoped to get medical advice. When he did so, he was told to have an operation as soon as possible. The British capital was as good a place as any for private treatment. On 8 October, he was admitted to the London Clinic.

The operation was risky in more ways than he realised. If it went wrong and his spinal cord was damaged, he could lose the use of his legs. Even if it was completely successful, he would need to spend several weeks lying flat in bed; flying back to Chile during that period would almost certainly be out of the question. Pinochet's family and the Chilean army advised against the operation, but he went ahead with it. Since surviving an assassination attempt twelve years earlier, when his motorcade was ambushed with anti-tank missiles outside Santiago and five of his bodyguards were killed, he had developed a steadily greater sense of his own invulnerability. Late on 9 October, Chilean radio reported that the general was recovering from his operation. For the next few days, he lay in his small expensive room high up on the eighth floor of the London Clinic, listening to the central London traffic through the double glazing, receiving the odd visitor, and sleeping.

By 13 October, Garzón had realised what an opportunity this was. He suggested to newspapers in Spain and Britain that there was now enough legal impetus for Pinochet to be detained and questioned in London. The British Home Office indicated to the Spanish that it would give permission for both to happen. The following day, the British police received formal faxes from Madrid requesting that they find Pinochet, prevent him from leaving the country, and arrange to interview him. News of a possible arrest reached the Chilean government the same day; the Chilean embassy in London hurriedly began inquiring about tickets for the next available flight to Santiago. But Pinochet's doctors at the London Clinic said he would not be safe to travel immediately. Anyway, the first plane the embassy tried was full. Pinochet stayed in his bed, thickly sedated.

On 15 October, the *Guardian* published an article headlined 'A Murderer Among Us', written by Hugh O'Shaughnessy, a longstanding pursuer of Pinochet in British newspapers, which called for the general's detention. Reading it, the idea still seemed somehow unlikely. It was easy to skim over the article, which was printed at the bottom of a page, as a ritual protest. And the day went by without an arrest; so did most of the next. The British government said nothing decisive. The Chilean government worried about flight schedules. Then, very late on the evening of 16 October, with the notion beginning to settle that Pinochet would be gone in a few days, leaving behind fretful doctors and frustrated human-rights lawyers clutching uncompleted paperwork, there were footsteps in the corridor on the eighth floor of the London Clinic. At first, Pinochet's Chilean bodyguards thought the British detectives had come to relieve them. But then the Chileans were asked to hand over their weapons. Pinochet was woken up and informed in English, translated for him by his bodyguards, that he was under arrest for crimes against humanity including torture, genocide and ordering disappearances.

He spent six weeks altogether inside the redbrick box of the London Clinic and at Grovelands nursing home, marooned in the far north London suburbs, watching the oaks in the grounds lose their leaves and his police guards pacing along the perimeter railings. Then he was moved to a more permanent British address. It was early December 1998 by now, and the initially frantic legal to-and-fro had settled into a slower rhythm. The Chilean government's attempts to have the general released immediately had failed. The House of Lords, the Chief Justice, and above all Jack Straw, the Home Secretary, with his Chilean memories, had all made their first ambiguous statements. Now the case had entered the British extradition system, with its seemingly infinite possibilities for appeals and counter-appeals. The waits lengthened for press conferences and announcements. The demonstrators, for and against the ex-dictator, established their British rituals. Obscure or long-forgotten arguments about Allende and 'disappearances' and the limits or otherwise of international arrest warrants became staples of radio phone-ins and newspaper controversialists, both broadsheet and tabloid. The Home Secretary received 70,000 letters and emails. A retired electrician from Cheshire speculated in the *Daily Telegraph* that a local campaign against pampas grass, involving warning notes and vandalism of gardens, might be 'a statement about Pinochet'. He explained, 'There's plenty of pampas grass growing in Chile.' Surprisingly quickly, it almost began to feel as if Pinochet had always been with us, so routinely was his name now mentioned. And most simultaneously strange and banal-sounding of all was the improvised prison where he was now confined: a detached house with a double garage in Surrey, called Everglades.

The general's supporters had wanted something grander. They had proposed to the police that he be allowed to rent a property in Eaton Square in Belgravia, across Green Park from Piccadilly and even more expensive. As an alternative, they had suggested a country retreat in Somerset. But the police vetoed both: Belgravia, it was argued, was too close to central London and would attract too many demonstrators; Somerset was too distant for court appearances. As a compromise, both sides settled on Wentworth in Surrey. From the first time I went there, it was easy to see why.

There was blossom and sunshine as the train left behind the western edge of London with its tower blocks and graffiti. Surrey, which is one of Britain's wealthiest and most right-wing counties, began to reveal its lanes and towpaths, its big executive lawns and cars, its cottage conversions and distant spires, a landscape like the deep-green England of tradition, but smartened and tidied and made more exclusive. The first sign of Wentworth was the international golf course, with its bunkers and silver-birch trees, then, through them, like dachas outside Moscow, were the outlines of large houses. The private estate where Pinochet was staying was threaded between the holes of the golf course, with everything maintained by the same management. Other residents included the comedian Russ Abbott and the actress Nanette Newman. When I called the estate office, they had breezily referred to the ex-dictator as 'General P'.

The train stopped at Sunningdale, the nearest station to Wentworth. The estate was two miles away, and there was no public transport to get there – another reason, perhaps, why Wentworth had been deemed suitable. I decided to walk. Before setting off, I crossed the station car park, with its Mercedes and Range Rovers pristine in the sun, and went to get a sandwich from the local supermarket, where Pinochet's bodyguards were sometimes seen buying sweetcorn and chicken to make *pastel de choclo*, a baked Chilean dish with a sweet crust. The supermarket was a Waitrose, the most upmarket British chain, and inside it was full of women with bony wrists, tans from skiing and bobbed haircuts. It felt like shopping in a rich part of Santiago, right down to the proud display of trimmed beef and the racks of Chilean wine.

Afterwards, as I walked along the A30 in the blast of the passing traffic, this feeling strengthened. The houses set back from the road, even before I got to Wentworth, were not like many English houses I had seen before. They had Spanish-style roofs, signs warning of private security, high locked gates and hedges like walls. In the gaps in the traffic, there was a hush in these compounds, just a breeze in the crowns of the trees in their gardens, high above. No one seemed to be around. I imagined the owners somewhere indoors, the victors of the free-market revolution begun by Pinochet and Thatcher, counting their winnings at their leisure.

When I got to the main gates of the Wentworth estate, there were no demonstrators. It was a weekday, and Pinochet's opponents were generally too busy with their jobs and lives to come here outside the weekend, except on days when fresh developments were expected. The rest of the time, the police barriers and cones stood by the roadside, looking insignificant, probably minor roadworks as far as most of the passing cars were concerned. Up closer, there were small signs of the current drama: footprints in the gatehouse flower beds, scraps of tape on the fence where placards had been fixed, stickers on lamp posts saying 'Extradite Now!' But it was a polite sort of debris. No one had been building barricades or throwing rocks, like they often did on anti-Pinochet protests in Santiago.

This time, no one had needed to. For the general's house, rather astonishingly, was in plain view across the road. Despite paying £10,000 a month, his supporters had secured a property on the most public side of the estate, only a hundred yards or so from the A30. You could see the chimney and steeply pitched roof of Everglades through a convenient dip in the perimeter fence. The fir trees in front of the house were not tall enough to screen it. Every chant and drum roll of the weekly demonstrations could carry straight across.

It was too tempting not to try and get a little closer. A single police car had driven past while I was outside the main gates to the estate; of the rest of Pinochet's much-publicised protective cordon there was no sign. I walked back towards Sunningdale for a few hundred yards, then quickly turned into a more minor entrance. There was a white wooden sign saying 'Private Residents Only' and another saying 'Golfers Crossing'; beyond them, a narrow tarmac road disappeared into the trees. There was no pavement, so I kept to the verges, which were as green and smooth as a billiard table. Behind them were more hedges and house outlines and warnings about private security. As the road dipped and climbed and curved and subdivided, confusingly after a while, the trees closed overhead like a tunnel. The sound of the A30 receded, but I tried to keep parallel to it, heading back in the rough direction of Everglades. I passed driveways and urns on gateposts, unused swimming pools and garages with thatched roofs, oversized homes in every style from mock-Tudor to 1970s Californian. Occasional golfers in the distance were the only other pedestrians; without a golf bag over my shoulder, I began to feel conspicuous. A few houses before Pinochet's, a large dog suddenly rushed up on the other side of the hedge I was skirting. Its lunging bark sounded deafening in the near-silence. Then a car drove slowly by, the first I had seen inside the estate; two middle-aged women in thick make-up stared across through the windscreen. Soon afterwards, another car appeared, with 'Premier Security' written down the sides. It crept past. I decided that today I would not risk the general's cul-de-sac.

Inside Everglades, I learned later, almost half the ground-floor rooms were occupied by armed policemen. There was an armed police check-point at the gates to the house, and another at the entrance to the cul-de-sac. There were additional patrols with dogs in the garden. Pinochet was initially forbidden to use it anyway; when this restriction was relaxed after a few weeks, he was often told to keep to a sliver of patio behind the house. His indoor escort of police officers, following in his shuffling foosteps day and night, would watch to make sure he did not stray far across the lawn.

In Chile, even in retirement, Pinochet had become accustomed to multiple residences: a great bunker of a house in eastern Santiago, and seaside homes in Iquique and Bucalemu, south of Valparaíso. Now he had a chilly hollow in Surrey instead of views of the Pacific and the Andes. His Chilean cook, his Chilean bodyguards and butler, Lucia and his other relations, visiting Chilean generals and British politicians – all of them had to squeeze into half a dozen rooms. There was just enough space for his exercise bike, his books and videos (he favoured action films), a computer, a television, and his possibly self-conscious spread of personal photographs, of Margaret Thatcher and his friends in the Santiago military mixed in with his grandchildren.

Such details, most frequently relayed by the British newspapers sympathetic to Pinochet, hardly added up to the kind of discomfort experienced at the Villa Grimaldi. Yet there was an indignity about being an ex-dictator in Everglades' badly proportioned rooms. One day, a television-licence inspector even called round. The name of the house itself sounded like something from a mocking sitcom. And then, above all, there was the humiliating, apparently unchanging truth of his situation: he was under house arrest. During the autumn of 1998 and the winter that followed, the general's British allies, old and new, began to refer to him without any irony as 'Britain's only political prisoner'.

Their shared taste for exaggeration aside, Pinochet's British supporters were an intriguingly eclectic group. There were right-wing polemicists such as Paul Johnson and Bruce Anderson, who both included Pinochet in personal lists of the twentieth century's 'greatest' politicians, within a month of each other, in their respective columns in the *Spectator*. There were the traditional public backers of extreme conservative causes, such as the zoo-owner John Aspinall and Taki the gossip columnist. There was the editor of the *Sunday Telegraph*, Dominic Lawson, who described the ex-dictator as 'articulate' and 'in many ways deeply impressive', and who was granted, together with a colleague, the only British newspaper interview with the captive general. It is vividly remembered at the *Sunday Telegraph* that Lawson returned from Wentworth with his hair newly slicked back, and wearing an unexpected pair of sunglasses.

With greater subtlety, the pro-Pinochet network of the 1970s and 1980s also reasserted itself. Apart from *The Economist*, all the old print backers of the dictatorship took up anti-extradition positions. Meanwhile, Tim Bell ran a public relations campaign for the general's release – 'we are in favour of reconciliation and not retribution' – just as his PR firm had once aided the campaign of Pinochet's protégé Hernán Buchi for the Chilean presidency. Charles Alexander, a prominent figure in the City of London who had encouraged foreign investors to return to Chile during the dictatorship, wrote a long article along the same lines in the *Daily Telegraph*. And Margaret Thatcher, naturally, came publicly to Pinochet's defence within days of his arrest, writing first to *The Times*:

Sir, I have better cause than most to remember that Chile, led at that time by General Pinochet, was a good friend to this country during the Falklands War. By his actions the war was shortened and many British lives were saved . . . There were indeed abuses of human rights in Chile and acts of violence on both sides of the political divide . . . [But] it is not for Spain, Britain or any other country to interfere in what is an internal matter.

There was one prominent British defender of Pinochet, however, who appeared to fit into neither of these two fairly predictable camps. Norman Lamont was a Conservative peer and former Chancellor. He had been previously best known for his mixed handling of the British economy in the early 1990s, and for a series of minor newspaper scandals during the same period involving his over-enthusiastic use of a personal credit card and his efforts to evict a dominatrix called Miss Whiplash from his basement. Now he unexpectedly became Pinochet's most regular advocate in Parliament and the British media. Lamont had not previously been associated with Chile, or with right-wing Conservative causes. His public persona was intense – he had a small troubled face and owlish eyebrows – and slightly accident-prone, but moderate by his party's standards. His autobiography, *In Office* (1999), which contained no mention of Pinochet, was noted for its modest sales and its unsensational, even rather boring account of government during the Conservatives' slow decline in the early 1990s. Lamont had lost his parliamentary seat in 1997 – 'I'm a fairly fatalistic individual,' he said afterwards, 'I didn't feel tremendous emotion at the moment of defeat' – and had since been a modest presence in the House of Lords. If anything, his career demonstrated the eventual political limits of the revolution begun by Thatcher and Pinochet in the 1970s. Privatisation and free-market reforms, in Britain at least, had not become sufficiently popular to keep their advocates in power.

Yet almost from the day of the general's arrest in London, Lamont suddenly resurfaced on television and in the press, making speeches and writing articles and posing parliamentary questions with the dogged tirelessness of an eager young backbencher. His stocky pinstriped figure became a familiar sight in Chilean newspapers. He repeatedly visited Pinochet at Wentworth. He defended the 1973 coup on radio phone-ins. He twice flew out to Chile for meetings with the Pinochet Foundation, a private trust set up by the military and business beneficiaries of the dictatorship in the early 1990s, which was coordinating the general's defence in Britain. In December 2000, after Pinochet had been spirited back to Chile, Lamont was awarded a 'Star of Merit' by the Foundation at a ceremony in Santiago. Days later, Pinochet was placed under house arrest on the orders of a Chilean magistrate, but Lamont received an invitation to lunch with the general regardless. 'There were pisco sours [a traditional Chilean cocktail] all round,' the former Chancellor recalled on his return.

A few months earlier, I met Lamont and asked him why his public life was taking this surprising tangent. It had first happened, he began, when he heard about the arrest at the London Clinic on television. 'I couldn't believe it!' he said, with a convincing trace of incredulity still in his smooth, ex-minister's voice. 'I found it unbelievable that a former head of state could be arrested in another country. I thought it was an affront to Chile. Slightly to my surprise . . .' – he paused, and a proud smile flickered between his full cheeks – 'I seemed to be the only person in England who took this view.'

Lamont folded his arms and leaned back behind his desk. We were sitting in an air-conditioned office with long windows overlooking Hyde Park. He had overseen his interests from here since leaving the House of Commons. Besides writing his autobiography, he had become a director of five companies, a consultant to two others, a lecturer abroad and the head of a think tank. Yet there was a sense, somehow, that he had time on his hands. A copy of *In Office* stood behind him on the window ledge, like a reproach for no longer being in government. He was an enthusiastic attender of the Lords. He was considering learning Spanish. Possibly writing another book . . .

The day after Pinochet was detained, Lamont rang the Chilean embassy. He spoke to the ambassador and offered his services. Almost instantly, he became the unofficial British spokesman – usefully respectable and well-known – for the anti-extradition cause. He found himself in a new and interesting milieu: 'I was rather impressed by the [pro-Pinochet] Chileans I met in television studios. These were mild-mannered, middle-class people – not rich, not military.' At first, he was more wary of the general himself. 'A lot of bad things happened under the military government,' Lamont admitted early in our interview, with slightly disarming candour. A few minutes later, he went further: 'Funnily enough, I know a person who was imprisoned. Well, not imprisoned. Put in the Santiago football stadium. He was a contemporary of mine at Cambridge in the 1960s. He was in the Communist Party, had been to Cuba. The Chileans took one look at his CV . . .' Lamont looked down at his desk. 'Mutual friends have told me he was extremely frightened.' Then he quickly added: 'I've never discussed it with him.'

Anyway, in the autumn of 1998, such thoughts soon evaporated in the rush to challenge Pinochet's arrest. 'It's the first time I've organised a campaign on anything. It took up a lot of my time. The more people were indifferent, the more I got riled.' Lamont was introduced to one of the general's sons, Marco Antonio, and found him 'a delightful chap'. Inevitably, the call came to meet Pinochet himself. As they sat in the narrow lounge at Wentworth, with the general in his preferred armchair at the end of the room, and Lamont and an interpreter on the sofas to either side of him, straining to catch his half-whispers, Lamont discovered, 'I did rather like him. We just had rather jolly talks. He was rather controlled . . . philosophical, more concerned about his grandchildren. There were people banging drums outside. I could never see why that was allowed. It would've driven me mad – I'm very sensitive to noise. He just shrugged and laughed.'

Lamont's knowledge of Chilean politics and history was then, and had remained, quite hazy. 'I'm vaguely aware of O'Higgins and Cochrane and all these people. I was working for a bank in the Argentine when Allende came to power. When I came back to Britain, I followed what he was doing in the papers. I regarded the coup . . .' – Lamont waved a hand – '. . . rather neutrally. Then I was vaguely aware of the free market there. The one thing one did know was that Chile had a very good system of privatised pensions. I thought I should learn more about it, but I never did . . .'

For Lamont, the issue in October 1998 and since was the old-fashioned conservative one of national sovereignty. 'I do not think you can live in a world,' he said, his words stiffening into public-speaking mode, 'where a middle-ranking judge can arrest anyone anywhere for something that happened twenty-five years ago. For diplomacy to work, you need immunity from prosecution for heads of state.' At the end of the twentieth century, however, after Hitler and Stalin, Pol Pot and the Nuremberg trials, this was quite a difficult argument to make. As 1999 went by, and Pinochet remained in Surrey, Lamont and other members of the campaign to free him began to worry that the ex-dictator would never leave Everglades.

'I think the low point was the latter part of the year,' Lamont said. 'Straw seemed to be implacable. The government seemed to hate Pinochet.' Among the general's Chilean and British supporters, Lamont admitted, 'There was a degree of tension.' A disagreement arose over whether to change the legal and historical emphasis of the campaign to a more emotional one, exploiting Pinochet's age and possibly fragile health. Charles Alexander remembers: 'I said on the first day after he was arrested, "He's got to get very ill, very quickly." But Tim Bell disagreed with me. He said, "Pinochet got rid of the commies, and that's our argument."'

Meanwhile, other Britons involved in the campaign became frustrated that it was not generally aggressive enough. Patrick Robertson, once a rising figure on the nationalist fringe of the Conservative Party and now the spokesman for the Chilean Reconciliation Movement, as the main pro-Pinochet group in London euphemistically called itself, argued that the general's supporters should lobby for Chilean trade sanctions against Britain and a break-off of diplomatic relations. Meanwhile, Fernando Barros, a long-standing Chilean ally of Pinochet, worried that the anti-extradition cause was becoming a vehicle for intrigue within the Conservative Party. 'I do not want this to be about Margaret Thatcher or British politics,' he told the *Observer*, a newspaper, significantly, without any ties to the Conservatives or the pro-Pinochet campaign. Not completely convincingly, Barros added, 'This is about Chile.'

To try to redirect these jostling energies more constructively, Lamont sought set-piece events where all aspects of Pinochet's case could be publicised equally. The first of these was a debate in the House of Lords in July 1999. It was a quiet time of year politically; attention was almost guaranteed. And Margaret Thatcher had agreed to give her first speech in the chamber for three years.

The debate was in the evening, with the daylight that struggles in through the stained glass fading, and the glow of the red benches and the gold surfaces even more heightened and unreal than usual. Thatcher, who was approaching her seventy-fourth birthday, looked like a waxwork. Her hair was teased up and enormous, and her strong nose was very pale. She sat waiting for a discussion about pensions to end with a slightly eerie stillness. Every now and again she would suddenly lean down to scrabble for something in her handbag.

The chamber was not full, but the few dozen people in the room were an unusual cross-section: a Chilean with a gloomy moustache in the public gallery, a reporter from the *Sun* in the press gallery, several senior Labour peers on the government benches and, sitting right next to Thatcher, Lord Howe, the former Conservative minister who, nine years before, had precipitated her removal as Prime Minister and party leader. Until the question of Pinochet had brought them together, they had barely talked since 1990.

Lamont got up to speak first. His waist looked wider and his hair much whiter than in his days as Chancellor of the Exchequer, but there was vigour and apparent conviction in his rhetoric. The detention of Pinochet had been 'worthy of the Borgias'. The general had been confronted by 'armed police' while 'under anaesthetic'. There had been 'many disquieting features about the arrest'. Skilfully, any sign of awareness that thousands of Chileans had suffered the same, or much worse, remained absent from Lamont's features.

Thatcher listened with a respectful look, gently bobbing her head. Then her turn came. Her voice was almost absurdly deep and grave. Pinochet had been arrested 'at dead of night'. He had been 'held illegally for six days'. The touch of foreboding that she once used to summon up for big ideological confrontations was in her words again. 'The organised international Left,' she said, 'are bent on revenge.' Why? Because the general had 'saved Chile' – at a time when 'communism was advancing through the hemispheres'. Now, the South American country was a place of 'thriving free enterprise', which had been jeopardised by the arrest at the London Clinic. 'This is the Pandora's box which has been opened,' Thatcher warned, apparently winding herself up for her conclusion. 'Unless Senator Pinochet returns safely to Chile, there will be no hope of closing it.'

Like the other speakers, she had been allocated four minutes. But she surged past the limit. At seven minutes, her sentences lengthening and growing more rhythmic, she was interrupted by a House of Lords official and told to stop. She refused, with a defiant rise in her voice. 'I very rarely use up my time,' she said, as if she had been saving her political energies for years for this moment.

That autumn, after British politics had been on its summer holiday, it was announced through the pro-Pinochet London newspapers that Thatcher and Lamont would be speaking publicly about the general again. This time, the audience present would be much larger, the publicity even wider than it had been after the Lords debate. For the first time since she had been forced from power, Thatcher planned to address the Conservative Party's annual conference.

It had been hoped, before this news, that the gathering in Blackpool would be an invigorating one for the party. William Hague, the Conservative leader then, was young and inexperienced but seemed to be becoming more assured. The Labour government, halfway through its term of office, was encountering its first major problems – not least over what to do about Pinochet. The next general election was probably less than two years off. Yet Thatcher's latest intervention over the Chilean, almost from the moment it was scheduled, threatened to blot all this out. For her to speak to the Conservative delegates at the main, official conference was considered too destabilising: like Pinochet in right-wing Chilean circles, she was still more of a draw than anyone else. So Lamont and his colleagues in the Chile Reconciliation Movement were forced to look for a venue on the fringe of the conference. They found a cinema, which did not sound terribly glamorous, except that it held approaching a thousand people, and a rumour about a live video link-up with the general himself had begun to circulate. When the day came, the queue for the evening rally had begun to form by teatime.

The ABC Cinema was inland from the seafront and the Winter Gardens, where the conference was taking place. 'Blackpool's Best Value Cinema', as it called itself, was a big graceless cube with worn paint-work. It dominated the bed-and-breakfasts and cheap businesses at this less profitable end of the resort: Popeye's Takeaway, Blackpool's Second Hand Scene, and a dark and noisy 'Tappas Bar and Disco' called Ricky's, which was directly opposite the ABC and advertised low-priced lager in the window. When I arrived outside the cinema in late afternoon, a cool October breeze had started coming in off the Irish Sea, which sat grey and already darkening in the distance, yet the door to Ricky's was wide open. It was a weekday, out of season, but inside young men in tracksuits were racing their pints.

At the entrance to the ABC, there were about forty people queuing beside a row of radio and television vans. None of the early arrivals looked Chilean. They all seemed to be Conservative Party delegates. I got talking to a man in a blazer from Northamptonshire. He said: 'Pinochet saved a thousand British lives in the Falklands.' And then: 'Every leader in the world has got blood on his hands.' The man introduced me to a pig farmer in front of him, who had been on television that day criticising the Labour government's rural policies. The pig farmer said, 'They ought to do with Blair what they're doing to Pinochet.'

The queue lengthened behind us. There were women, almost all middle-aged or older, in scarves and gold jewellery. There were slightly younger men, frequently in pinstriped suits. Everyone seemed cheerful, even boisterous. It was halfway through the party conference, with another evening in Blackpool's overheated restaurants approaching, and Margaret Thatcher speaking in three quarters of an hour. No one was talking much about Chile. 'Who's this General Pinochet chap, then?' someone asked me, half-seriously. 'He seems to be very popular.' At that moment, a big modern coach pulled up outside the cinema. Another cluster of conservative-looking people got out. But there was something different about them: their clothes were better cut, their dyed hair was more ambitious, and their faces were Mediterranean rather than pinkish. They were ushered straight inside. The Chile Reconciliation Movement had arrived.

In the cinema lobby, the posters for upcoming releases had been taken out of their frames and replaced with giant printed slogans: 'Free Pinochet', 'Britain's Only Political Prisoner'. Lying on every seat cushion in the auditorium, there was a small Chilean flag attached to a miniature flagpole. Up on the screen was a picture of Pinochet in the garden at Wentworth, surrounded by grandchildren, with the sun shining and a smile softening his huge face. It was the same photograph that had recently accompanied his interview in the *Sunday Telegraph*.

Outside in the street, with about half an hour to go, another group of Chileans arrived, this time darker-skinned and less groomed. They were directed by the police towards a set of crowd barriers that had been set up outside Ricky's. The anti-Pinochet protesters had driven over from Manchester. Some of them had brought their children. They immediately unrolled banners and started chanting: 'Extradition, the only right decision! Extradition, the only right decision!' The police filmed them with a small camera they had attached to a pole. A passing red Sierra honked in support. A few of the regulars from Ricky's came out to see what was happening. A very thin woman with a drinker's complexion did a little dance in time with the chants. As the Chileans switched to 'Now is the time to pay for your crimes!' a black Jaguar drew up opposite and Margaret Thatcher stepped out. She had chosen an electric-blue suit. She smiled for a moment at all the noise, then turned for the cinema. At the lobby stairs, she was helped, still smiling, up towards the projection room, where the Chile Reconciliation Movement were making their final preparations.

The projection room, like the rest of the interior of the ABC, had a red-and-blue spotted carpet and a ceiling of off-white tiles. It looked like an ancient nightclub. Yet inside, through the open doorway, Lamont was standing, leaning slightly forward in his concentration, rereading some notes. The Chileans, who included several senators and Marco Antonio Pinochet, were straightening their clothes. Then a voice came from the corridor outside: 'Have you got them all in a line?' Lamont put down his papers. The speakers formed into single file, and he led them out. On their way to the auditorium, each of them was handed a formal script by one of the smart young Pinochet activists, not all of them Chileans, who had suddenly materialised around the lobby stairs. Lamont was biting his bottom lip a little as he passed me, trailing a cloud of strong eau de cologne.

In the auditorium, every seat had been occupied for some time. Crashing military music was coming through the cinema speakers. Lights played over a black podium. As the speakers walked on stage, a standing ovation was already forming. The audience became a forest of waving plastic flags, as if it was the Last Night of the Proms. The music and the clapping and the special roar when Thatcher stepped out into the lights all seemed to fuse into one. The journalists in the room looked disbelieving, or appalled, or exhilarated. I wondered if this was anything close to what fascism felt like.

The next two hours were riveting and laboured in equal measure. British speakers alternated with Chileans. The usual arguments were made about Allende's malice and Pinochet's good intentions. The ex-dictator's giant features glowered down from the screen above. The jolting realisation came and went that these were mainstream British politicians on stage in his defence. Passages of long-dead Cold War rhetoric came dustily back to life. There were references to the Cuban revolution of the 1950s, to continents 'going communist'. A professor of Chilean history said with great certainty of the 1970s, 'Socialists, then as now, ruled throughout Europe.' The Santiago military were commended for their 'professionalism' during the coup. One of the senators directly compared 'President Pinochet' – no one called him General – to Margaret Thatcher, 'whose difficult decisions, risking unpopularity, saved Britain from decline'. There was near-deafening applause. Marco Antonio Pinochet, before he spoke, crossed the stage to shake her hand. And when it was finally her turn, Lamont took the microphone like the master of ceremonies at a boxing match: 'Ladies and gentlemen. We now come to the most important moment of this meeting. She's back. Lady Thatcher! . . .'

She did not speak well. Her voice was so deep this time, it sounded cracked and slurred. But her defence of Pinochet was much broader than she had previously dared. It ended with an almost utopian depiction of Chile under the dictator: 'More people were housed . . . medical care was improved . . . infant mortality plummeted . . . life expectancy rose . . . highly effective programmes against poverty were launched . . .' She concluded:

The Left lost the Cold War in Chile, as they lost it everywhere else. For our Home Secretary, who visited Chile as a young left-wing activist, that must have been very distressing. It can hardly have been much pleasanter for our Prime Minister, who recently described Allende as his 'hero'. The Left in Chile, and in Britain, had to abandon all the rhetoric, and most of the policies, of socialism in order to get power. But what they couldn't and wouldn't abandon was the poisonous prejudices they harboured in their youth. And this, of course, was the situation when a trusting, elderly, former Chilean ruler chose to pay one too many visits to his beloved Britain last autumn.

Afterwards, the delegates clapped with their Chilean flags clamped under their arms. Then the Conservative activists poured out of the cinema, still holding them. Some of the activists shook their flags at the anti-Pinochet demonstrators across the road. 'Go back to Chile!' one of the delegates shouted. 'We'll lynch you!' shouted another.

But the demonstrators had Chilean flags of their own, tied to the police barriers and crackling in the wind. After the delegates had dispersed, downhill towards the seafront and the neon of the town centre, the two dozen protesters stood and waited. They began to attract attention again from people in Ricky's and from passers-by. Two teenage boys holding drinks and slices of pizza had arrived to go to the cinema. They had been told to be patient by the police: Thatcher and the other Chileans were still inside. The boys shuffled in behind the barriers for warmth and sipped their drinks. 'My film starts at eight-forty. I don't really care about Maggie Thatcher,' said one. 'What's she doing, signing books?' said the other. Out of the hot doorway of Ricky's, an old man with a pot belly and several other teenagers appeared. There were still television cameras outside the ABC, and these had started filming the protesters. The people from the bar flicked Vs at the lenses. Then they picked up some spare placards that were lying on the pavement, and waved them in the air. Each of the placards had a grainy black-and-white photograph mounted on it of someone who had 'disappeared' under Pinochet; but the drinkers did not see. They grinned and laughed and chanted for the cameras. One of them pointed at a flag: 'What country is that? Is it Greece?'

The Chileans did not seem to mind. A couple of very young mothers with prams joined them behind the barriers. Then there was someone

in a wheelchair. Quick Lancastrian and South American accents min-
gled in the cold air. From the cinema, the crowd now looked quite thick
and forbidding.

Shortly after nine, the cars came for Lamont and Thatcher. There
were boos when the two of them emerged. He hurried out through a
side exit like a court defendant. She came out of the main door escorted by Denis Thatcher, who looked across the street, mouth open, with
an expression that might have been shock or incomprehension. When
the coach reappeared for the right-wing Chileans, they tried to look
nonchalant, mock-applauding the protesters. But the chanting –
'Assassin! Assassin!' – was too loud, and the wait to get on the coach
slightly too long. As it drove off, the drinkers from Ricky's flicked more
V-signs. And then they went back inside for another.

After Blackpool, the campaign to free Pinochet quietened down. Its
more exotic, probably counterproductive themes – the menace of
Allende, the virtues of the Pinochet dictatorship, the conspiracy against
him of 'the international Left' – were finally abandoned in favour of
the single, apolitical focus of his health. It had got him into trouble in
Britain, and it would get him out of it.

Helpfully, the British government was thinking along similar lines.
On the one hand, the Prime Minister continued to let it be known that
he regarded the ex-dictator as 'unspeakable'. Tony Blair said so in his
speech to the Labour Party's own annual conference in September
1999. By mid-January 2000, his official spokesman still maintained,
'He holds exactly the same view'. However, this did not necessarily
mean that the Blair government wished to detain Pinochet for years,
while the slow British extradition process took its course – let alone see
the Chilean die in Wentworth. The humiliation of his arrest, followed
by a few months' confinement, with all the attention these brought to
his past cruelties, was arguably punishment enough. If the general then
returned to Chile a diminished figure, this argument went on, anti-
Pinochet sentiment would at least be partially satisfied, while the damage done to diplomacy and trade with South America would only be
fleeting. Such a strategy was a Third Way, if you liked, between the two
impulses that had previously dictated official British attitudes to
Pinochet: either outraged hostility or admiring cooperation. This new,
classically Blairite compromise was also roughly what happened.

For much of 1999, while all the shocks and spectacles and ideological battles went on around the case, there were discreet discussions between London and Santiago, and the Spanish government in Madrid, about how Pinochet's health might secure his release. The Chileans and Spanish, if anything, were even more worried than the British that the general might never leave Surrey. The Chilean administration was facing a general election, a population sharply divided over Pinochet's treatment, and a restive military: senior officers were making regular public pilgrimages to Wentworth. In Madrid, there was a right-wing government, the first since Franco. Since taking office, it had worked hard to appear moderate, a break from the past; it did not wish to spark any associations with Spain's own recent dictatorship.

As the relevant telephone calls were made between the three capitals, and meetings took place at neutral locations under cover of international conferences on other matters – Robin Cook, the British Foreign Secretary, met his Chilean counterpart Juan Valdes in Rio de Janeiro and in Wellington in New Zealand, for example – Pinochet's supporters in Britain were publicising plenty of possible health-related justifications for an eventual deal. The planned link-up with him from Blackpool, it was suggested, had not taken place because he had felt unwell. The general, after all, was now in his mid-eighties. Despite his exercise bike, and the pride in his fitness that had caused him, in his more active days, to have his morning routine broadcast to Chileans on breakfast television, he was inevitably deteriorating physically. Exactly how fast was disputed. A fresh ailment always seemed to appear whenever there was a new legal move against him. And there was a suspiciously precise choreography to the way his friends and relations would rush from Santiago to his bedside at Wentworth every few months. News of these emergencies – on at least one occasion Pinochet was reported as close to death – tended to appear first in the British papers that supported his release.

Yet, for all this likely bluffing, it was clear by the start of 2000 that house arrest did not agree with him. In early January, after long negotiations between the Chilean government, the general's expensive British lawyers, and the Home Office, it was arranged that he should have a medical examination, to see whether he was fit to be extradited and put on trial in Spain, or to be kept under foreign arrest at all. The panel of doctors chosen for the task by the Home Office appeared to find both ambiguous and definite evidence for an acceleration in Pinochet's decline since he had been imprisoned:

For the last eight to nine months he has noted difficulty in walking and can now only cover 200 yards before his legs become too weak to continue. He now walks with a stick. Numbness of the soles of his feet has also progressed over that time.

Over the last ten months he has noticed a gradual progression of problems with his memory . . . He has difficulty in remembering people's names and in recalling dates and events . . . He has been reported as talking as if he had difficulty in turning ideas into speech.

On 9 September 1999 Senator Pinochet was walking in the garden and developed sudden headache and imbalance. Other episodes suggestive of transient cerebral dysfunction reported to us include once failing to recognise his wife and once failing to register that his son had visited him. He also recalls an episode in which his vision became dim for a short period.

When seen by Dr Thomas [Pinochet's doctor at Wentworth] on 14 September Senator Pinochet . . . was small-stepped with instability on turning . . . When reviewed later by Dr Thomas . . . a definite increase in parkinsonian features was noted, with parkinsonian speech difficulty, deterioration in handwriting, inability to dress himself, and needing help with rising from a chair . . .

Since then the Senator has had two further falls, one in the garden and one in the bathroom . . . His voice noted as quiet in October has also deteriorated.

There is a history of urinary symptoms – hesitancy, poor stream, urgency and occasional incontinence. He can generally stay in bed until early morning but thereafter may have to void three or four times.

Senator Pinochet was depressed last summer . . . He still feels homesick and bored and frustrated . . . He wakes frequently at night. In recent months he has lost interest in his former activities. He used to read and use the computer but now tends to sit watching television and says he has forgotten how to use the computer. Letter writing has become a chore and his handwriting less legible. Recently he has developed difficulty in shaving without cutting himself.

He has been troubled in recent months with aching pain in both buttocks, and his knees hurt in cold weather.

The indignity of all this was a kind of justice, of course. The medical report was supposed to remain confidential, yet its main findings were soon leaked to the international media. And then there was the fact that the actual examination had taken place not at the London Clinic or some other spotless private facility, but at a crowded, draughty public hospital. Northwick Park was even less glamorous than Grovelands. It was back in the droning outer suburbs of the capital, a patched-together complex of clinics of different ages, people pushing trolleys along cracked pathways and ambulances looking for parking spaces. It perfectly exemplified the wheezing National Health

Service that Margaret Thatcher and her Chile-inspired policies had helped create. The wing where Pinochet was seen was no different from the rest. It had tape over holes in its windows, chipped and banging doors, bare wires hanging from the walls. The general arrived in a wheelchair, and was interviewed by three doctors while lying in bed. He had to use a hearing aid. His strolls around Piccadilly before his arrest might as well have been decades before.

Yet if Pinochet's reputation as an invincible leader was now ruined and absurd, there was a consolation. The doctors, all revered specialists, declared him unfit to stand trial. Physically, they decided that Pinochet would be able to endure it. But not mentally: his 'memory deficit', his 'limited ability to comprehend', his 'impaired ability to express himself' and his 'easy fatiguability' would combine to make a fair hearing impossible.

At once, there were claims from Pinochet's opponents and others that he had fooled the doctors. Since his arrest, the general had been looked after part of the time by his own Chilean medical staff; it was alleged that coaching in how to manufacture symptoms had taken place during the extended run-up to the tests. But a British neuropsychologist who had tested Pinochet independently, Dr Maria Wyke, agreed with the Home Office's panel. 'General Pinochet's pattern of performance,' she wrote to them in early January, 'never suggested that he was attempting to fake disability.' Soon afterwards, Jack Straw announced that he was 'minded' not to allow Pinochet's extradition to Spain. At the end of January, a Chilean Air Force jet arrived in Britain. It was assumed that Pinochet would be leaving at any moment.

But then the process seemed to stall. There were no more statements from the British government on the Pinochet case for several weeks. The plane sat, fat and helpless in the Oxfordshire mist. This had happened before. Back in November 1998, on the day of his eighty-third birthday, Pinochet had waited at Grovelands with his bags packed, confidently expecting that the judges in the House of Lords who were considering his case at that stage were about to vote in favour of his immediate release. Yet, by three votes to two, they did not; and the ex-dictator had been thrown into one of his blackest moods. A few days later he was sent into his Surrey exile.

Pinochet had not been alone in his misjudgement in November 1998. In fact, at regular intervals throughout his detention, a general expectation had built up in Britain that he was about to be freed. Few people had anticipated his arrest, after all. Then there was the unprecedented nature of the case. And the sheer freakishness of the circus around it. Most British political and legal commentators reacted to all this as if it was a kind of dream, from which the country would very soon awaken.

Even the anti-Pinochet protesters seemed to share this view at times. Outside Bow Street Magistrates' Court in London one morning, while the usual crush formed to get into the public gallery, and the police shoved back a rare group of Pinochet supporters who were taking up too much room, a woman from the Chile Committee for Human Rights said to me, 'We're going from miracle to miracle.' When we got inside the building, the public gallery turned out to be a tiny, separate courtroom up many flights of stairs, with two large televisions linked to the proceedings downstairs. From a lot of the room's narrow benches, it was hard to see the screens. The sound was too low. Pinochet's lawyer rustled his papers, took endless sips of water, and slowed down his sentences with legal pleasantries, as if determined to say as little as possible. Yet once a court official began to read out the charges against Pinochet, the small brown room we were in, full of people struggling to concentrate after queuing outside almost since dawn, suddenly felt like a startlingly clear lens onto three decades of evasions and cruelties. The court official struggled with the names of the dictatorship's victims, but the glimpses of what had happened to them lingered horribly:

. . . severe electric shocks . . . beating him and depriving him of sleep . . . inserting a tube into his anus . . . forcing him to imbibe hallucinogenic drugs . . . making threats about her nine-year-old daughter . . . interfering with her breathing . . . confining him in a small cage . . . allowing him to hear the infliction of severe pain on others . . . depriving him of food and water . . . damaging his sight . . . suspending him repeatedly . . . forcing him to rape her sister . . .

The general, with his contempt for legal restrictions and elected politicians and all the other complicated public processes of democracy, was now being snared and exposed by them – and in particular, by the version of these processes that operated in the country he thought he loved. The ironies and satisfactions in this were almost infinite. The Chileans in the public gallery at Bow Street held their heads absolutely still as they listened and watched, as if in a trance.

On other occasions, simply waiting for news seemed its own reward for Pinochet's opponents. In Chile, on politically charged days, there can still be tear gas and truncheons; in London, the days that Pinochet court verdicts were due, the open spaces outside the cold British official buildings were seething and warm and expectant as the best sort of football crowd. When the Lords had been deliberating, the gathering place was Parliament Square: a rectangle of clipped Whitehall grass, usually sterile and traffic-bound, suddenly invaded by middle-aged Chileans and Chileans in their twenties, men in Allende glasses and men with radios, people greeting each other and embracing, people smiling, absurdly I thought, before the verdict had even been broad-cast. All around, beyond the crowd, was the stern Victorian skyline of official London. Hundreds, probably thousands of causes and protests had come and gone in this square mile. The great looming clock-face of Big Ben inched towards the appointed hour. People called in Spanish for silence in the crowd. A small ring formed round each radio. Ear-phones were pressed in and held. People looked at their shoes or up at the drifting clouds. The hush, the tensing of postures as the opinion of each Law Lord was announced, was like following some distant but monumental penalty shoot-out. Then someone shouted, 'Six-one!' Everyone was shrieking and leaping. Someone was blowing bubbles. A tiny old lady was shaking her fists.

That was in March 1999. Exactly a year later, Pinochet was gone. 'I have today decided,' Jack Straw stiffly declared on 2 March, in a state-ment distributed on the steps of the Home Office shortly after eight o'clock in the morning, 'that I will not order the extradition of Senator Pinochet to Spain.' The statement continued: 'The only factor militat-ing against the extradition . . . is the state of his health.'

At a quarter to ten, the general's inglorious little convoy edged down the drive in front of Everglades, through the electric gates, up the cul-de-sac, and into the maze of roads of the Wentworth estate. Pinochet and his wife sat behind tinted glass in a people carrier, also the pre-ferred mode of transport of the Blair family. The ex-dictator's posses-sions followed in a transit van. The motorcade avoided the protesters and journalists lined up, as usual, by the main gates, and left the estate by an unattended exit. For the next hour and a quarter, Pinochet and his entourage vanished, somewhere in the thick belt of roads that sur-rounded the capital. At eleven o'clock, the people carrier and its police outriders were finally spotted by a television news crew in a helicopter. The general was processing up the A1.

With a greater shrewdness than he had exhibited previously on this particular visit to Britain, Pinochet had agreed to be flown out of the country from a Royal Air Force station a long way from where most British journalists were based. At five o'clock that morning, the Chilean jet that had been waiting for him for over a month had taken off from Oxfordshire, and headed 150 miles north to RAF Waddington in Lincolnshire. Appropriately, this was a base that had been used during the Falklands. During the morning, British military police closed off all the roads around it. No protesters appeared.

A single car with two British television journalists on board pursued Pinochet up the A1. But when they caught up with him, somewhere in Cambridgeshire, they were soon spotted and pulled over by the police. On his last day in Britain, it seemed, some of the general's accustomed protections were finally being restored to him. Just before one o'clock, his motorcade drove into Waddington. The Chilean Air Force jet had already turned on its engines.

A cargo hoist had to be used to lift Pinochet into the plane. There was then a small delay. A present had arrived for the general from a well-wisher. As television crews began to gather beyond the perimeter fence, it had to be carried out to the aircraft. The gift was a signed silver plate: a reproduction of those cast in 1588 to commemorate Sir Francis Drake's victory over the Spanish Armada. No one could accuse Margaret Thatcher of lacking a sense of history.

16

His Eighty-fifth Birthday

Three months after Pinochet had gone back to Chile, I took the train again to Wentworth. It was a glowing early summer day, as if winter had never happened, and the golf course was thick with players. Outside the gates of the estate, the lamp posts had been repainted where the protesters had slapped their cheap stickers. There were only the smallest shreds of paper and tape still attached to the fence along the A30. The empty roadside smelt of spilled oil and passing traffic. Ants were reclaiming the verges.

I walked straight into the estate, along a shaded perimeter road for a few minutes, and turned into Pinochet's old cul-de-sac. There were three or four large houses, a great thick curve of hedge, and then, at the end of it, a new signpost. Everglades had been renamed 'Savannah'. The electric gates were shut, but there was a builder's van in the driveway. I looked across the gravel at the house, with its imitation Georgian windows, its broad-as-possible façade, its pediment over the front door, none of which quite concealed the medium-sized rental property behind it all. Then the gates opened; the van was leaving. Before they closed again, I stepped onto the drive and walked in as businesslike a manner as I could manage towards the front door.

The garden either side of the drive was well kept and large but almost barren: there was a lawn with barely a flower bed, a single spindly rose growing up the side of the house, an outdoor trestle table of the kind you see outside pubs, and a satellite dish. The flash of trucks rattling along the A30 was easily visible through the trees. When I got to the front door, it was ajar. Inside there was a cramped sunless hallway, and rooms with low ceilings leading off it. Everything, including the carpets, was in pale neutral colours. It felt like the sort of place a tabloid might hide away someone whose story it had paid for, or, in a different era, where a defector might have been brought to be debriefed. As I was peering into the hall, a tall and very tanned woman, middle-aged and authoritative-looking, suddenly appeared. I muttered something about Pinochet and my having been given this address. She listened for a moment, then said in a smart Home Counties accent, 'They're long gone. We're just curtain-fitting. Barton and Wyatt are the estate agents, in Virginia Water, if you're interested.'

Two houses away, an older woman answered when I knocked and started asking questions about having Pinochet as a neighbour. 'It was pretty grim,' she said, keeping the chain on. 'There were police dogs in our garden. The police cars ruined the grass verges. We had a party that first Christmas, and we had to give the police a list of the guests. And then there was the drumming every Saturday from two until six, the obscenities . . .' She glared out from the crack in the door, thin and immaculate in a trouser suit at eleven in the morning. In a deep, scornful voice reminiscent of Margaret Thatcher, she continued, 'I thought it was *disgraceful*. We want a residents' association covenant to stop this happening again. We've got a lot of covenants here, you know.' What had she thought of Pinochet himself? Her eyes lightened a little. 'My doctor said he was a charming man. I've been to South America. I'm quite interested in Chile. And Pinochet was a leader, like Margaret Thatcher. You don't want a weakling.' The old woman gave an almost wistful smile. 'Only Margaret had the courage to go and see him.'

I decided to get a broader selection of local opinions before going back to London. In a smaller house right on the edge of the estate, facing straight onto the A30, I did find one much younger man, wearing a rowing club T-shirt and holding on to a golden retriever, who thought that the anti-Pinochet protesters were 'probably as well behaved as you're going to get'. He gazed from the porch of his thatched cottage towards where they used to gather, perhaps thirty yards away. 'When it was our little girl's birthday, they sang "Happy Birthday", then went back to singing against Pinochet.' The man lowered his voice. 'Anyway, how bad would it have been in Chile if it had gone socialist? I don't think I would have liked to live under Pinochet. If someone took my child away, I'd be like those [Chilean] women were across the road.'

But the owner of the house nearest Everglades was more typical. It was a flashy white split-level with a pool. He said his children used to

wave to the ex-dictator when he was out in the garden. The ex-dictator would wave back. 'You'd see him sitting out there,' the man said,
thickset in his polo shirt, as his wife parked the Mercedes. There was a
hint of admiration, probably rare, in his curt Essex syllables: 'With his
butler serving him drinks.'

The question of Pinochet retained a certain level of interest in Britain
during 2000. The manner of his return to Chile in March – a military
band at Santiago airport, senior officers present without the approval
of the government, the general delightedly abandoning the wheelchair
to which he had been believed to be confined – received a great deal of
attention. Every subsequent picture of Pinochet taking the sea air at
Bucalemu or walking, apparently in reasonable comfort, in the Chilean
sunshine, would prompt a brief fury of letter writing to British newspapers, even to those not noted for their interest in foreign affairs. The
revelation of the legal and policing costs of the general's detention,
which were in the low millions, drew a similar response. Intermittently, there was news of less favourable developments for Pinochet in
Chile. His happy return had been deceptive. In August 2000, the
Chilean Supreme Court removed his immunity from prosecution.
Cases against him brought by relatives of his victims began surfacing
on an almost weekly basis. In December came his house arrest. At least
some of Pinochet's British critics began to feel that his arrest in London, for all its chance and half-heartedness, had been worthwhile.
Even Dick Barbor-Might and Sergio Rueda, at moments during our
interviews, when the talk moved on to the more recent stages of
Pinochet's political career, would permit themselves a passing smile.

To those less involved, though, the former dictator of Chile went
back to being a marginal figure, most likely, as soon as he was home
and 8,000 miles away from Britain. During the summer of 2001, a play
about the Pinochet case called *Sick Dictators* ran for a few weeks at the
Jermyn Street Theatre in Piccadilly, very appropriately just along from
where the general had liked to buy his ties. But the critics were unin-
terested or, at best, unimpressed, and the production did not tour. A little more enduring was the use of Pinochet's name as a sort of
free-floating symbol for slyness or intimidating cruelty. 'Doing a
Pinochet' was adopted by some newspapers as a phrase for getting ill
when politically useful. A year after he had left Britain, I saw 'Pinno-
chet' in the middle of a knot of freshly sprayed boasts and taunts on a

wall in east London. A year and a half after the general had slipped away, I saw a new Swedish film in London, set in the mid-1970s, with a scene where giggling children 'played Pinochet' by pretending to electrocute each other. The film had a lot of jokes, but that one got the cinema roaring.

More subtly, the dictator remained a presence in British politics – not as a controversy or a problem any more, but as the influence on government policy he had been since the late 1970s. The Blair administration may have condemned him and permitted his arrest and confinement, but some of its initiatives in other areas – allowing private companies to take over state schools, eagerly recruiting businessmen into the government, arranging the construction of new public roads and hospitals through very generous 'partnership' deals with profit-making corporations – carried a distinct whiff of Chile in the 1980s. The connection was rarely mentioned, except in the more historically inclined pamphlets from right-wing think tanks such as the Adam Smith Institute, and in the more esoteric speeches of the unconventional Labour MP Frank Field, who once made a trip to Chile to study its privatised pensions. You could say that the Chicago Boys and the notions they started putting into practice have become so much part of the modern political landscape that almost everyone has ceased to notice.

In Santiago, not far along the Alameda from the presidential palace, there is a small well-kept square where students hang about. I was walking past it on my very first afternoon in Chile when one of them came up to me. He was wearing new dark jeans and a white polo shirt, New Balance trainers and a Fiorucci rucksack. He had sharp darting eyes and was in his early twenties. He invited me to sit down with him under one of the palm trees. We talked for five or ten minutes; he told me he was studying gynaecology at the University of Chile, that his father was a socialist and had had 'trouble' under Pinochet, and that both his uncles were exiles in Canada. Then he gave me a short, fluent lecture on privatisation and poverty in Chile since 1973. As well as studying, he said, he worked at one of Santiago's remaining public hospitals, trying to ease things for the poor. 'I am a socialist,' he said, 'But a modern socialist.' Then he asked me for money.

I took out a thousand pesos. 'That's only two dollars,' the student said without a blink of embarrassment. 'I need 350 dollars a month just for university fees.' I gave him a few thousand pesos more. He reached into his rucksack and took out a small piece of paper. He handed it to me; it was a poem, neatly word-processed. He had a whole sheaf of them, tucked in next to his lecture notes. Looking across the square, I realised that so did all the other students: they were constantly jumping up from the benches and the grass, approaching passers-by, and exchanging pieces of paper for cash after a few minutes' chat. As my temporary friend got up to leave, his original politeness restored, he asked me a parting question. He knew that Pinochet and Thatcher were friends, and that Britain had followed Chile's lead on some social issues. But did we have to pay university fees? I said we did; and as he walked off into the sunshine, his situation suddenly seemed rather less foreign.

It was easy to think, in Chile in December 1999, that Pinochet had really won. Of course, he was still being held in Britain, but his release was nearing and his political work was done. Both countries, and many others besides, had been changed for good – whether they recognised the originator of the free-market revolution of the last quarter of a century or not.

Yet when I went back to Chile the following year, it was clear that, in another sense, Pinochet had lost. His reputation – after his groggy arrest in London, his weeks convalescing in a nursing home, his months watching television in a rented living room, and, finally, his pleas for mercy on grounds of feeble health – was no longer the unchanging, intimidating thing it had been. His old subordinates in the military were now testifying against their former commander-in-chief. The judicial system, which had always been considered full of toothless Pinochet appointees, appeared to be taking all the allegations against him seriously. A judge from a good conservative family called Juan Guzman was poking around in the mass graves from the 1970s, and looking for more in the country's forgotten corners. His talk about putting Pinochet on trial was sounding less and less like a gesture. The general's usual delaying tactics of public frailty, legal obstructiveness and plain defiance seemed to be working less well than they had in Britain. By the end of 2000, there seemed a real chance that he had escaped Jack Straw and the Spanish for something worse.

This new conventional wisdom about the Pinochet case, as ever, unravelled soon afterwards. His house arrest lasted only a few weeks. In March 2001, the charges against the ex-dictator in Chile were drastically scaled down: to covering up his regime's violent acts rather than ordering them. In July, the Santiago Appeals Court ruled that Pinochet was mentally unfit to stand trial. Bodies continued to be dug up, accusations continued to multiply against him, but the case as a whole seemed frozen. Rather than a decisive – and divisive – resolution, you could say that Chile was now simply waiting for Pinochet to die.

On the day after his eighty-fifth birthday, I was down in Valdivia, looking for Cochrane. That evening, in the echoing old hotel towards the edge of town where I was the only guest, I put on the television in my room. It was the news. After a couple of other items, there was a five-minute biography of Pinochet. Most of it was archive footage: Pinochet as a severe-looking boy in Valparaíso, as a young officer in a pith helmet in Iquique, as a steadily more senior soldier, his moustache and chest getting bigger; then the juddery black and white of the coup; then Pinochet in a succession of increasingly ornate dictator's uniforms, then him in his tweedy civilian clothes, trying to look like a grandfather. But what struck me more than any of this, even more than the film of riots and buried civilians that was irreverently mixed in throughout, was the final few seconds of the item. It used recent pictures of the ex-dictator, and they were not flattering.

He seemed barely able to walk. His big grey head drooped forward. A terminal stiffness slowed his every movement. His eyes were down. All of this could perhaps have been faked for the cameras. Yet, when Pinochet did lift his head, his eyes and open mouth looked aghast at the world.

17

London Boys

While I was in Chile, there was another face I kept seeing. Or rather, a set of faces, in slightly blurred colours, that were always appearing on posters stuck to telephone boxes and walls. The first time was in Santiago, as I was walking uphill into the middle-class suburbs. The graffiti and fly-posting of the city centre had given way to scrubbed shopfronts. The people on the streets were older. The side roads were full of tall hedges and a gathering, contented silence. Yet someone had slapped a lone poster on a fire hydrant. Unusually for Chile, the poster was in English. 'London Boys', it read along the top, then underneath, 'The Best Of Morrissey, Brett Anderson, Jarvis Cocker, Jim Kerr, Depeche Mode . . .' Beside each name there was a postcard-sized portrait: one of a man with big earrings, one of a man with a quiff, one of a man with truculent thin lips, and so on. Finally, there was a Santiago address and an upcoming date. To the initiated, all this meant something very specific: somewhere in the capital of Chile, there was a nightclub for people who liked their pop stars to be fading and British.

I had left for Valparaíso by the time the date arrived. But around the port, among all the Cochrane statues and museums, there were more posters advertising local versions of the same kind of evening. The cheaply printed photographs and names had been pasted up so frequently, in the same places, that the posters were in thick, flaking layers. Morrissey and Depeche Mode were always mentioned, and so, now, were more specialised British names and genres: 'Portishead . . . The Prodigy . . . The Cure . . . Britpop/Acid/House . . .' Musicians from other countries were never included, and the club nights seemed to happen every weekend.

That Saturday evening, I waited on the clifftop terrace of the

Brighton Bed & Breakfast for Valparaíso harbour to turn from blue to black, via a strange glassy silver at dusk that seemed to suspend the ships like tabletop ornaments. Then the noises of the port after dark started to drift up: the shouts and smashing of bottles that had been heard since British sailors and merchants first made Valparaíso rowdy and bursting in the 1820s; the newer sounds of speeding cars in the tight streets; and the throb of music from nightclubs waking up. In quick succession, I recognised three songs, from the 1970s, the 1980s, and the late 1990s. They were all British.

Down in the town centre, everyone was walking around eating chips. As usual, it was quite cold by now, with a mist coming in off the sea, like an evening in Newcastle. There was a square full of take-aways, hot air coming out of their doors, where people seemed to congregate. Most of them were in their teens or twenties, and were drinking bottles of Chilean lager. At the far end of the square, a road disappeared round a corner; every now and again, groups of boys and girls would break away from the square and follow this narrow curve uphill and out of sight.

The road, once you walked up it, was a steepening S-shape, lit like a stage set by yellow-bulbed streetlamps and lined with tall, almost Georgian nineteenth-century houses, which were made of stone rather than the standard wood and corrugated iron. Their upper storeys were dusty but still elegant. At ground level, virtually every building was a bar: a doorway with neon above and music blasting out. The first one I went into had the biggest sign of all. It was called Valparaíso Liverpool.

Outside, the four bowl-haired heads of the Beatles, circa 1966, glowed in illuminated silhouette. Inside, with a line of young Chileans sitting at it, there was a bar made of mock-Tudor panelling. There was English bitter and cider. Behind the beer pumps, there was a City of Liverpool crest mounted on a plaque on the wall. There were postcards for sale of Liverpool streets. There was a photograph of a Liverpool football team from the late 1980s, kneeling triumphantly with a trophy. There was a recent picture from a British music magazine of Liam Gallagher of Oasis reading the *Daily Mirror*. And as the long dark room came into focus, there was more. Past the bar, a low stage jutted out, under a banner reading 'John Lennon Corner'. Next to the stage, stairs led up to a large wooden balcony, built in the style of an English medieval minstrels' gallery. A mural in psychedelic greens and yellows wobbled along the back wall. Ringo Starr appeared as a giant crab, leading a column of Chileans past a grasping, monstrous octopus – perhaps it was Pinochet – towards a sign saying, 'To London'.

I stayed for a glass of Tetley's while one of the long-haired Chilean boys got on stage and did a tentative version of 'Imagine'. Then he came back to the bar, looking pleased with himself, and a DJ started playing hits by the Police to the half-empty room. No one was dancing, so I moved uphill to the next bar. It was plainer, without any British kitsch. But the music playing was still familiar: a single from the late 1980s by Siouxsie and the Banshees, from Bromley in Kent, then something, inevitably, by Depeche Mode, from the flat concrete suburbs of Essex. As the songs droned and stuttered in their English way, and girls dragged their boyfriends on to the dance floor for the most melancholy ones, I sat at a small table between Chilean couples, thinking self-conscious thoughts about what the British had given Chile and vice versa. And then, after midnight, I walked back to the Brighton Bed & Breakfast, along the cobbled alleyways where Cochrane and North and Barbor-Might and Balmaceda and the young Pinochet and Allende in his days as a Valparaíso politician might have been. It all seemed quite romantic, the old port and its traffic in the infamous and the idealistic, the unlikely alliances formed here between two such distant countries. The next morning, on cue, there was a picture of John Lennon in the local paper. But when I went on a boat tour of the harbour that afternoon, I still found myself looking at the British-built warships riding at anchor, with the sun on their blank hulls and their tiny portholes, and wondering which of them had been used for torture.

Acknowledgements

In roughly chronological order, I would like to thank James Davidson and David Godwin for welcoming the idea of this book in the first place; Walter Donohue at Faber for being enthusiastic at the prospect of editing it; and my superiors at the *Guardian* for letting me have the time to research and write it. I would like to thank the friends and colleagues who gave me ideas, contacts, and encouragement from the early stages onwards: Giles, Charlotte, Jonathan, Simon, Mark and Rob; Dan and Olly; Stuart and Conrad; and Sarah. I would like to thank all the staff of the British Library, and in particular those of Humanities Reading Room 2, for providing a perfect base for the project, and the diverse inhabitants of St Pancras and Kings Cross for reminding me that an outside world still existed. I would like to thank the journalists whose reporting from Chile educated me and got me excited: Richard Gott, Malcolm Coad and Hugh O'Shaughnessy. And the eye-witnesses to events there during the seventies who talked to me at such patient length: in particular, Dick Barbor-Might and Sergio Rueda. Their hospitality, and that of the North family and Vera Proctor, was welcome and generous. More specific but valuable help came from Dennis Heathcote at Greenwich University, Calum Laird at D. C. Thomson, and Bob Somerville at Rolls-Royce in East Kilbride. Peter Strafford kindly lent me books. Paul Laity and the *London Review of Books* let me try out some ideas. Lisa Darnell gave me one when I had none. Bernard Taper at the University of California gave me confidence, long-distance. Richard Kelly and Rachel Alexander at Faber, and Katie Levell at David Godwin Associates, gave me momentum in the later, slightly weary stages. Throughout, my family gave me more support than even they may have realised. And Sara, while doing so much for this book, reminded me that there is more to life than writing.

Bibliography

This is a selection of the books and other sources that have been helpful. Some were background reading, some were useful for several parts of the book, and some simply illuminated a single chapter. I have grouped them, though, by the chapter to which they seem most relevant.

1 THE NITRATE KING
Anonymous, *Chile: A Remote Corner on Earth*, Empresas Cochrane, 1992
Hinde, Thomas, *An Illustrated History of the University of Greenwich*, James and James, 1996
Shorney, David, *Teachers in Training 1906–1985: A History of Avery Hill College*, Thames Polytechnic, 1989

2 THE MYSTERY OF GENERAL PINOCHET
Anderson, Jon Lee, 'The Dictator', *The New Yorker*, 19 October 1998
O'Shaughnessy, Hugh, *Pinochet: The Politics of Torture*, Latin America Bureau, 2000

3 A SCOTSMAN IN VALPARAISO
Coad, Malcolm, 'Pacific Port which still Remembers the Maverick Naval Hero Britain Forgot', *Guardian*, 13 June 1992
Cochrane, Thomas, Earl of Dundonald, *Narrative of Services in the Liberation of Chili, Peru, and Brazil from Spanish and Portuguese Domination*, Ridgway, 1859
Collier, Simon, and William F. Sater, *A History of Chile 1808–1994*, Cambridge, 1996
Grimble, Ian, *The Sea Wolf: The Life of Admiral Cochrane*, Blond & Briggs, 1978
Harvey, Robert, *Cochrane: The Life and Exploits of a Fighting Captain*, Constable, 2000

Thomas, Donald, *Cochrane: Britannia's Sea Wolf*, Andre Deutsch, 1978
Tute, Warren, *Cochrane: A Life of Admiral the Earl of Dundonald*, Cassell, 1965

4 'The England of the Pacific'
Allende, Isabel, *Daughter of Fortune*, Flamingo, 1999
Anonymous, *Antony Gibbs and Sons Limited: Merchants and Bankers 1808–1958*, Wilfred Maude, 1958
Ferguson, Niall, *The House of Rothschild: The World's Banker 1849–1998*, Weidenfeld, 1998
Graham, Maria, *Journal of a Residence in Chile, During the Year 1822*, London, 1824
Kynaston, David, *The City of London*, Volume One: *A World of Its Own: 1815–1890*, Chatto & Windus, 1994
Kynaston David, *The City of London,* Volume Three: *Illusions of Gold: 1914–1945*, Chatto & Windus, 1999
Smith, W. Anderson, *Temperate Chile: A Progressive Spain*, Black, 1899

5 Desert Capitalism
Anonymous, *The Life and Career of Colonel North: From Apprentice Boy to Millionaire*, Kent District Times Company, 1896
Blakemore, Harold, *British Nitrates and Chilean Politics 1886–1896*, London, 1974
Booth, John Bennion, *Palmy Days: Reminiscences of Victorian London*, Richards Press, 1957
Castle, Captain W. M. F., *Sketch of the City of Iquique (Chili, S. America) during the Last Fifty Years with Notes on the Nitrate Ports and Railways*, Plymouth, 1887
Hervey, Maurice H., *Dark Days in Chile: An Account of the Revolution of 1891*, E. Arnold, 1891
North, John, *Life and Career of the Late Colonel North: How He Made His Millions, as Told by Himself*, Leeds, 1896
O'Brien, Thomas F., *The Nitrate Industry and Chile's Crucial Transition: 1870–1891*, New York University Press, 1982
Rojas, Ernesto Zepeda, *Humberstone*, Chilean government pamphlet, n.d.
Rojas, Ernesto Zepeda, *The Fertile Desert: The Old Nitrate Mines of Santiago Humberstone and Santa Laura*, Chilean government pamphlet, n.d.
Russell, William Howard, *A Visit to Chile and the Nitrate Fields*, London, 1890

6 Jack Straw and the 'Revolution in Liberty'
Sigmund, Paul E., *The Overthrow of Allende and the Politics of Chile 1964–1976*, University of Pittsburgh Press, 1977

7 ALLENDE

Allende, Salvador, *Chile's Road to Socialism*, Penguin, 1973

Anonymous, *The Popular Unity's Programme*, National Planning Office Republic of Chile, 1970

Horne, Alistair, *Small Earthquake in Chile*, Macmillan, 1972

Moss, Robert, 'The Santiago Model : Revolution within Democracy?', *Conflict Studies*, January 1973

Moss, Robert, 'The Santiago Model 2: Polarisation of Politics', *Conflict Studies*, January 1973

Moss, Robert, *Chile's Marxist Experiment*, Forum World Features, 1973

Terry, Walter, 'This Chile Nonsense', *Daily Express*, 14 May 1974

Zammit, J. Ann, ed., 'The Chilean Road to Socialism: Proceedings of an ODEPLAN-IDS Round Table, March 1972', Institute of Development Studies, Sussex University, 1973

8 THE COUP

Anonymous, 'The End of Allende', *The Economist*, 15 September 1973

Guzmán, Patricio, *The Battle of Chile*, Parts 1–3, Patricio Guzmán Producciones, 1975–9

Luttwak, Edward, *Coup d'Etat: A Practical Handbook*, Allen Lane, 1968

9 IN THE NATIONAL STADIUM

Jara, Joan, *Victor: An Unfinished Song*, Jonathan Cape, 1983

10 A STORY ON THE RADIO

Cassidy, Sheila, *Audacity to Believe*, Collins, 1977

Cassidy, Sheila, *Sharing the Darkness*, Darton, Longman and Todd, 1988

11 SOLIDARITY IN EAST KILBRIDE

The London Programme, London Weekend Television, 16 May 1976

'A Study in Exile: A Report on the WUS (UK) Chilean Refugee Scholarship Programme', World University Service, 1986

12 'THATCHERITE BEFORE THATCHER'

Asher, Mukul, Karl Borden and Eamonn Butler, *Singapore versus Chile: Competing Models for Welfare Reform*, Adam Smith Institute, 1996

Bethell, Leslie, ed., *Chile since Independence*, Cambridge, 1993

Clark, Alan, *Diaries*, Weidenfeld, 1993

Cockett, Richard, *Thinking the Unthinkable: Think Tanks and the Economic Counter-Revolution, 1931–1983*, HarperCollins, 1994

Congdon, Tim, *Economic Liberalism in the Cone of Latin America*, Trade Policy Research Centre, 1985

Guzmán, Patricio, *Chile, Obstinate Memory*, Patricio Guzmán Producciones,1997

Hurtado, Alvaro Garcia, *The Political Economy of the Rise and Fall of the Chicago Boys*, Cambridge University Press, 1983

O'Brien, Phil and Jackie Roddick, *Chile: The Pinochet Decade*, Latin America Bureau, 1983

Pinera, Jose, and others, 'The Pensions Problem', *Journal of the Institute of Economic Affairs*, March 1998

Thatcher, Margaret, *The Downing Street Years*, HarperCollins, 1993

Thatcher, Margaret, *The Path to Power*, HarperCollins, 1995

13 A British Pinochet?

Butler, David, and Dennis Kavanagh, *The British General Election of February 1974*, Macmillan, 1974

Chalfont, Lord, 'Could Britain be Heading for a Military Takeover?', *The Times*, 5 August 1974

Crozier, Brian, *A Theory of Conflict*, Hamish Hamilton, 1974

Crozier, Brian, *The Minimum State: Beyond Party Politics*, Hamish Hamilton, 1979

Crozier, Brian, *Free Agent: The Unseen War 1941–91: The Autobiography of an International Activist*, HarperCollins, 1993

Dorril, Stephen, and Robin Ramsay, *Smear!: Wilson and the Secret State*, Fourth Estate, 1991

Finer, S. E., *The Man on Horseback: The Role of the Military in Politics*, Pall Mall Press, 1962

Gould, Tony, *Imperial Warriors: Britain and the Gurkhas*, Granta, 1999

Hall, Stuart, and Martin Jacques, eds, *The Politics of Thatcherism*, Lawrence and Wishart, 1983

Hall, Stuart, and others, *Policing the Crisis: Mugging, the State, and Law and Order*, Macmillan, 1978

Haseler, Stephen, *The Death of British Democracy: A Study of Britain's Political Present and Future*, London, 1976

Hutber, Patrick, *The Decline and Fall of the Middle Class - And How it can Fight Back*, Associated Business Programmes, 1976

Kitson, Brigadier Frank, *Low Intensity Operations: Subversion, Insurgency, Peace-keeping*, Faber, 1971

Leigh, David, *The Wilson Plot*, Heinemann, 1988

Moss, Robert, *The Collapse of Democracy*, Temple Smith, 1975

Mullin, Chris, *A Very British Coup*, Hodder & Stoughton, 1982

Pocock, Tom, *Fighting General: The Public and Private Campaigns of General Sir Walter Walker*, Collins, 1973

Strachan, Hew, *The Politics of the British Army*, Oxford University Press, 1997

Walker, Christopher, 'The Mood of Britain: Senior Officers Concerned about Subversive Forces', *The Times*, 23 May 1972

Walker, General Sir Walter, *The Bear at the Back Door: The Soviet Threat to the West's Lifeline in Africa*, Valiant, 1978

Walker, General Sir Walter, *Fighting On*, New Millennium, 1997

Whitehead, Phillip, *The Writing on the Wall: Britain in the Seventies*, Joseph, 1985

Wright, Patrick, *The Village that Died for England,* Jonathan Cape, 1995

14 QUITE HELPFUL TO US IN THE FALKLANDS

Anonymous, *Beagle Channel Arbitration between the Republic of Argentina and the Republic of Chile*, Her Majesty's Stationery Office, 1977

Campbell, Duncan, 'The Chile Connection', *New Statesman*, 25 January 1985

Darwin, Charles, *The Voyage of The Beagle*, E. P. Dutton & Co., 1955

Hickman, John, *News from the End of the Earth: A Portrait of Chile*, C. Hurst & Co., 1998

West, Nigel, *The Secret War for the Falklands*, Little, Brown, 1997

15 PINOCHET IN PICCADILLY

Guzmán, Patricio, *The Pinochet Case*, Patricio Guzmán Producciones, 2001

Harris, Robin, *A Tale of Two Chileans: Pinochet and Allende*, Chilean Supporters Abroad, 1999

Lamont, Norman, *In Office*, Little, Brown, 1999

Robertson, Geoffrey, *Crimes against Humanity: The Struggle for Global Justice* (revised pbk edn), Penguin, 2000

16 HIS EIGHTY-FIFTH BIRTHDAY

Ensalaco, Mark, *Chile Under Pinochet: Recovering the Truth*, University of Pennsylvania Press, 2000

17 LONDON BOYS

Alegria, Fernando, *Allende: A Novel*, Stanford University Press, 1993

Index